The Power of Poetry

Second edition

Jo Eshuys

Vic Guest

Glendon Lewer

Cathy Crawley

NELSON
CENGAGE Learning™

Australia • Brazil • Japan • Korea • Mexico • Singapore • Spain • United Kingdom • United States

The Power of Poetry
2nd Edition
Jo Eshuys
Vic Guest
Glendon Lewer
Cathy Crawley

Editor: Juliet West
Project editor: Kelly Robinson
Publishing editor: Jane Moylan
Managing designer: Sharon Hall
Text designer: Rose Keevins
Cover designer: Rose Keevins
Illustrator: Irena Zdraveska
Photo researchers: Karen Forsyth @ Copper Leife and Gillian
    Cardinal
Indexer: Russell Brooks
Production controller: Deepa Travers
Reprint: Jess Lovell
Typeset in Vega regular 11pt by Sardine Design

Any URLs contained in this publication were checked for currency during the production process. Note, however, that the publisher cannot vouch for the ongoing currency of URLs.

For product information and technology assistance,
in Australia call **1300 790 853**;
in New Zealand call **0800 449 725**

For permission to use material from this text or product, please email
aust.permissions@cengage.com

National Library of Australia Cataloguing-in-Publication Data
The Power of Poetry.

2nd ed.
For secondary students.
ISBN 978 0 17 012485 0.

1. Poetics – Textbooks. I Guest, Vic, 1941 –.

808.1

Cengage Learning Australia
Level 7, 80 Dorcas Street
South Melbourne, Victoria Australia 3205

Cengage Learning New Zealand
Unit 4B Rosedale Office Park
331 Rosedale Road, Albany, North Shore 0632, NZ

For learning solutions, visit **cengage.com.au**

Printed in China by China Translation & Printing Services.
7 8 9 10 11 12 13 15 14 13 12 11

Contents

Contents

Contents

Acknowledgements

The authors and publisher would like to gratefully credit or acknowledge the following:

Photographs

AbleStock, p. 131; APL/Corbis/© Robbie Jack, p. 2, /© John and Lisa Merrill, p. 78, /© Roy McMahon, p. 112, /© Penny Tweedie, p. 239, /Underwood & Underwood, p. 246, /Hulton Deutsch, pp. 250, 277, 287; Auscape International/Jean-Marc La Roque, pp. 48–9, 92, /Wayne Lawler, p. 245; Bridgeman Art Library for *The Scream*, 1893 (oil, tempera & pastel on cardboard), Edvard Munch, Nasjonalgalleriet, Oslo, Norway. Oil, 91 x 73.5cm, p. 62, *The Scream*, c.1893 (engraving), Munch, Edvard, private collection, 19th century, p. 64; Corbis RF, p. 152; *Plum-trees by Water* by Eitoku, 16th century, Juko-in, Kyoto. Reproduced by permission of Kodansha, Ltd., p. 80 (middle); Getty Images/Image Bank, p. 46, /Photographer's Choice, p. 71, /Tony Stone, pp. 111, 184, /TimeLife Pictures, p. 143, /Iconica, p. 202, /Taxi, p. 220, /Image Bank, pp. 231, 238; *Ballad of the Drover*, Pro Hart, oil on hardboard, 14" x 18", 1973. Reprinted by kind permission of Pro Hart, p. 99; Istockphotos, pp. 14–15, 17, 19, 22, 29, 35, 37, 38, 39, 45, 72, 74, 76, 82, 105, 109, 119, 126, 129, 142, 146, 159, 188, 190, 197, 198, 208, 209, 210, 213, 214, 226–30, 233, 235, 252, 259, 260, 263, 268, 270-2, 281, 284, 285, 288, 293, 297; Liquid Library, pp. 118, 148, 183; Jude Morrell for cover design, *The Simple Gift* by Steven Herrick, University of Queensland Press, 2000, p. 135; *Bird on Branch* by Miyamoto Musashi (Niten), 1584–1645, 37 13/16 x 10 11/ 16 inches, Ink on paper; mounted as a hanging scroll, Philadelphia Museum of Art: Purchased with the Fiske Kimball Fund and the Marie Kimball Fund, 1968. Photo by Graydon Wood, p. 80 (right); Newspix, pp. 108, 189, 256, 289; Photolibrary.com, pp. 8, 32–3, 54 (both), 58, 60, 95, 130-1, 167 (bottom), 185, 204, 212, 230–1, 236, 237 (both), 282; Photos.com, pp. 4–5, 5, 7 (all), 12, 20–1, 24, 44, 47, 51, 66, 73, 79, 88, 106, 114, 130, 141, 151, 155, 158, 164, 173, 182, 192-93, 195-6, 201, 222, 232, 261, 267, 291, 296; Mitch Reardon/Lonely Planet Images, pp. 42–3; *Autumn Landscape* by Sesshu, inc and colour on paper, late 15th century. Reproduced by kind permission of the Tokyo National Musuem, p. 80 (left); Simon Pulse, New York, for cover, *The Simple Gift* by Steven Herrick, 2004, p. 136; Smart Digital Australia, p. 155; StockXchange, pp. 85, 89, 110, 181; Stock Photos/Zefa, p. 83; *Flight into Egypt* © 2002 by John August Swanson, Serigraph 38½" x 12 1/8" www.johnaugustswanson.com, p. 168; Carol Walker/Nature Picture Library, p. 104; Wildlight/Penny Tweedle, p. 49.

Acknowledgements

Text

'It is a Puzzle' from *Please Mrs. Butler*, by Allan Ahlberg (Kestrel, 1983), Copyright © Alan Ahlberg, 1983, p. 203; 'One-parent family', © Moira Andrew, first published by Blackwell, 1985, p. 232; 'Tarentella' from *Sonnets and Verse* by Hilaire Belloc (Copyright © The Estate of Hilaire Belloc 1923) is reproduced by permission of PFD www.pfd.co.uk on behalf of the Estate of Hilaire Belloc, p. 46; 'Remembering' and 'School' by Tallace Bissette, pp. 182, 191; Andrew Bolt for 'Indecision', p. 212; Use of the poem 'The Questions' from *In Her Strapless Dresses* by Lily Brett reprinted by permission of Pan Macmillan Australia Pty Ltd. Copyright © Lily Brett 1994, p. 251; 'Lambing time' and 'Forgotten' by Margaret Brusnahan, by permission of Magabala Books, pp. 48, 239; 'Snail' by David Campbell from *Collected Poems*, by permission of HarperCollins Publishers, p. 89; 'The Child Who Walks Backwards' take from *The Garden Going on Without Us* by Lorna Crozier. Used by Permission of McLelland and Stuart Ltd, p. 284; Roald Dahl, 'Jack and the Beanstalk' from *Revolting Rhymes*, Jonathan Cape Ltd & Penguin Books Ltd, by permission of David Higham Associates, Ltd., pp. 72, 104; Bruce Dawe for poems 'Gulf War' from *Mortal Instruments: Poems 1990–1995*, 'Katrina's Wedding' and 'Mementos', from *This Side of Silence: Poems 1987–1990*, 'Pleasant Sunday Afternoon', from *Sometimes Gladness: Collected Poems 1954–1987*, by permission of Pearson Education Australia, pp. 112, 173, 252; 'The country dog' by Max Fatchen, © Max Fatchen, by permission of Johnson and Alcock, p. 104; 'Killing a whale' by kind permission of David Gill. First published in *The Pagoda and other Poems*, Chatto & Windus, p. 294; 'Christmas Thank You's' by Mick Gowar, HarperCollins, London, 1981. Reprinted by permission of HarperCollins Publishers Ltd. © Mick Gowar 1981, pp. 292–3; Steven Herrick, University of Queensland Press for 'The meaning of art' and 'The Ten Commandments', and 'Marriage' from *Poetry to the Rescue*, © 1998, 'To my son Joe', 'Toenails', from *My Life, My Love, My Lasagne*, © 1997, 'Kiss the Dog', 'Looking', 'Old Bill', 'All that Knowledge', 'Old Bill and the Ghosts', 'Need', 'The Afternoon Off', 'A Man', 'Simple Gift', 'The Hobo Sky', 'Champagne', 'Westfield Creek' and 'Sleep', from *The Simple Gift*, © 2000, 'A Gated Community' and 'Tom and Cleo', from *Tom Jones Saves the World*, © 2002, 'The Earthquake' from *Love Ghosts and Nose Hair*, © 1996, 'For Once in My Life' and 'Emma and the Right Way' from *A Place Like This*, © 1998, 'A Poem for Darcy' from *Waterbombs*, © 2000, pp. 7, 110, 121, 127–32, 137, 260, 264, 268, 269, 285; 'Alex, on holiday?' (from *Naked Bunyip Dancing*, Allen & Unwin Publishers, 2005),

Acknowledgements

'The Colour of My Town', 'One Sunday at a Time', and 'Directions Out' (from *By the River*, Allen & Unwin Publishers, 2004) by Steven Herrick, by permission of Allen & Unwin Publishers, pp. 235, 258, 267; From *Witness* by Karen Hesse. Copyright 2003 by Karen Hesse. Reprinted by permission of Scholastic Inc., pp. 140–3; 'Ballad of the Landlord' by Langston Hughes, from *The Collected Poems of Langston Hughes*, Vintage, by permission of David Higham Associates, p. 287; 'Kimberly' (from *Three Has Gone*, Blackie Children's Books/Penguin Group, London, 1994) and 'The Father's Off Inventions' (from *Action Replay: Anecdotal Poems*, Ed. Michael Rosen, Penguin Group, London) by Jackie Kay. Reprinted by permission of PFD on behalf of Jackie Kay, pp. 205, 225; 'Summer Full Moon' by James Kirkup, p. 30; 'Angry rap' by Komninos, reproduced by permission of University of Queensland Press, p. 45; 'The Scream', © B.C. Leale and the Calder Educational Trust, 2005, p. 66; 'I can feel my lip throbbing' by Tanya Lintzeris, p. 147; 'Growing Up' by Wes Magee. Reproduced by permission of Wes Magee, p. 297; 'Spiritual song of the Aborigine' by Hyllus Maris, from *Inside Black Australia*, ed. Kevin Gilbert, Penguin Group Australia Ltd., p. 42; 'Reynard the Fox' by John Masefield, published by permission of the Society of Authors as the literary representative of the Estate of John Masefield, pp. 290–1; Ray Mather for 'Ordering words' and 'Remember me', pp. 11, 204; 'Tap' by Peter McFarlane from *Doing Bombers off the Jetty*, Macmillan Education Australia, Melbourne, 1997. Reproduced by permission of Macmillan Education Australia, p. 109; 'First Lesson' from *Times Three* by Phyllis McGinley, published by Secker & Warburg. Reprinted by permission of The Random House Group Ltd., p. 227; Roger McGough for 'Streemin' and 'First Day at School' from *In the Glassroom*, 'Two Haiku' from *Waving at Trains*, 'The Leader' from *Sky in the Pie*, and 'An Apology' from *Holiday on Death Row*, © Roger McGough 1976, 1982, 1983, & 1979, reproduced by permission of PFD (www.pfd.co.uk) on behalf of Roger McGough, pp. 6, 78, 108, 112, 289; VINCENT, Words and music by Don McLean, © MCA Music/Universal Music Publishing Australia P/L. Printed with permission. All rights reserved, p. 59; 'Nice work' by Judith Nicholls, p. 18; 'Hawk' by Catherine Noack from *Floating on Clouds: The Dorothea Mackellar Poetry Awards, 1998–2001*, reproduced by permission of the Dorothea Mackellar Memorial Society, p. 35; 'Colour Bar' by Oodgeroo of the tribe Noonuccal, from *My People*, 3e, The Jacaranda Press, © 1990, Reproduced by permission of John Wiley & Sons Australia, www.jaconline.com.au, p. 49; 'Best Friends' by Sharon Olds from *The Dead and the Living*, copyright © 1987 by Sharon Olds. Used by permission of Alfred A. Knopf, a division of Random House, p. 202; Copyright © Gareth Owen 2000. From *Collected Poems for Children*, Gareth Owen, published in 2000 by Macmillan. Reproduced by permission of the author c/o Rogers, Coleridge & White Ltd., 20 Powis Mews, London W11 1JN, p. 197; 'Little Poem' by Ron Padgett, used by permission of Ron Padgett, p. 211; 'Yesterday' courtesy of Patricia Pogson, p. 222; 'Mort Aux Chats' by Peter Porter, by permission of the author, p. 115; 'Press bulbs flash round the suspect' by Ron Pretty, p. 85; 'Life Lesson' and 'Adversity'

Acknowledgements

by Don Raye from *Like Haiku*, Charles E. Tuttle Co., Inc of Boston, MA and Tokyo, Japan., pp. 78, 81; 'Don't talk about your childhood' by Vicki Raymond, from *Selected Poems*, reprinted by permission of Carcanet Press, p. 190; 'Slowly' by James Reeves, pp. 21, 39; Extract from *All Quiet on the Western Front* by Erich Maria Remarque, published by Jonathan Cape. Reprinted by permission of The Random House Group Ltd., p. 249; Rony Robinson for 'Who Is You', Reprinted by permission of PFD on behalf of Rony Robinson. © Rony Robinson, p. 219; Michael Rosen for 'In the playground' from *When Did You Last Wash Your Feet?*, (© Michael Rosen 1986), 'Going through old photos', from *Quick, Let's Get Out of Here*, (© Michael Rosen 1983), 'George' and 'The car trip', from *The Hypnotiser*, (© Michael Rosen 1988), 'Mart's advice' and 'Rodge said', from *You Tell Me*, (© Michael Rosen 1979), all reproduced by permission of PFD (www.pfd.co.uk), on behalf of Michael Rosen, pp. 6, 111, 119, 235, 237–8, 243; 'Aeroplane' by Ingrid Ryan, to my father, who always encouraged me to write, p. 79; 'Attack' by George Sassoon. Copyright Siegfried Sassoon by kind permission of George Sassoon, p. 248; I WAS ONLY 19, Words and music by John Schumann, © M.C.A./ Universal Music Publishing P/L. Printed with permission. All rights reserved, pp. 279–80; Modesto Silva for 'Miriam', p. 214; 'Freedom to Breathe' from *Stories and Poems* by Alexander Solzhenitsyn, published by Bodley Head. Reprinted by permission of The Random House Group Ltd., p. 146; 'People' by Bobbi Sykes, by permission of University of Queensland Press, p. 189; 'Update' by Joyce Trickett, by permission of the estate of Joyce Trickett, p. 71; 'Curio' by Fleur Tiver, p. 104; 'Mirror' by John Updike from *The Carpentered Hen and Other Tame Creatures*, copyright © 1982 by John Updike. Used by permission of Alfred A. Knopf, a division of Random House, p. 88; 'Mary's Plea' by Daisy Utemorrah, from *Inside Black Australia*, Penguin Group Australia Ltd., p. 5; 'Coming Late' by Barrie Wade, reprinted by permission of Barry Wade, p. 198; 'Ode to Uluru' by Michelle Williams from *Tapestry* ed. by Michelle Williams, John Wiley & Sons Australia, © 2004, Reproduced by permission of John Wiley & Sons Australia, www.jaconline.com.au, p. 152; Michelle Williams for 'Pop', p. 282; 'A Voyage of a Poem' by Gillian Wilson from *Floating on Clouds: The Dorothea Mackellar Poetry Awards*, 1998–2001, reproduced by permission of the Dorothea Mackellar Memorial Society, p. 12; Judith Wright: 'Legend' from *A Human Pattern: Selected Poems* (ETT Imprint, Sydney 1999), pp. 36–7; 'Sunnyside Up' and 'Beyond de Bell' from *Talking Turkeys* by Benjamin Zephaniah (Viking, 1994). Copyright © Benjamin Zephaniah, 1994, pp. 8, 240–1.

Every attempt has been made to trace and acknowledge copyright holders. Where the attempt has been unsuccessful, the publisher welcomes information that would redress the situation.

About the authors

Jo Eshuys and **Vic Guest** have co-authored over 50 text books. They have previously won the APA award for the best textbook series of the year and are shortlisted regularly. They were both educated in Victoria, graduating from Melbourne University. They taught in Victoria before travelling overseas and finally settling down in Queensland where they teamed up to become one of the most formidable writing teams in Australian education. Their involvement in the classroom and on curriculum boards has kept them abreast of the latest trends in education in the fields of Humanities, English and Physical Education. Vic and Jo are known for creating innovative texts. They believe that poetry can be a powerful form of communication in all aspects of life.

Glendon Lewer is a senior teacher of English and Special Education at Miami State High School. Glendon is a published poet and was a major contributing author to the 1st edition of *The Power of Poetry*. Her involvement in teaching students with special needs has led to a particular interest in visual literacy, and developing cross-curricular programs which cater for diverse learning styles and multiple intelligences.

Cathy Crawley is the Head of Department in English at Miami State High School. She has a special interest in critical literacy and has acted as a literacy advisor to primary and secondary schools. She has also advised on and written government policies on literacy, leading to the introduction of whole school literacy programs and reading frameworks in schools. Cathy is currently studying her Masters degree in Professional Communication.

Chapter 1

'Mary's plea' by Daisy Utemorrah

What is poetry?

Poetry is a way of giving others a glance at what's in your head and heart. It is the oldest form of literature. Poetry and poets were prized in ancient times. The ancient Greeks used poetry to write powerful plays. The early Arabs fought over it, the Egyptians used it to worship the gods, while the rulers of India provided a lavish lifestyle for the best poets. In more recent times, famous writers such as Chaucer, Shakespeare and Goethe wrote all their work as poetry, exploring the most powerful beliefs and feelings of their time. Even today, knowing the work of our famous poets is still the mark of an educated person.

All the world's a stage
And all the men and women merely players:
They have their exits and their entrances;
And one man in his time plays many parts,
His acts being seven ages . . .

William Shakespeare, from *As You Like It*

Many poets use poetry as a medium to make a social comment. Poetry can question the world and its people and challenge the values and attitudes of our society and culture. Poets may have experienced injustices due to their age, race, class or gender, and may write poetry as a means of expressing their emotions and sharing their opinions or experiences with the reader.

Through poetic language, the reader is affected by the poem and its message and may become more aware of the world around them. Poetry, then, can be seen as a way to make changes in the world by educating people and encouraging them to make a difference.

What is a poem?

Poems are different from other types of writing. They look different because of the way the lines are structured. They sound different because of the way they flow. They have more sound patterns, more imagery and more rhythm than other text types.

A poem is:
- unique to the person who wrote it
- not necessarily 'difficult' or 'challenging' but can explore deep and complex human experience
- a form of art and therefore represents something of the world in which it is created
- written within the particular culture, time period and from the personal experience of the writer. This shapes its style, its form and the beliefs expressed in it
- a way to have a strong impact, positive or negative, on the audience that reads it.

Poetry is different from other types of writing because we can say things in our own way without having to follow the rules for sentences and paragraphs. The only rule of poetry, according to the famous poet S.T. Coleridge, is that we use 'the best possible words in the best possible order'.

Why write poetry?

We all have powerful feelings and opinions that we need to get out. Some people can do it through music or art, but all of us can do it through poetry. Words of sadness or happiness can be the beginning of a poem, no matter how short, simple or personal it might be.

There is no need to struggle with trying to achieve regular patterns of rhyme or rhythm. Many popular poets reject such patterns because these patterns can make their words sound forced or artificial.

A poem is like a letter – it's the message that counts, not the letter itself. It doesn't matter if every reader sees a different message. The strength of a poem is the impact it has on the poet or the audience.

Australian poet Judith Wright was once asked why she wrote poetry:

I pull at an idea in my head, but what's attached to it I don't know until I pull it out. By writing it down I can discover what the ideas in my head really mean. It's a bit like exploring. I know what general direction I want to go in but I don't know the detailed path. The more I write, the more my ideas become clear.

Another well-known writer, C. Day Lewis, said:

I do not sit at my desk to put into poetry something that is already clear in my mind. If it were clear in my mind I wouldn't have a need to write about it. We don't write in order to be understood; we write in order to understand.

Lewis was pointing out that poetry should not just be something clever to impress an audience. It should help us understand something about our own lives.

Often, when we write, we are listening to our inner voice, that special part of us that knows who we truly are. And no matter who we are, we sometimes feel inadequate or lonely.

Mary's plea

Where am I
You, my people
Where am I standing.
Take me back
    and hold my hand
I want to be with you.
I want to smell
    the smoke
    of burnt grass.

Where are you
    my people
I am lost;
I've lost everything; my culture
    that should be my own.

Where am I
The clouds
    o'er shadow me
    but my memories are there.
But I am lost,
    my people,
Take me back
And teach the things
I want to learn.

Is it really you my people,
The voices,
the soft voices that I hear.

Daisy Utemorrah

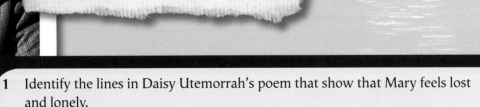

1   Identify the lines in Daisy Utemorrah's poem that show that Mary feels lost and lonely.

2   Suggest to whom Mary is speaking when she says, 'You, my people'.

3   In this poem, Mary is lost and lonely because she feels her culture has been silenced. In pairs, discuss the reasons that are suggested by the poem for Mary's unhappiness. Write your answer in a paragraph. Choose one person from each pair to report to the class.

Activity **1.1**

Teachers, and the classroom in general, have been the subjects of many poems. The following two poems present a light-hearted, yet truthful comment on some aspects of school life.

Streemin

Im in the botom streme
Which meens Im not brigth
dont like reading
cant hardly write

but all these divishns
arnt reely fair
look at the cemtery
no streemin there

Roger McGough

Rodge said

Rodge said,
'Teachers – they want it all ways –
You're jumping up and down on a chair
or something
and they grab hold of you and say,
"Would you do that sort of thing in your
own home?"
So you say, "No."
And they say,
"Well don't do it here then."
But if you say, 'Yes, I do it at home.'
they say,
"Well, we don't want that sort of thing
going on here
thank you very much."
Teachers – they get you all ways',
Rodge said.

Michael Rosen

The Meaning of Art

Sarah said to her teacher,
'I like green, it's my favourite colour.'
Ms Ginola replied,
'What shade of green?
The green of the trees?
The green of the grass?'
'No,' said Sarah, 'just green.'
'You mean, the green of the leaves?'
    said Ms Ginola.
'The green of moss? Olive green perhaps?'
'No,' said Sarah. 'Just green. Green green.
That's what I like.'
'Green like your school uniform?'
    asked Ms Ginola.
'Green like the deep ocean?
Green like a lime, or a glossy green apple?'
'No,' said Sarah. 'Just green. My green!'
'Maybe green like your eyes.
Or green like a traffic light.
A bright smart green, is that it?'
    asked Ms Ginola.

'No,' said Sarah. 'I like blue.'

Steven Herrick

The audience

There are times when we want to write only for ourselves. Often, however, a poem is written for someone else. You may not directly identify the people or person you are writing for – there is an implied audience. As the poet you may not be writing your personal opinions but write as though you are someone else – the implied writer. For example, in Roger McGough's poem 'Streemin' the implied writer is the student, not McGough himself.

There are many different audiences to aim at. An effective poem will be written in a way that suits the intended audience. Above all, the message has to be clear.

1   a   The three poems on pages 6–7 use the language of children. Why do you think the poets have chosen to write this way?

    b   Identify the implied writer in each poem and the implied audience.

2   Explain what the poem 'Streemin' says about equality in society.

3   Imagine you're writing an article for a student newsletter. The purpose of your article is to describe to teachers and parents how students would like to be treated at school. Use the poems on pages 6–7 to stimulate your thoughts.

The following poem is included just for pleasure. It is written in a humorous tone, even though the subject is quite serious.

Sunnyside up

When people
See people
Reading up
Side Down,
They think,
Maybe,
The reader
Can't read,
But
You should
Smile now,
Because you
Have found
A poem
That's out
To mislead.

Benjamin Zephaniah

'A voyage of a poem' by Gillian Wilson

Poetic techniques

The power of words

Just like a scientist might use a formula, or a chef follow a recipe, poets use particular language techniques to help convey a certain message or emotion. Poets use poetic devices such as metaphors, similes and personification to reveal thoughts and feelings. Poets also influence the reader through the use of sound devices such as rhyme and rhythm, and the use of particular vowel or consonant sounds to create a desired effect.

When you write poetry, the words you choose will be very important. If you use poetic techniques, the effect of your poem could be even more powerful. However, finding the right words to express yourself isn't always easy. It often takes several drafts to change your words and phrases until the poem begins to come alive for the reader.

Activity 2.1

1   Here are a few activities to help you find the words you want for a poem about yourself.

   a   Think of something that happened to you in the past. Picture the event in your mind: for example it could be the first time you rode a bike. On the right-hand side of your page, write down five words that describe that picture. Sometimes these five words alone can be like a short poem.

   tyres
   brother
   falling
   dad
   bitumen

   b   Now develop your poem by putting three descriptive words in front of each word in your list.

rubber, thick, charcoal	*tyres*
mimicking, know-all, annoying	*brother*
speeding, stumbling, lurching,	*falling*
quiet, helpful, supportive	*dad*
close, rough, scary	*bitumen*

   c   Now add a comment, a noise or a bit of rhyme to finish off your poem.
   Hold on . . . I can't . . . keep pedalling . . . I can't . . . crash!

   d   Repeat this activity on another topic – for example, your first day at high school. Concentrate on finding the best words to get your meaning across.

Ordering words

Attention   all
      you   words,
GET INTO LINE!
I've had enough of you
Doing what you w
       ill,
   STAND STILL!
There are going to be a few changes
Around here.
From now on
You will do
What I want,
THAT   WORD!
You heard,
Stay put.
Youcomeouttoofast
Or per   ulate
     amb
GET IT STRAIGHT!
You are here to serve me.
You are not at ease
To do as you please.
Whenever I attempt to be serious
You make a weak joke.
Always you have to poke
       fun.

AS YOU WERE!
Don't stir.
If ever I try to express
My feelings for someone
You refuse to come out
Or come out all wrong
So sense make none they can of it,
Yet you're so good once they've gone!
Well,
I'm in charge now
And you will say what I tell you to say.
No more cursing
Or sarcasm,
Just state my thoughts clearly
Speak what's on my mind.
Got it?
Right,
F
  A
   L
    L   OUT.

Ray Mather

Activity 2.2

1 Describe what is being 'ordered about' in Ray Mather's poem.

2 Identify some of the problems that Mather has with words.

3 Which of the following statements do you think he would agree with? Explain your answers.
   a Words can be easily controlled.
   b Words never really seem to sound the way you intend.
   c It's easy to find the right word.
   d Words are there to serve us.

4 The poet uses military style language. Choose two phrases or words that show this. Why do you think the poet has used this particular style of language?

A voyage of a poem

Poems are soothing, so soft and gentle,
Or rising up strong then crashing back down on earth.
Sometimes so vigorous like a volcano erupting.
Sometimes so sweet like a baby sleeping.
Reading a poem is like taking a trip to a place you've never
Been before.
It's like floating on clouds to a faraway place,
Or being chased by thunder and lightning.
Weaving in and out of words, pausing, whispering, taking deep breaths.
Sending chills down your spine, or making your heart beat faster than ever.
Poems send you on the journey of your life.

Gillian Wilson

Activity 2.3

1 Read 'A Voyage of a Poem' again and list all the effects that poetry has on the reader.

2 Sketch the most powerful images from the poem, using suitable colours.

3 Identify the lines that suggest that poetry is to be connected with nature.

The thought-fox

I imagine this midnight moment's forest:
Something else is alive
Besides the clock's loneliness
And this blank page where my fingers move.

Through the window I see no star:
Something more near
Though deeper within darkness
Is entering the loneliness:

Cold, delicately as the dark snow,
A fox's nose touches twig, leaf:
Two eyes serve a movement, that now
And again now, and now, and now
Sets neat prints into the snow

Between trees, and warily a lame
Shadow lags by stump and in hollow
Of a body that is bold to come
Across clearings, an eye
A widening deepening greenness,
Brilliantly, concentratedly,
Coming about its own business
Till, with a sudden sharp hot stink of fox
It enters the dark hole of the head
The window is starless still: the clock ticks,
The page is printed.

Ted Hughes

Writing 'The thought-fox'

This poem does not have anything you could easily call a meaning. It is about a fox, obviously enough, but a fox that is both a fox and not a fox. What sort of a fox is it that can step right into my head where presumably it still sits . . . smiling to itself when the dogs bark? It is both a fox and a spirit. It is a real fox: as I read the poem, I see it move. I see it setting its prints. I see its shadow going over the irregular surface of the snow. The words show me all this, bringing it nearer and nearer. It is very real to me. The words have made a body for it and given it somewhere to walk.

If, at the time of writing this poem, I had found livelier words, words that could give me much more vividly its movements, the twitch and craning of its ears, the slight tremor of its hanging tongue and its breath making little clouds, its teeth bared in the cold, the snow-crumbs dropping from its pads as it lifts each one in turn, if I could have got the words for all this, the fox would probably be even more real and alive to me now, than it is as I read the poem. Still, it is there as it is. If I had not caught the real fox there in the words I would never have saved the poem. I would have thrown it into the waste-paper basket as I have thrown so many other hunts that did not get what I was after. As it is, every time I read the poem the fox comes up again out of the darkness and steps into my head. And I suppose that long after I am gone, as long as a copy of the poem exists, every time anyone reads it the fox will get up somewhere out in the darkness and come walking towards them.

Ted Hughes

1   Hughes talks about how he makes the fox come to life in his poem.
    Write or sketch the particular images that show a realistic picture of the fox.

2   Describe what you think a 'thought-fox' might be.

Activity 2.4

Choosing the right word

If your poem is going to show exactly how you feel, then it's important to choose the right word.

City blues

Sunday dawn in a November city
the bully ⟨ light / sun ⟩ wades in
sets glass aflame
⟨ slams / puts ⟩ ⟨ dark / hard ⟩ shadows on anything
not big enough to take it.
The wind ⟨ strips / unzips ⟩ trees
makes them tittletattle
harsh small talk
⟨ puts / drives ⟩ their leaves into a lurch
somewhere.
A sheet of paper
⟨ followed / chased ⟩ by a coke can
takes ridiculously to the air
⟨ floats / flaps ⟩ into the sunlight

is a ⟨ swan / bird ⟩
tumbles
knows its place
as the less fortunate should.
In the ⟨ shadow / shade ⟩
this ⟨ miniscule / small ⟩ steeple
comes to the point
which is more than can be said
for the big-time ⟨ corporations / companies ⟩
and their ⟨ skyscrapers / sky-spoilers ⟩
⟨ napalmed / lit up ⟩ by that
lousy sun.

Mike Hayhoe

Activity 2.5

1   Look at the poem 'City Blues' and see how Mike Hayhoe has given the reader alternative words to choose from. Rewrite the poem with your own choices.

2   In pairs, compare the different versions you chose. How did these choices affect the meaning of the poem?

3   Describe how the particular choice of words changes the mood of the poem.

A family of words

Nouns, verbs, adjectives and adverbs belong to a family of words. Used well, they can make your poems come alive.

Poetic nouns

The words we use to name things are called nouns. They can name a person, a place, a thing, an event, an idea or a feeling.

   It is important to choose the right noun because it makes your poetry strong and clear. Try to use nouns that give more meaning to your poetry. For example, a noun such as *dog* doesn't tell your readers as much as the nouns *doberman* or *poodle*. You can see that nouns such as *tree, fish, car, clothes* and *athlete* do not tell your readers as much as *willow, barramundi, Porsche, gown* or *gymnast*.

Activity 2.6

1 Alter the nouns (in italics) in these sentences to give a clearer picture.
   a The *man* walked slowly towards the *room*.
   b Racing ahead, the *girl* ran past the *boys* and won the *event*.
   c The *woman* wore a *flower* on her *dress*.
   d The *dog* lay in the shade of a *tree* near the *water*.

Best things

Coke from the fridge,
Bananas, cherries,
Mum when she's had
A couple of sherries;
Ice cream and jelly,
Nearly everything on telly:
Cartoons, westerns,
Comedy, pop –
Start on that
I'll never stop;
The taste of parsley,
Vinegar, mustard,

School chocolate pudding
With green custard;
Waking up
On a Saturday morning:
Weekend thoughts dawning;
Old jeans –
Who cares if I get a rip in?
The taste of a Cox's Orange Pippin;
Sailing in a boat;
The smell of creosote;
Chips all squashy
From the shop in town,

Or Mum's chips, crisp
And golden brown;
Great blobs of candy floss
And hotdogs at the fair,
My bed, my new bike,
My favourite chair . . .

I could go on forever
If I wanted to –

And so, I expect, could you.

Eric Finney

Activity 2.7

1 **a** List ten nouns Eric Finney uses to describe his 'best things'.
   b Choose ten nouns of your own and use them to create a brief poem about 'The things I like'.
   c A lot of the images in the poem relate to our senses. In a table like the one below, list all the nouns Finney uses according to what sense they appeal to.

Touch	Taste	Smell	Sight	Sound

   d Now fill in your own noun chart with your favourite senses and translate them into a short poem about yourself.

Poetic adjectives

The aim of the adjective is to add colour and meaning to what you are speaking or writing about. Using adjectives in poetry is one way of describing your deepest reactions, feelings and thoughts.

An adjective is linked to a noun and can make that noun much more interesting.

- Adjectives can describe how something looks:
  the *thin* basketballer.
- They can describe an action:
  the *dunking* basketballer.
- They can be used to compare two or more objects:
  the *tall* basketballer
  the *taller* basketballer
  the *tallest* basketballer.
- Sometimes you will need to use 'more' or 'most':
  the *powerful* basketballer
  the *more powerful* basketballer
  the *most powerful* basketballer.

An adjective game: Doctor Doris's Dog. The aim of this game is to get you to think of as many adjectives as you can that all start with the same letter of the alphabet.

First, choose a letter of the alphabet. Then, going round the class, each person in turn has to think of an adjective beginning with that letter. For example, if you chose the letter A, the first person might say 'Doctor Doris's dog is an angry dog', and the next person might say 'Doctor Doris's dog is an active dog'. You keep on going until the person whose turn it is can't suggest an adjective. Any adjectives will do. For example, Doctor Doris's dog might be described as 'accurate' or 'alluring'!

Activity **2.8**

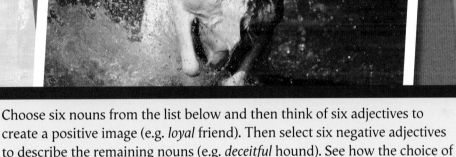

1 Choose six nouns from the list below and then think of six adjectives to create a positive image (e.g. *loyal* friend). Then select six negative adjectives to describe the remaining nouns (e.g. *deceitful* hound). See how the choice of adjective can affect our perception of feelings.

- friend
- tree
- hound
- motorbike
- teacher
- owl
- singer
- mother
- flower
- burglar
- dancer
- pool

Activity **2.9**

2 Choose nouns from the list below, and use adjectives to describe a feeling you have about them (e.g. *eerie* ghost).

- ghost
- meal
- sport
- accident
- thunder
- holidays
- detention
- drought

3 Using some of your answers to questions 1–2, and any other adjectives you wish, create a powerful poem. Alternatively, look at the photo on page 18 to stimulate your imagination, and write a poem about the feelings it gives you. Describe how the colours reflect the mood of the poem.

Activity 2.10

1   List five things you can see in the image below (e.g. rainforest, tall trees). Then change the adjectives or nouns you have used to create either a negative or positive feeling about the image (e.g. *threatened* rainforest).

2   Sketch and colour in a forest of your own to give it a different feeling.

Nice work

Never use the word NICE, *our teacher said.*
It doesn't mean a thing!
Try . . .
beautiful, shining, delicious,
shimmering, hopeful, auspicious,
attractive, unusual, nutritious –
the choice is as long as a string!
But please, *never* use the word NICE,
it just doesn't mean a thing!

(*She's nice, our teacher.*)

Judith Nicholls

Activity **2.11**

1   Add another five adjectives to Judith Nicholls' list of words to use instead of *nice*. You may need to use a thesaurus.

2   Now colour code your adjectives into categories such as colour, visual or tactile.

3   According to your list of adjectives, what things could never be described as *nice*? Explain your answer.

Poetic verbs

Verbs are the action members of the word family. *Read, cry, laugh, jump* and *run* are all examples of verbs. The aim of a verb is to add action to what we say and write.

When writing poetry we must be able to use verbs effectively, because the verb is the central action of any poem. By choosing the right verb you can create a more powerful word picture. For example, instead of *The elephant made a noise*, say *The elephant trumpeted*.

Activity **2.12**

Write out the sentences below and change the verbs (in italics) to create a clearer picture of the action.

a   The teacher *spoke* to the class.
b   The snake *moved* to the rock.
c   The dog *walked* in the water.
d   Grandma *ate* the food.
e   The baby *cried*.

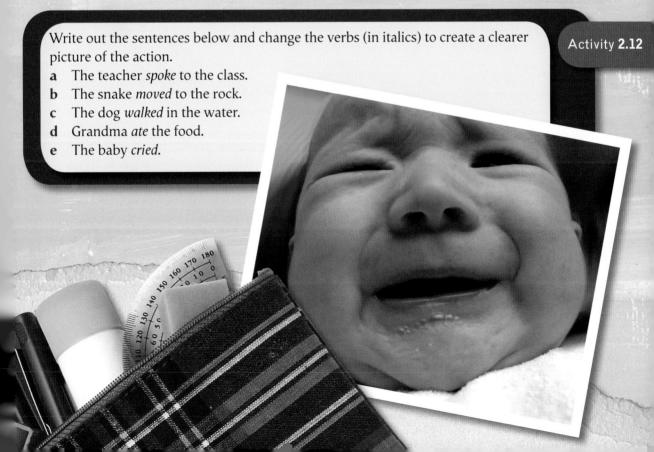

The tomcat

At midnight in the alley
A tomcat comes to wail,
And he chants the hate of a million years
As he swings his snaky tail.

Malevolent, bony, brindled,
Tiger and devil and bard,
His eyes are coals from the middle of hell
And his heart is black and hard.

He twists and crouches and capers
And bares his curved sharp claws,
And he sings to the stars of the jungle nights
Ere cities were or laws.

Beast from a world primeval,
He and his leaping clan,
When the blotched red moon leers over the roofs,
Give voice to their scorn of man.

He will lie on a rug tomorrow
And lick his silk fur,
And veil the brute in his yellow eyes,
And play he's tame, and purr.

But at midnight in the alley
He will crouch again and wail,
And beat the time for his demon's song
With the swing of his demon's tail.

Don Marquis

Activity 2.13

1 a List five verbs Don Marquis uses in 'The tomcat' to describe the tomcat's nature.
   b Sketch the cat as you see it.

2 Don Marquis helps to build up an impression of the tomcat by his choice of descriptive words. Find the verbs he uses to bring to life the features listed below, and discuss why they are so effective:
   a his song   d his claws
   b his tail   e his nature.
   c his movements

3 a This poem creates a negative image of cats. What words are used to suggest the tomcat is evil?
   b Change the words to make the cat likeable.

Poetic adverbs

An adverb is any word that adds to the meaning of a verb, telling you when, how or where an action takes place.

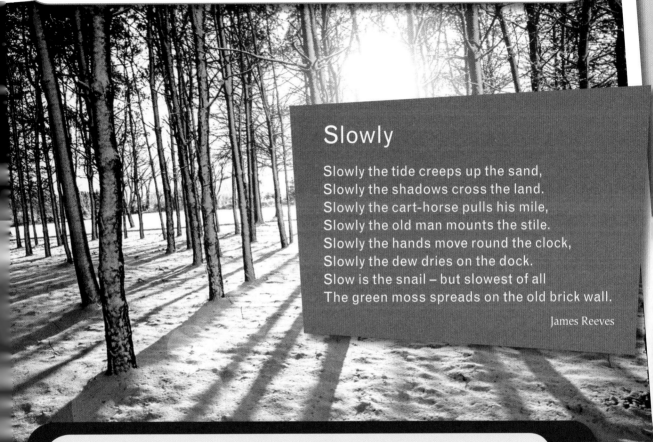

Slowly

Slowly the tide creeps up the sand,
Slowly the shadows cross the land.
Slowly the cart-horse pulls his mile,
Slowly the old man mounts the stile.
Slowly the hands move round the clock,
Slowly the dew dries on the dock.
Slow is the snail – but slowest of all
The green moss spreads on the old brick wall.

James Reeves

Now it's your turn to write a poem that uses adverbs. Either choose an adverb yourself or use one of these: *quietly, softly, swiftly, brightly, gently, lightly, loudly, proudly*.

Draw a mind map like the one below. Place your chosen adverb in the middle and fill in the surrounding boxes with actions or events relating to your adverb.

Activity **2.14**

From the ideas in your mind map, write an adverb poem like the one above.

London snow

When men were all asleep the snow came flying,
In large white flakes falling on the city brown,
Stealthily and perpetually settling and loosely lying,
Hushing the latest traffic of the drowsy town;
Deadening, muffling, stifling its murmurs failing;
Lazily and incessantly floating down and down;
Silently sifting and veiling road, roof and railing
Hiding difference, making unevenness even,
Into angles and crevices softly drifting and sailing.

from 'London snow' by Robert Bridges

Activity 2.15

1   In 'London snow' describe the effect the snow has on the town.

2   Pick out the line that most clearly allows you to picture the snow falling on the sleeping town. Say why.

3   Draw an image that you think best suits the poem or mime the events in the poem, trying to emphasise the verbs used.

4   Remembering to choose your verbs and adverbs carefully, write a poem on one of the following topics: a windy night; a thunderstorm; a cyclone; an earthquake.

The family of words working together

Before you read the poem 'Picture of childhood', brainstorm its title in pairs, thinking of all the pictures of childhood you have in your mind. Now, look at the striking verbs, adjectives, adverbs and nouns that the Russian poet Yevgeny Yevtushenko uses in his poem.

Picture of childhood

Elbowing our way, we run.
Someone is being beaten up in the market.
You wouldn't want to miss it!
We put on speed, racing to the uproar,
scooping up water in our felt-boots
and forgetting to wipe our sniffles.

And stood stock-still . . . In our little hearts something tightened,
when we saw how the ring of sheepskin coats,
fur-coats, hooded coats, was contracting,
how he stood up near the green vegetable stall
with his head pulled into his shoulders from the hail
of jabs, kicks, spitting, slaps in the face.

Suddenly someone from the right by the handcart pushed his teeth in,
Suddenly someone from the left bashed his forehead with a chunk of ice.
Blood appeared – and then they started in, in earnest.
All piled up in a heap they began to scream together,
pounding with sticks, reins,
and iron pins out of wheels.

In vain he wheezed to them: 'Mates, you're my mates – what's the matter?'
The mob wanted to make a job of it.
The mob were quite deaf. They were raging.
The mob grumbled at those who weren't putting the boots in,
and they trampled something that looked like a body
into the spring snow that was turning into mud.

They beat him up with relish. With ingenuity. Juicy.
I saw how skilfully and precisely
one man kept putting the boots in,
boots with greasy tags on them,
right under the belt of the man who was down,
smothered in mud and dungy water.

Their owner, a bloke with an honest enough mug,
very proud of his high principles,
was saying with each kick: 'We won't let you get away with it!'
booting him deliberately, with the utmost conviction,
and, sweat pouring, with a red face, he jovially called to me:
'Come on, youngster, be in it!'

I can't remember – how many there were, making a din, beating him up.
It may have been a hundred, it may have been more,
but I, just a boy, wept for shame.
And if a hundred are beating somebody up,
howling in a frenzy – even if for a good cause –
I will never make one hundred and one!

Yevgeny Yevtushenko

powerful verbs
powerful nouns
powerful adjectives
powerful adverbs

Activity 2.16

1 Summarise in your own words what is happening in the poem 'Picture of childhood'.

2 Explain what you feel is the poem's message.

3 Find other examples in the poem of powerful nouns, verbs, adjectives and adverbs.

4 In pairs, describe what this poem says about people and violence in society.

5 If you could say three things to the people in the poem, what would they be?

7 Write a poem combining powerful nouns, verbs, adjectives and adverbs. Choose a topic with plenty of action: for example, a football clash, two dogs fighting, a motor race . . . or a topic of your own choice.

Using powerful language to express feelings

Sometimes it's hard to find the right words to express ourselves. Exploring poetry can help you to expand your language and voice your feelings in more interesting and stimulating words and phrases. Poetry is about using emotive words, sounds and images to help bring a poem to life. Using poetic techniques in your own writing will make you a better writer.

Look at how this poem uses powerful language to get across the theme of rejection and insincerity.

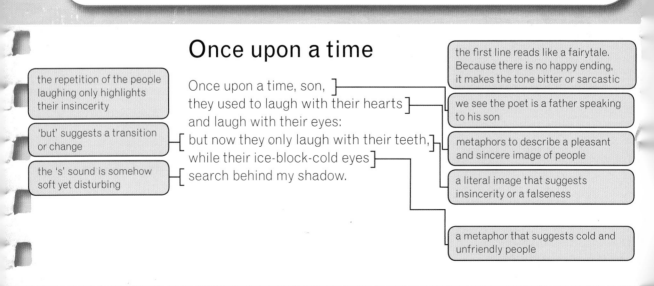

Once upon a time

the repetition of the people laughing only highlights their insincerity

'but' suggests a transition or change

the 's' sound is somehow soft yet disturbing

Once upon a time, son,
they used to laugh with their hearts
and laugh with their eyes:
but now they only laugh with their teeth,
while their ice-block-cold eyes
search behind my shadow.

the first line reads like a fairytale. Because there is no happy ending, it makes the tone bitter or sarcastic

we see the poet is a father speaking to his son

metaphors to describe a pleasant and sincere image of people

a literal image that suggests insincerity or a falseness

a metaphor that suggests cold and unfriendly people

There was a time indeed
they used to shake hands with their hearts:
but that's gone, son.
Now they shake hands without hearts
while their left hands search
my empty pockets.

> the poet is highlighting how people can have two faces or change their opinion about people

'Feel at home'! 'Come again':
they say, and when I come
again and feel
at home, once, twice,
there will be no thrice –
for then I find doors shut on me.

> the sound of a door shutting is quite powerful and suggests a finality

So I have learned many things, son.
I have learned to wear many faces
like dresses – homeface,
officeface, streetface, hostface,
cocktailface, with all their conforming smiles
like a fixed portrait smile.

> the repetition of the face image emphasises how people wear many masks. The adjectives used to describe the masks are associated with the city. Perhaps the poem is showing how city life and its people are impersonal? Negative adjectives are used to describe the smiles

And I have learned too
to laugh with only my teeth
and shake hands without my heart.
I have also learned to say 'Goodbye',
when I mean 'Good-riddance':
to say 'Glad to meet you',
without being glad; to say 'It's been
nice talking to you', after being bored.

> again, showing how people are two-faced, even in the language they use

But believe me, son.
I want to be what I used to be
when I was like you. I want
to unlearn all these muting things.
Most of all, I want to relearn
how to laugh, for my laugh in the mirror
shows only my teeth like a snake's bare fangs!

> the image of the mirror reinforces having two faces

So show me, son,
how to laugh, show me how
I used to laugh and smile
once upon a time when I was like you.

Gabriel Okara

> this last line makes you question why the poet has changed. Perhaps it is because he has grown up? Has city life destroyed his innocence? Has he learned to conform to society? Again, the 'once upon a time' likens the poem to a fairytale

> likening his smile to a snake's bared fangs suggests the poet has become two-faced like everyone else. It is a frightening and disturbing image and gives a negative mood to the poem

Activity 2.17

Quote the powerful words and phrases which strengthen the following emotions in the poem, using a table like the one below. An example has been done for you.

Emotion	Supporting quote
regret	
hope	
disappointment	
pretence	*I have learned to wear many faces...*
sadness	

Happiness

Emotive words

Language is an important part of our culture. Different words can portray particular images or emotions. Emotive words are used to create strong feelings in poems.

To help you choose a word that gives the emotional effect you want, use your thesaurus. For example, in the thesaurus the words *slim, thin, lean, slender* and *bony* are all listed together. Some of these create a positive or negative feeling, whereas others are neutral. These feelings are often determined by particular cultural expectations in our society.

Being described as:
- *slim* is positive
- *scrawny* is negative
- *thin* is neutral.

By selecting the right words you can influence the emotional response of your reader.

Copy and complete the following table by adding a positive and a negative term to each neutral one listed. Two examples have been done for you.

Positive	Neutral	Negative
obedient	does as asked	crawler
hound	dog	mongrel
	educated	
	strong	
	horse	
	casual appearance	
	thin	
	death	
	working together	
	spends money freely	

Yen-Ha Chau, a young student, wrote an emotive poem about death – the death of a child on a refugee boat sailing to Australia.

Do you believe that a child can die in the middle of the Pacific Ocean?

Do you believe that a child can die
in the middle of the Pacific Ocean?
His boat in the middle of the ocean
the whole ocean surrounding him
while we have a soft drink
coffee or beer.
We say this coffee is too sweet
it's not very good for our health
but he hasn't got a cup of sweet coffee
even a drop of water.
His mother's tears can't save him.
He looks like a dried tomato
He holds his little hands tightly.

He dies with his eyes open.
God can't even save him.
Nobody can save him.
You can hear
the sea wave's cry and the wind call his name.
You can see
Hell waving to him.
He is dying
without a drop of water.
He is dead
in the middle of the Pacific Ocean.

Yen-Ha Chau

1   In 'Do you believe that a child can die in the middle of the Pacific Ocean?' Yen-Ha Chau writes as though the child is dying right now, yet we know it happened in the past. Why is this technique effective?

2   List some of the emotive words and phrases in this poem, and say how each of them makes you feel.

3   Suggest why you think Yen-Ha Chau doesn't use the child's name.

4   Explain how this poem makes the reader sympathise with the refugees.

5   In a newspaper or on the Internet, find an article that reports the case of some refugees. Transform the story into a short poem using powerful language.

6   Illustrate the poem you wrote in question 5.

The sound of poetry

Clang, clatter, bang, whisper, scratch, grind, clunk, wham, ding – all of these words bring a sense of sound when we say them. Words have their own special sounds: long, short, sharp, soft, loud, harsh or interesting sounds. There are many ways in which sound effects can be included in poems.

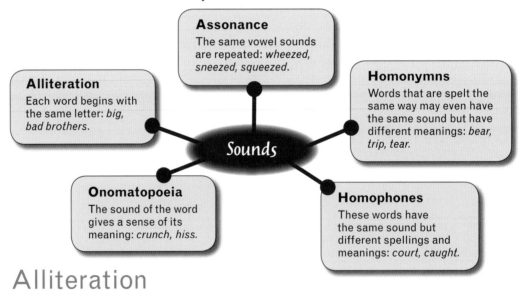

Assonance
The same vowel sounds are repeated: *wheezed, sneezed, squeezed.*

Homonymns
Words that are spelt the same way may even have the same sound but have different meanings: *bear, trip, tear.*

Alliteration
Each word begins with the same letter: *big, bad brothers.*

Sounds

Onomatopoeia
The sound of the word gives a sense of its meaning: *crunch, hiss.*

Homophones
These words have the same sound but different spellings and meanings: *court, caught.*

Alliteration

Alliteration is the repetition of the same sound in different words for effect. It usually happens at the beginning of the word, and can add humour or power to poetry. It can also create a particular mood or feeling and can help the flow or movement of language. Some alliterative sounds create a soft, calming effect like *l*, *s* and *f*, while some sounds can be hard and abrupt like *b* and *d*.

Write alliteration words for these letters. One has been done for you.

Big
lack
ears
ite
rothers

H M

T R L

Spring

Nothing is so beautiful as spring –
    When weeds, in wheels, shoot long and lovely and lush;
    Thrush's eggs look little low heavens, and thrush
Through the echoing timber does so rinse and wring
The ear, it strikes like lightnings to hear him sing;
    The glassy peartree leaves and blooms, they brush
    The descending blue; that blue is all in a rush
With richness; the racing lambs too have fair their fling.

What is all this juice and all this joy?
    A strain of the earth's sweet being in the beginning
In Eden garden. – Have, get, before it cloy,
    Before it cloud, Christ, lord, and sour with sinning,
Innocent mind and Mayday in girl and boy,
    Most, O maid's child, thy choice and worthy the winning.

Gerard Manley Hopkins

1   Read this poem aloud to a partner.

2   Write down five examples of alliteration. Discuss with your partner why alliteration makes this poem effective.

3   In pairs, write a short poem about your favourite season that uses alliteration in every line.

Assonance

Assonance is the repetition of the same or similar vowel sounds. For example: *Joe drove home so slowly.* The following example, by Tennyson, is particularly effective because it uses both assonance and alliteration. The repeated vowels are in bold.

All day the wind breathes
l**o**w with the mell**o**wer t**o**ne
Through every h**o**ll**o**w cave
and alley l**o**ne . . .

Alfred, Lord Tennyson, *from The Lotos-Eaters*

the same sounds
but with different
spellings

Summer full moon

The cloud tonight
is like a white
Persian cat –
It lies among the stars
with eyes almost shut,
lapping the milk from
the moon's brimming dish.

James Kirkup

Both assonance and alliteration are powerful ways to:
- allow the poem to flow more quickly as the sounds are repeated
- slow the poem down as each word is emphasised
- create clear images
- add emotions or feelings
- create a certain mood or atmosphere – heavy or light, quick or slow, positive or negative.

Friendships

The teacher forced alliances –
Tried to teach 'awareness'.
We were made to expose likes and dislikes,
    thoughts and feelings.
We played name-games, face-games, voice-
    games,
Formed outer shells of friendship:
Thin skins, surface gloss, shallow shine,
Veneer!
Plywood performances and laminex laughter
A furniture-display arranged
By her, for her.
And then she left.

The polish dulled . . .
Smeared with embarrassment.
Each face a flimsy chair
Separate
No more the matching suite.
Tentative questions emerged.
I observed, listened, thought and dropped
    cautious words.
One girl was eager, alert and witty.
I edged closer . . .
    and conversed.

Similar likes! Similar dislikes! Similar
    opinions!
There *were* irritations
But minor.
Minor became major.
When someone else appeared she
reflected
    their ideas . . .
A mirror.
Changing to fit her company
As a beanbag moulds around a rear.

She did *not* think for herself –
She meekly just agreed . . .
A coat-hanger for others' whims.
Very pretty upholstery,
Comfortable padding,
But no firm foundation.
No sound support from supple springs
Thus crumpling under pressure.

I'm secure, I'm dramatic, I'm aggressive.
I need someone who bounces back . . .

A trampoline?

Erika Fryberg (student)

---

1 Read 'Friendships' and see how Erika Fryberg has used alliteration and assonance for emphasis and imagery.

Activity **2.22**

2 Identify five examples of assonance and five of alliteration. Select one example of each and explain why you think they are effective.

3 Describe the poet's opinion of friendships. Support your answer with examples from the poem.

4 List Erika's reasons for liking and disliking the girl in the poem. Do you think her reasons are justified? Explain.

Onomatopoeia

Sound words echo and imitate the natural sounds of objects, things, people and actions. When the sound of the word is similar to its meaning, for example, the 'buzz' of a saw, this is known as onomatopoeia. Poetry that uses onomatopoeia is most successful when it is read aloud. Onomatopoeia helps to bring the poem to life and adds realism.

Breakfast in bed

Click, clatter, bustling movement, scuff, crinkle,
Wrestle, bang, tinkle,
Enter aroma, sweet, sweet aroma.
The rasping of toast being spread with butter,
And the sweet smelling aroma.
It started with a high note, singing down the scale
Until the cup was full, then the aroma,
My stomach juices move in anticipation,
Water from the tap
Dripping.
She enters, softly, a gleam of light enters with her,
She smiles at me and places the source of activity next to me,
Music floats to my ears and oh, the sweet, sweet aroma.
Quick sharp crackle of newspaper, and oh, the sweet,
Sweet aroma.

William Rutherford

Activity 2.23

1   With a partner, read alternate lines of the poem 'Breakfast in bed'.
2   Choose the five words you think make the best sounds.

Buzzsaw

The buzzsaw
grinds its teeth.
The growl deep in its throat
breaks free as it
writes across the greengum
paying no attention to grammar.

Albert Holt

Hail

The hail
tinkles onto
the tin roof,
a tiny timpani
of tintinnabulation.

Albert Holt

Noise

I like noise.
The whoop of a boy, the thud of a hoof,
The rattle of rain on a galvanised roof,
The hubbub of traffic, the roar of a train,
The throb of machinery numbing the brain,
The switching of wires in a overhead tram,
The rush of the wind, a door on the slam,
The boom of the thunder, the crash of the waves,
The din of a river that races and raves,
The crack of a rifle, the clank of a pail,
The strident tattoo of a swift-slapping sail –
From any old sound that the silence destroys
Arises a gamut of soul-stirring joys.
I like noise.

Jessie Pope

Activity 2.24

1   As a class, read the poem 'Noise' out loud, stressing the sound words.

2   *Whoop* and *thud* are two of the sound words in the poem. Write out five more.

3   In pairs, write a short poem about pleasant sounds containing some onomatopoeia. Create an illustration for your poem.

Activity 2.25

1   Read through the cartoon above, then write down the sound words.

2   Write down what is happening in each frame.

3   Find an interesting picture from a magazine. Write down five onomatopoeic words to accompany the image.

4   Sit quietly in the classroom or another calm area of the school for five minutes. Write down all the sound words you hear and what you think made the noise. Use your words to write a poem called 'The sounds of school'.

Visual imagery

Creating images in the mind of the reader is the most powerful way to communicate. The four main ways of doing this are through similes, metaphors, personification and symbolism.

Similes

A simile is a type of image or verbal picture made by comparing two things, using the words *like* or *as*. For example: *As sharp as a laser beam* or *He roared like a lion*.

Activity 2.26

1   The similes game. Work with a partner. The object of the game is to give you a chance to produce imaginative similes. Match the two different halves of the similes given in columns A and B.

Choose any interesting possibilities. When you've finished, choose your favourite simile, and explain why you think it's effective.

A	B
as sharp as . . .	a tiger's roar
the ballerina moves like . . .	a leaping tuna
a roll of thunder is like . . .	a slab of concrete
the rain is like . . .	a surgeon's knife
as cunning as . . .	a drifting cloud
as slippery as . . .	a block of ice
as cold as . . .	a graceful swan
a young dancer is like . . .	an eagle's eye
the snake's skin is like . . .	a snorting bull
as bright as . . .	a white curtain
the furious teacher is like . . .	the howl of a hungry wolf
as dangerous as . . .	a steel spike
as noisy as . . .	a prowling leopard
as frightening as . . .	a shivering shadow
a dinosaur's tooth is like . . .	a wasp's sting

2   Write some similes to suit the following images:
   *   the sky during a thunderstorm
   *   the pavement on a hot day
   *   the skin of a snake
   *   the taste of ice-cream.

Lost

Desolate and lone
All night long on the lake
Where fog trails and mist creeps,
The whistle of a boat
Calls and cries unendingly,
Like some lost child
In tears and trouble
Hunting the harbour's breast
And the harbour's eyes.

Carl Sandburg

The laundry basket

My shirtsleeve hangs
over the rim of the laundry basket
like a limp human arm
from the jaws of a crocodile.

Chris Hereward

Hawk

Blue expanses of the sky,
A hawk circled above a tree
Like a delicate charcoal whisper,
On an endless turquoise canvas,
   Riding the air currents
   In great gliding curves,
Then round and slowly round again,
Till the sunset flamed across the sky.

Katherine Noack

Activity 2.27

1 **a** If 'the whistle of a boat' sounds 'like some lost child', what comes into your imagination when you read this simile?

  b Is the sound short and sharp, or long and low? Why?

2 **a** These three short poems make comparisons by using *like*. Using the title of the poems as headings, write out the similes in each.

  b Which poem do you like most? Give reasons.

3 Draw an image of the hawk using information from the poem.

Legend

The blacksmith's boy went out with a rifle
and a black dog running behind.
Cobwebs snatched at his feet,
rivers hindered him,
thorn branches caught at his eyes to make him blind
and the sky turned into an unlucky opal,
but he didn't mind,
I can break branches, I can swim rivers, I can stare out any spider I meet,
said he to his dog and his rifle.

The blacksmith's boy went over the paddocks
with his old black hat on his head.
Mountains jumped in his way,
rocks rolled down on him,
and the old crow cried, You'll soon be dead.
And the rain came down like mattocks.
But he only said
I can climb mountains, I can dodge rocks, I can shoot an old crow any day,
and he went on over the paddocks.

When he came to the end of the day the sun began falling.
Up came the night ready to swallow him,
like the barrel of a gun,
like an old black hat,
like a black dog hungry to follow him.
Then the pigeon, the magpie and the dove began wailing
and the grass lay down to pillow him.
His rifle broke, his hat blew away and his dog was gone
and the sun was falling.

But in front of the night the rainbow stood on the mountain,
just as his heart foretold.
He ran like a hare,
he climbed like a fox;
he caught it in his hands, the colours and the cold –
like a bar of ice, like the column of a fountain,
like a ring of gold.
The pigeon, the magpie and the dove flew up to stare
and the grass stood up again on the mountain.

The blacksmith's boy hung the rainbow on his shoulder
instead of his broken gun.
Lizards ran out to see,
snakes made way for him,
and the rainbow shone as brightly as the sun.
All the world said, Nobody is braver, nobody is bolder,
nobody else has done
anything to equal it. He went home as bold as he could be
with the swinging rainbow on his shoulder.

Judith Wright

Activity 2.28

1   Write down the three similes from the poem 'Legend' that you think are the
    most effective. Which simile do you like most? Why?

2   Summarise the overall message of the poem.

3   Explain the title of the poem.

4   Look up the definition of the term 'legend'? Do you think this poem matches
    the definition? Explain.

5   On a time line, map out the blacksmith's boy's day with ten separate events
    from the poem.

Beware of the cliché

A cliché is a simile which has become boring through overuse. Here is a list of
some that have become so common that the reader knows what's coming and
gets bored:

- as cold as ice
- as green as grass
- as sharp as a razor
- as cool as a cucumber . . .

If you want to make your reader interested in and excited by what you have
to say, then steer clear of cliché similes. The trouble is, you may not realise a
particular simile has become a cliché. There's a way to find out on the following
page.

Activity 2.29

1   Write down two similes that you have heard many times. Share yours with others in the class. Write them all down, and make a mental note not to use them unless you want to use a cliché on purpose.

2   Create five new similes by completing the following. The first is done for you.
    a   as hot as *a dragon's kiss*
    b   as cold as . . .
    c   as thin as . . .
    d   happiness is like . . .
    e   as bright as . . .
    f   hunger is like . . .
   Share your similes with others in the class.

You!

You!
Your head is like a hollow drum.
You!
Your eyes are like balls of flame.
You!
Your ears are like fans for blowing fire.
You!
Your nostril is like a mouse's hole.
You!
Your mouth is like a lump of mud.
You!
Your hands are like drum-sticks.
You!
Your belly is like a pot of bad water.
You!
Your legs are like wooden posts.
You!
Your backside is like a mountain-top.

From the Igbo people of Nigeria

Activity 2.30

Using the words 'You' or 'Your' write a poem to someone else in which you create original similes about that person.

Metaphors

A metaphor is another way of creating a powerful image in which a comparison is made between two things. Whereas a simile says one object is *like* or *as* another, a metaphor actually says one object *is* another object. Here are some examples of metaphors:

- A ship's anchor is an iron claw.
- A mirror is a deep pool.
- A mobile phone is a teenage tracking device.

The sea

The sea is a hungry dog,
Giant and grey.
He rolls on the beach all day.
With his clashing teeth and shaggy jaws
Hour upon hour he gnaws
The rumbling, tumbling stones,
And 'Bones, bones, bones, bones!'
The giant sea-dog moans,
Licking his greasy paws.
And when the night wind roars

And the moon rocks in the stormy cloud,
He bounds to his feet and snuffs and sniffs,
Shaking his wet sides over the cliffs,
And howls and hollos long and loud.

But on quiet days in May or June,
When even the grasses on the dune
Play no more their reedy tune,
With his head between his paws
He lies on the sandy shores,
So quiet, so quiet, he scarcely snores.

James Reeves

Using metaphors

When your mood
Is a black storm,
Or your fingers
Are the clamps
Around my heart,
Or the river
Snakes through the valley –
You are using
Metaphors.
Something is not just
Like something else
But actually
Is something else.
The truck becomes
The roaring dragon,
The crying child becomes
A screeching gull,
Your whisper becomes
The wind in the trees.

1   Suggest reasons why James Reeves has chosen a dog to represent the sea.

2   Do you feel he made a good choice? Explain why or why not.

3   Write a poem about the sea using metaphors of your own.

4   While the poet uses a dog as a metaphor for the sea, you could use other animals to describe things. Try to think of something these animals could represent and give reasons for your answer.

Animal/metaphor	Represents	Reasons
elephant		
cat		
snake		
horse		
spider		

Personification

Personification is a metaphor in which human characteristics are given to non-human things. It can give great power to poetry.

The wind is angry

The wind is angry –
he's been in a rage all night,
stamping his feet, bellowing
and finally breaking out.
In morning light he gallops,
at full tilt, round the house
charging at the walls,
pulling at the thatch
and beating with clenched fists
against the windows.

Even now, he's thrusting
icy fingers through crevices
and under doors.

The house is tired
and slightly bored;
she watches with listless eyes,
sighs – settles on her haunches
and entrenches herself still more.

Adrienne Brady

Chapter 2 Poetic techniques

Activity 2.32

1   Suggest why you think Adrienne Brady chose to make the wind male and the house female.

2   Rewrite the poem, reversing the roles. Describe the difference this makes.

3   Again rewrite the poem, this time leaving out the personification. What effect does this have on the poem?

The fog

Slowly, the fog,
Hunch-shouldered with a grey face,
Arms wide, advances,
Finger tips touching the way
Past the dark houses,
And dark gardens of roses.
Up the short street from the harbour,

Slowly the fog,
Seeking, seeking;
Arms wide, shoulders hunched,
Searching, searching.
Out through the streets to the fields,
Slowly, the fog –
A blind man hunting the moon.

F.R. McCreary

Activity 2.33

1   Describe the type of person the poet chose to be the fog. Do you think this was a good choice? Explain.

2   Identify the line that creates the clearest picture in your mind. Describe the picture that it creates.

3   Write a short poem using personification. Here are a few ideas to start you off.
    The storm raised his dark head . . .
    The sun wrapped warm arms around us . . .
    Fear wrapped her fingers around my throat . . .

4   Illustrate the poem, using your imagination.

Symbolism

Your poems can become more intriguing and more powerful if you give your words and phrases a double meaning. Perhaps a dark cloud could signify anger, a rose could signify love, a child could signify innocence. This is called using symbols. Symbols can be determined by culture. For example, in western society, white is a symbol of purity, while black is a negative symbol.

Activity **2.34**

Suggest what the following symbols represent to you:
a   a horseshoe   e   the colour red
b   a pitchfork   f   a champagne glass
c   a cross   g   a hearth.
d   skull and crossbones

For Aboriginal people, the environment is not just something to be lived in. It gives meaning to life, through the land, trees, rivers, valleys and even the rain and wind. Aboriginal poetry is therefore filled with symbols.

Spiritual song of the Aborigine

I am a child of the Dreamtime people
Part of this land, like the gnarled gum tree
I am the river, softly singing
Chanting our songs on my way to the sea
My spirit is the dust-devils
Mirages, that dance on the plain
I'm the snow, the wind and the falling rain
I'm part of the rocks and the red desert earth
Red as the blood that flows in my veins
I am eagle, crow and snake that glides
Through the rainforest that clings to the mountainside
I awakened here when the earth was new
There was emu, wombat and kangaroo
No other man of a different hue
I am this land
And this land is me
I am Australia.

Hyllus Maris

1 Identify some of the symbols used to describe Aboriginal people in this poem.

2 Explain how one of these symbols helps to describe an Aboriginal person and their culture.

3 When you combine all of these symbols, what do you feel Hyllus Maris is describing?

4 Think up five symbols of your own.

5 Now write a poem using symbols. Start your poem with *'I am . . . .'*

Look at how William Blake has used a growing apple tree to symbolise his growing anger.

A poison tree

I was angry with my friend:
I told my wrath, my wrath did end.
I was angry with my foe:
I told it not, my wrath did grow.

And I watered it in fears,
Night and morning with my tears;
And I sunned it with smiles,
And with soft deceitful wiles.

And it grew both day and night,
Till it bore an apple bright;
And my foe beheld it shine.
And he knew that it was mine,

And into my garden stole
When the night had veiled the pole:
In the morning glad I see
My foe outstretched beneath the tree.

William Blake

Activity **2.36**

1 Identify the part of the poem 'A poison tree' that talks about expressing anger to a friend.

2 Describe what Blake says will happen if you don't express your anger.

3 Suggest why you think he chose an apple tree as his symbol.

4 Transform the poem into a flow chart that shows the events in the poem.

5 Use the flow chart to construct a short news bulletin or news story.

Rhythm

The rhythm is the flow and beat of the poem. It is used to help create the mood. Rhythm is created by the stress you place on certain words or parts of words when you read. (See also pages 102–103.) To show which words are to be stressed, you can use the mark / for a heavy beat and × for a soft beat.

Read the two lines below, putting a stress on the heavy beats marked /. Read them several times until you get the feel of the rhythm. Tap the rhythm with your finger.

```
  ×     /     ×     /     ×      /     ×     /
The   wind  and  rain  and  sleet  and  hail
  /     ×     /     ×     /      ×     /
Lashed  the  boat  and  ripped  the  sail
```

Activity **2.37**

In groups, read the poem 'angry rap'. Read it with a rap beat. Try reading a line each. Just feel the rhythm by reading it over and over. If you have a drummer in your class, add a drum beat.

angry rap

won't somebody listen,
listen to us please,
give us what we ask for,
give us what we need.

when i was at school
i was treated like a fool
i tried to be cool
but i broke all the rules.
keep in line
get to class on time
being is a crime
submit and you'll be fine.
sonny where's your tie.
give me twenty reasons why
boy, i wish you'd try
couldn't wait to say goodbye.

in this society
no one listens to me
the bureaucracy
doesn't recognise me.
haven't i got rights
do i have to fight?
they say go fly a kite
i think i just might.
at the end of the queue
makes ya wanna spew
we are people too
just trying to get through.

at home it's the same
i'm always to blame
life is just a game
where parents reign.
be seen and not be heard
feel like a caged-up bird
they have the last word
it really is absurd.

speak when spoken to
we have opinions too
always tell me what to do
don't give a hoot for you.

i went to work
i was treated like a jerk
nearly went berserk
work, work, work.
do this, do that
don't talk, don't chat
the boss gets fat
that's where it's at.
lift heavy weights
no smoko breaks
no coming in late
no talking to your mates.

Komninos

In 'Tarantella', Hilaire Belloc takes a musical idea and expresses it in words. He remembers an inn where, with his past love, he danced the tarantella – a rapid, whirling southern Italian dance.

Tarantella

Do you remember an Inn,
Miranda?
Do you remember an Inn?
And the tedding and the spreading
Of the straw for a bedding,
And the fleas that tease in the High
    Pyrenees,
And the wine that tasted of the tar?
And the cheers and the jeers of the young
    muleteers
(Under the dark of the vine verandah)?
Do you remember an Inn, Miranda,
Do you remember an Inn?
And the cheers and the jeers of the young
    muleteers
Who hadn't got a penny,
And who weren't paying any,
And the hammer at the doors and the Din?
And the Hop! Hop! Hap!
Of the clap
Of the hands to the twirl and swirl
Of the girl gone chancing,
Glancing,
Dancing,

Backing and advancing,
Snapping of the clapper to the spin
Out and in –
And the Ting, Tong, Tang of the guitar!
Do you remember an Inn,
Miranda,
Do you remember an Inn?
Never more,
Miranda,
Never more.
Only the high peaks hoar:
And Aragon a torrent at the door,
No sound
In the walls of the Halls where falls
The tread
Of the feet of the dead to the ground.
No sound:
Only the boom
Of the far Waterfall like Doom.

Hilaire Belloc

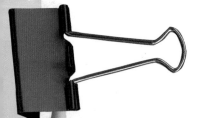

Activity 2.38

1 In groups, read the poem aloud and clap out the beat to get a feel for the rhythm.

2 Allocate alternate lines to the people in your group and perform the poem for the class.

Rhyme

Words that sound the same, or almost the same, are likely to make us notice them. There is something about words that echo one another in a poem that makes us pay attention and helps us to 'hear' the poem. Many poets use rhyme, which is the repetition of sounds.

Why use rhyme?

Rhyme can make your poem dance
Rhyme can make it race and prance
Rhyme can give it quite a bite
Rhyme can make it cute and tight
Rhyme can make your poem a hit
Rhyme can help you remember it.

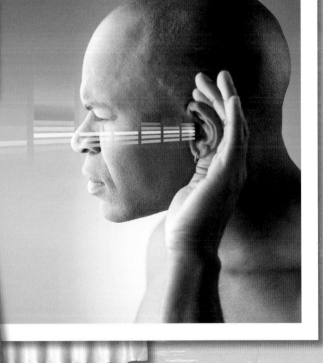

Rhyme

The trouble with rhymes
that you find sometimes
is that once they are found
you find you are bound
just because of the sound
to use them and then
you do not know when
to stop.

Pie Corbett

Activity **2.39**

1   Choose one of the above poems and write out the words that rhyme.

2   With a partner, read the poem 'Rhyme' aloud.
    a   Discuss how the rhyming pattern gives the poem pace.
    b   What is the effect of the short last line?

3   Make up a short rhyming poem about something you like, such as food, sport, TV, animals or music. Share your poem with others in the class.

Lambing time

I was travelling alone on a train one day	**a**
And I heard a white woman to another one say,	**a**
'Oh! Look at the newborn lambs by the tree;	**b**
They always bring back such memories to me.	**b**
'When I was a child we had a young lamb	**a**
And used to bottle-feed it by hand.'	**a**
Well, I smiled to myself at what I had heard	**b**
But went on with my reading, not saying a word.	**b**
My mind raced back to when I was a kid,	**a**
And what the sight of new lambs did.	**a**
It meant that night when we had tea,	**b**
There'd be lambs' tails for the family and me.	**b**
Thrown on the coals and cooked to a turn,	**a**
Poked now and then so they didn't all burn.	**a**
All wishing aloud as the last were gone,	**b**
That lambs had two tails instead of one.	**b**
She smiled at me as she left the train	**a**
And I laughed out aloud as I saw it again,	**a**
Her with bottle-fed lamb by the tree	**b**
And me with sweet little lamb feeding me.	**b**

Margaret Brusnahan

Activity 2.40

1   Read the poem 'Lambing time' aloud to a partner.

2   Describe the effect that reading it aloud has on the poem.

3   Summarise the message in the poem.

4   Do you think the poem is humorous or serious? Explain your answer.

Notice how the rhyming pattern in the next poem forces you to pause at the end of each second line. The poet's anger comes through passionately this way.

Colour bar

When vile men jeer because my skin is brown,
This I live down.

But when a taunted child comes home in tears,
Fierce anger sears.

The colour bar! It shows the meaner mind
Of moron kind.

Men are but medieval yet, as long
As lives this wrong.

Could he but see, the colour-baiting clod
is blaming God

Who made us all, and all His children He
Loves equally.

As long as brothers banned from brotherhood
You will exclude,

The Christianity you hold so high
is but a lie,

Justice a cant of hypocrites, content
With precedent.

Oodgeroo of the tribe Noonuccal (formerly Kath Walker)

Activity 2.41

1   Describe the rhyming pattern in the poem 'Colour bar'.

2   Explain why Oodgeroo becomes so angry when 'a taunted child comes home in tears'.

3   Describe your feelings when you read this poem.

4   This poem carries a powerful message about racism and prejudice in society. Explain the feelings of the poet and the reasons for these feelings.

Using the tools of poetry

Practise using poetic tools to improve your writing and understanding.
*   Can you unlock the door to your real self?
*   Can you untangle one idea from the million thoughts in your head?
*   Can you find the right words?
*   Can you put it all together?
*   Does it make sense?
*   Will people understand?

Activity 2.42

Write a poem of your choice. There are different ways you can do this. Here are some ideas:
*   Think of a main word.

    concrete
*   Add another word that reminds you of the main word.

    concrete
    asphalt
*   Now add some more words, each one reminding you of the word before.

    concrete
    asphalt
    playground
    black
    night
    vampire
    blood
    suck
*   As you progress, you can add phrases and sentences. A poem will begin to suggest itself to you.
*   Redraft your list so that it begins to take the shape of a poem.

Writing poetry for an audience

There are three stages involved in writing a poem:
- scribbling
- drafting
- listening.

Scribbling

Have you ever had a great idea which was lost because you didn't get it down at the time? Keep a notebook to scribble down ideas when they hit you – feelings when they are strongest and words that seem just right. Jot them down so they won't be gone forever! You can express your feelings about simple things or about more complex issues.

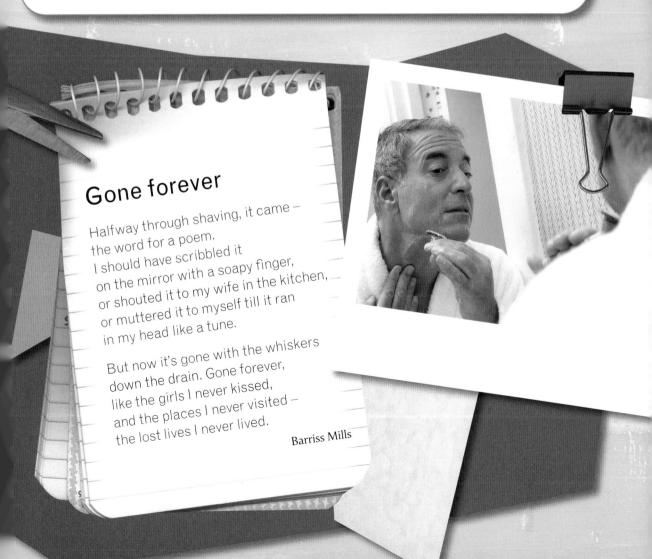

Gone forever

Halfway through shaving, it came –
the word for a poem.
I should have scribbled it
on the mirror with a soapy finger,
or shouted it to my wife in the kitchen,
or muttered it to myself till it ran
in my head like a tune.

But now it's gone with the whiskers
down the drain. Gone forever,
like the girls I never kissed,
and the places I never visited –
the lost lives I never lived.

Barriss Mills

Drafting

If you've got a powerful idea or feeling to express, let your first draft flow as strongly and quickly as you can. Get it down in any way that suits. Use all your energy in being creative; correctness can come later.

On your second time through, work on your draft to make it more powerful. Look for words to make it different. Cut out the unneccessary words to make it tight. Look for ways to make it more visual and more rhythmic.

Try to step outside your own feelings and consider your reader. Will the poem make sense to someone else? Will they understand? Will they feel what you feel?

Now go over it all again, and when you're happy that your poem is just the way you feel inside, sit back and breathe a sigh of relief!

Listening

Writing poems is also about listening. First, learn to listen to your own inner voice – whether in the quiet of a special place or in the roar of a crowd.

Second, tune in to someone else by listening to their poem. Is it the idea that matters or is it the rhythm? Are the images the key or is it the story? Is it about sounds or about emotions? Have they effectively conveyed their opinion or the message that needs to be heard? Does it make a particular social comment? Or is it all of these?

If you learn to listen to yourself, you can hear others too.

Activity 2.43

1   Choose one of the poems you have written.
2   Read this chosen poem to yourself.
3   Address the questions asked above.
4   Do the same with a friend's poem.

Chapter 3

'Vincent' by Don McLean

Pictures and poetry

You have probably heard the saying, 'a picture paints a thousand words'. Pictures can be the source of great inspiration. Many poets have written about images that have aroused in them particular emotions or feelings. Paintings, photos, films, sketches, cartoons and computer images can be the inspiration for a poem.

We understand poets through their written or spoken language, whereas with artists and photographers we understand their messages by 'reading' their visual images. Just as it is important to understand written and spoken language, you can also be aware of how images carry messages. Visual literacy, therefore, is the ability to understand the meaning and components of an image.

When you want to analyse an image, ask yourself the following questions:

- What is happening in the picture?
- What objects can you see?
- When and where is the picture located?
- What are people in the image doing?
- What do the facial expressions, body language or clothing suggest?
- Why do you think this image was created?
- What is the artist or creator trying to tell you?
- What structures, buildings or environment are in the image and what is their significance?

Activity 3.1   In pairs, look at the self-portrait of van Gogh on page 58 and analyse the image by discussing and brainstorming the questions above.

Visual elements

Visual images communicate through using a variety of **visual elements**.
These elements include:

Shapes

Shapes are part of our world. We grow up learning what shapes mean and share
that meaning with others in a type of 'picture language'. Think of a young child's
drawing of a house. Most children will draw a circle for the sun, a square for the
house and a rectangle for the roof, with perhaps a triangle-shaped tree in the
garden. A circle tends be calm and relaxed, like other curvy images. A square
can be stable, but also dull and less natural, while a triangle is seen as signifying
action or conflict. Artists love to play with shapes.

Direction

When we look at an image, our eyes move across the image in certain ways. We
tend to look at the vertical image first, followed by the horizontal. The diagonal
direction can give a feeling of movement or change. The direction of curves can
be either unstable or safe depending on the sharpness of the curves. Triangles can
'trap' our eyes and draw attention to a certain image.

Lines

Lines can give a feeling of motion across a visual space. A line has a definite
direction. The horizon or a horizontal line can provide a feeling of balance and
stability. Diagonal lines attract the eye.

Dots

Dots can act as the pointer or marker of space.

Texture

Texture is the surface of an image or an effect created by the artist. Certain
features may appear rough or smooth and this will add to our understanding
of and relationship with the image.

Hue

The colour of something is its hue. Hues can be divided into warm and cool
colours. Colours are important in expressing moods and feelings. Red represents
anger, pain and love. Blue is cool and calming and is often used to represent
truth, authority and stability. In many cultures black represents evil, whereas
white is associated with innocence. Yellow is cheerful and warm.

Saturation

The colour within images can be saturated, that is to say, deeper or brighter, to create a different feeling or mood.

Value

Value is the positioning of light and dark within an image to express emotions, light, space and movement.

Scale

Scale is the relative size of objects in the image. Often there is an illusion of depth. Scale can make some objects appear inferior or superior.

Dimension

This is the feeling of being close to or far away from an image. Light, shadow and perspective can create a feeling of dimension.

Motion

Visual images can carry an illusion of motion. A feeling of movement can be achieved through the elements above.

The combination of these elements helps to communicate an emotion or feeling to the observer of the image, just like poetry can create emotions.

Vincent van Gogh

Songwriter Don McLean was so inspired by van Gogh's masterpiece *The Starry Night* (1889) and by the troubled existence of the artist, he wrote a song called 'Vincent'. After you have read the story of van Gogh's life, the words of the song on page 59 will become more meaningful.

Biography of Vincent van Gogh

On 30 March 1853, a young minister's wife in southern Holland gave birth to a tiny baby with red hair. Little did his proud parents know that this child would be a lost and lonely soul tortured by powerful emotions for his entire life. And little did they know he would become one of the world's most famous artists.

As a child, Vincent was very sensitive, excitable, often moody and sad. His best friend was his younger brother Theo, the one member of the family who seemed to understand him.

At the age of 12, Vincent was sent off to boarding school, but he did not do well and was very isolated and unhappy. However, he developed a love for books and paintings, especially those depicting poor, downtrodden people struggling to survive.

At 16, Vincent left school and began working as a clerk for his uncle, a well-known art dealer. At first he worked in the London office and during this time he fell deeply in love with his landlady's daughter. She did not return his feelings, and this rejection shattered him. He left in a state of deep depression and lived alone, rarely seeing anyone. His letters to his brother Theo were filled with sadness and pain, and yet we can sense his anxious search to find a meaning to life. 'We are not on this earth just to be happy, but to achieve great things and rise above the ordinary existence that almost all of us have to suffer. We must overcome the darkness in our souls.' This belief became the driving force for the rest of his life, even though very few people understood his struggle to achieve it.

Eventually, he returned to Holland, where he became very religious, giving away his belongings and living in poverty. He spent his days helping poor farmers and coalminers, sharing what little food he had and even giving away his clothes. Somehow, he wanted to stop the pain of their poverty by taking it on himself. But he could not offer much and his own health suffered.

In 1880, at the age of 27, he decided that his mission in life was to become an artist. He gave himself to his drawings and paintings – lovingly, frantically and destructively. But everyone thought his paintings were weird and uninteresting. They wanted heroes, whereas for him the real world was the world of ordinary people, poor people struggling to survive.

Everyone other than Theo thought Vincent was irresponsible, unreliable, childish and even crazy. He had no money and relied entirely on his brother Theo to support him. His family and friends were at first disappointed, then saddened, and finally angered by his behaviour. They did not understand what he was searching for. Gradually, his art began to communicate for him: if he could not improve the harsh life of the Dutch peasants at least he could show it in his paintings.

Again Vincent fell in love, this time with a young widow. Again he was rejected, but this time he would not give up. She was so overwhelmed by his passion that in the end her only escape was to attempt suicide. This in turn

Vincent van Gogh

pushed Vincent to madness, as though nothing could ease the turmoil in his soul. His paintings were filled with blues and greys: cold, desperate colours.

He wrote to Theo: 'There is scarcely any colour that is not grey.' In 1886 he left for Paris, but found it too depressing and stifling, and so moved to the south of France where he painted furiously. Impressions crowded in on him, and he felt he must get them all down: the people, the cafes, the streets, the bridges, the farms, the orchards, the flowers. Animating all of these subjects was the sun, giving them gorgeous, brilliant colour. The bright yellow of the sunflower was echoed in countless blossoms and was spilt in great patches over the fields of grain.

In the space of twelve months he produced over 200 paintings and countless drawings. His work was to establish him as a giant of the art world. But at what cost? What had this emotional outpouring done to him? His haunting self-portraits tell us so much about how he saw the world.

Vincent became more and more overwrought and, on the verge of a mental breakdown, cut off one of his ears. On his release from hospital, he found the local townspeople had turned against him. Goaded by the taunts and jeers of small boys calling for his other ear, he cracked and was taken to a mental asylum in nearby St Remy.

Between fits of depression, he achieved an enormous amount of painting for one so ill. He still found the fields as colourful as ever, but the cypresses came to obsess him. He painted them as no-one else ever had – in a flaming torment of movement, of dark colour, of twisting coils. People, however, saw only his insanity. They could not see the beauty – or hear the cry of pain – in his paintings.

In 1890, life finally became too much for him. After a reunion with his family he recovered a little, but in July he shot himself and died in his brother's arms a few days later. He was 37 years old. At the time of his death, Vincent had only ever sold one of his paintings, for a sum equivalent to $80. Over a hundred years later, art dealers around the world scramble to buy a van Gogh and prints of his colourful paintings are seen everywhere. Recently, one of his paintings, *The Sunflowers*, was sold for $35 million.

Vincent van Gogh, *Self Portrait*, 1890
63 × 53 cm, Paris, Louvre

Vincent

Starry, starry night, paint your palette blue and grey,
Look out on a summer's day, with eyes that know the darkness in my soul.
Shadows on the hills, sketch the trees and the daffodils,
Catch the breeze and the winter chills,
In colours on the snowy linen land.

And now I understand what you tried to say to me,
How you suffered for your sanity,
How you tried to set them free.
They would not listen, they did not know how, –
Perhaps they'll listen now.

Starry, starry night, flaming flow'rs that brightly blaze,
Swirling clouds in violet haze reflect in Vincent's eyes of China blue.
Colours changing hue, morning fields of amber grain,
Weathered faces lined in pain,
Are soothed beneath the artist's loving hand.

And now I understand what you tried to say to me,
How you suffered for your sanity,
How you tried to set them free.
They would not listen, they did not know how, –
Perhaps they'll listen now.

For they could not love you,
But still your love was true,
And when no hope was left in sight on that starry, starry night,
You took your life, as lovers often do;
But I could have told you, Vincent,
This world was never meant for one as beautiful as you.

Starry, starry night, portraits hung in empty halls,
Frameless heads on nameless walls, with eyes that watch the world and can't forget.
Like the strangers that you've met, the ragged men in ragged clothes,
The silver thorn of bloody rose,
Lie crushed and broken on the virgin snow.

And now I think I know what you tried to say to me;
How you suffered for your sanity,
How you tried to set them free.
They would not listen,
They're not list'ning still, –
Perhaps they never will.

Don McLean

1   After reading the song (or listening to a recording of it), summarise what you think is the meaning of each verse.

2   Describe or sketch the three images in the poem that stand out in your mind. Write them down and explain why they stand out. For example:

'swirling clouds in violet haze reflect in Vincent's eyes of China blue.'

This is powerful because the image is one of a swirling loss of control like the sky in the painting. His eyes could be a mirror to the uncontrollable pain in his mind.

3   **a**   Explain how McLean wants us to feel about Vincent.
    b   Quote three lines which support your view.

4   Three references are made to Vincent's eyes in the poem: 'with eyes that watch the world and can't forget'; 'eyes that know the darkness of my soul'; 'reflect in Vincent's eyes of China blue'.
    a   Explain why you think McLean has made so many references to Vincent's eyes.
    b   Look at the self-portrait on page 58. How would you describe Vincent's eyes?

Vincent van Gogh, *The Starry Night*, 1889. Oil on canvas, 73.7 × 92.1 cm.
New York, The Museum of Modern Art. Acquired through the Lillie P. Bliss Bequest.
Photograph © 1997 The Museum of Modern Art, New York

1   Look at the painting, *The Starry Night*.
  a   Scan the image carefully for 60 seconds. Cover the picture. Write down
    as many features (buildings, colours, shapes, etc.) as you can remember.
  b   Consider all the visual elements on pages 55–56. How has van Gogh used
    lines to show movement, particularly in the cypress tree and the clouds?
  c   List the various shapes in the painting.
  d   The cypress tree resembles flames reaching across both earth and sky.
    This tree has traditionally been associated with graveyards and mourning.
     i   How does the cypress tree enhance the mood of the painting?
     ii   Why do you think van Gogh chose the cypress?
     iii   How do the diagonal lines of the cypress disturb the equilibrium
      of the horizon?
     iv   Why is the cypress such a dominant image in the painting?
     v   How does our eye tend to travel through the image?
  e   Has van Gogh created a feeling of texture? Explain.
  f   Colours (hue, saturation and value) help to create a particular feeling.
    The dots of yellow highlight the power of the stars and the sky, while the
    darkness of the cypress tree is somewhat threatening. Comment on the
    use of blue in the picture, against the colours of the cypress.
  g   Describe how light and shadow have added dimension.
  h   How has Don McLean captured van Gogh's visual elements in his song
    'Vincent'?

2   a   Match as many lines from the song as you can to parts of the painting.
  b   Choose a word in the song that best describes the sky.
  c   What does the painting tell us about Vincent's state of mind?
  d   Do you think van Gogh has succeeded in capturing the 'darkness in his
    soul'? Explain.

3   The song 'Vincent' is made more meaningful to us because of the information
  we have about the artist. Copy the table below and list the lines from the song
  which loosely relate to the information given in the biography. Some examples
  have been done for you.

Biography	Poem
'We must overcome the darkness in our souls'	*With eyes that know the darkness in my soul*
'Somehow he wanted to stop the pain of their poverty.'	
'They wanted heroes, whereas for him the real world was the world of ordinary people.'	

Biography	Poem
'They could not see the beauty – or hear the cry of pain – in his paintings.'	*They would not listen, they did not know how*
'Goaded by the taunts and jeers of small boys.'	
'There is scarcely any colour that is not grey.'	
'Impressions crowded in on him – the bright yellow of the sunflower.'	*Flaming flowers that brightly blaze*
'He painted them as no-one else had – in a flaming torment of movement, of dark colour, of twisting coils.'	*swirling clouds in violet haze*
'His haunting self-portraits tell us so much about how he saw the world.'	

4 In pairs, create your own song lyrics about Vincent van Gogh.

The Scream

The Scream, 1893, oil and pastel on cardboard, 91 × 73.5 cm, Oslo, National Gallery

The Scream (1893), by Norwegian artist Edvard Munch, is one of the most famous modern paintings. Munch describes the feelings and motives behind the image:

> I was walking along a path with two friends – the sun was setting – suddenly the sky turned blood red – I paused, feeling exhausted, and leaned on the fence – there was blood and tongues of fire above the blue-black fjord and the city – my friends walked on, and I stood there trembling with anxiety – and I sensed an infinite scream passing through nature.

The Scream expresses the loneliness felt by Munch as he looks at the blood red sky. He realises that the earth and nature are more powerful than humans and is haunted by how small and insignificant he feels.

1   In pairs, write down your initial feelings about and reactions to the painting, as well as any other elements that may have contributed to these feelings. Use a spider diagram like the one below.

Activity **3.4**

The Scream

2   Look at how the man screaming is placed at the foreground of the picture. Why do you think Munch did this?

It has been suggested that the 'man' in the painting is not a man at all, but a strange creature probably inspired by a Peruvian mummy that Munch saw at the 1889 Exposition Universelle in Paris. The mummy was crouched in a foetal position with its hands against its face. The hollow mouth and staring eyes in the painting are very powerful images.

Activity 3.5

1   Usually, we are reassured by the image of a face. Munch has shattered this reassurance. How?

2   **a**   What does the body language of the man suggest?
    b   Sketch the man in *The Scream* and label his facial expressions.
    c   Describe how these expressions make you feel.

3   The curved brush strokes tend to 'trap' the man in the painting. What is the effect of this?

4   Lines are very important in this painting. Look at the straight line of the bridge and how it appears never-ending. Suggest how this may relate to the scream of the man.

5   The colours used are very powerful. Comment on why Munch used such dramatic colours.

The Scream, 1895, lithograph, 35 × 25 cm, Oslo, Munch Museet

Munch did four versions of the painting and in 1895 he translated *The Scream* into a black-and-white lithograph that could be reproduced all over the world. This began the process of turning the original artwork into a mass-produced cultural object. *The Scream* has become an influential part of our culture. It has inspired T-shirts, movies and even coffee mugs.

Many people in society have been influenced by *The Scream*. Andy Warhol, the pop artist famous for his prints of Marilyn Monroe and Campbell soup cans, designed a series of silkscreen prints that were influenced by Munch and *The Scream*. In the movie *Home Alone,* Macauley Culkin imitated the figure. The image has also influenced a series of horror movies by Wes Craven, where a Halloween mask resembles the face of the screaming figure.

In 1991, American Robert Fishbone began selling inflatable dolls of the figure in the painting and has now sold hundreds of thousands of them. Some critics say people like Fishbone have destroyed the meaning of *The Scream* by taking the central figure out of the painting.

Activity 3.6

1 a Do you feel the painting needs the central figure of the screaming man? Explain.
   b Describe what the effect of the painting would be without the figure.
   c Give your opinion on whether the screaming figure is a successful image on its own without the background.

2 Look at the black and white lithograph of *The Scream* opposite. The lithograph has very distinct and bold lines compared to the softer lines of the coloured version.
   a Suggest how this helps to draw our attention to certain features.
   b Describe how the shadowing differs in each image.
   c Explain the effect this has on the mood of the painting.

Poets too have been affected by the painting.

The Scream

A jetty
spiders out of the sea.
The sky's blood-vessels break.

A sound from the unbuilt future
rises with whining shrillness –
its hot needle presses
through the base of the solitary head.

Hands valve down onto ears. Sound
earths in nerves of terror.

B. C. Leale

Notice how Leale has immediately focused on the jetty and how it intrudes into the picture, just as in the painting your eye tends to notice the jetty first.

Activity 3.7

1   a   Describe the feelings you get from the metaphor 'A jetty spiders out of the sea'.
    b   Do you think this matches the feelings you get from the painting? Explain.

2   Look at the line 'The sky's blood-vessels break'. How well do you think this describes the sky in Munch's painting? (Think particularly about shape and colour.)

3   Sketch your interpretation of 'A jetty spiders out of the sea. The sky's blood-vessels break.'

4   While Munch uses visual elements to help us imagine the scream of the man, Leale describes the sound of the scream with powerful and descriptive language. Explain why 'A sound from the unbuilt future' is so frightening.

5   The scream 'rises with whining shrillness'.
    a   Describe what you think this means.
    b   Suggest an instrument or object you think could make this sound.

6   Describe the mood of Leale's poem. You may choose to answer by drawing, discussing in groups or writing your own poem or song.

7   Imagine a musical interpretation of Edvard Munch's *The Scream* and B. C. Leale's poem.
    a   Suggest a style of music you would use.
    b   What particular musical instruments could highlight the mood?

8   Overall, how well do you think Leale has interpreted the emotions of Munch's painting? Does the poem match your feelings about the painting? Explain.

Chapter 4

A single raindrop
Slides silently down the leaf.
Still waters ripple.

Forms of poetry

Limericks

A limerick is a poem of five lines, which is meant to be absurd and witty. It is often thought of as 'nonsense' verse, and tells of unlikely events.

- the first, second and fifth lines rhyme and have the same number of beats

- the third and fourth lines rhyme and have the same number of beats. These lines are shorter than the others

- the rhyme scheme is a, a, b, b, a

- the rhyme depends on sound, and not necessarily on spelling

- the humour is contained in the 'punch line' – the last line – of the limerick

- you can create humour by playing with words and 'forcing' rhymes

There was a young man of Bengal
Who went to a fancy-dress ball.
He went, just for fun,
Dressed up as a bun,
And a dog ate him up in the hall.

A greedy young maiden named Firkins   **a**
Would recklessly gorge on raw gherkins   **a**
Till one day on a spree   **b**
She consumed eighty-three   **b**
And pickled her innermost workin's.   **a**

A right-handed fellow named Wright,
In writing 'write' always wrote 'rite'
Where he meant to write right.
If he'd written 'write' right,
Wright would not have wrought rot writing 'rite'.

There was an old man of Blackheath,
Who sat on his set of false teeth.
Said he, with a start,
'O dear, bless my heart!
I've bitten myself underneath.'

A thrifty young fellow of Shoreham
Made brown paper trousers and woreham;
He looked nice and neat
Till he bent in the street
To pick up a pin, then he toreham.

1 Complete the following limericks by matching the stem (the first two lines) from a–e with a suitable response (the last three lines) from i–v. Rewrite each limerick in your notebook.

a There was a young lady of Ryde
   Who ate a green apple and died.
b A sea-serpent saw a big tanker,
   Bit a hole in her side and then sank her.
c There was a young lady of Lynn
   Who was so excessively thin
d There was an old person of Crewe
   Who found a dead mouse in his stew.
e A wonderful bird is the pelican
   His beak can hold more than his belican.

i It swallowed the crew
   In a minute or two,
   And then picked its teeth with the anchor.
ii Said the waiter: 'Don't shout
   And wave it about,
   Or the rest will be wanting one too!'
iii He can take in his beak
   Enough food for a week,
   I'm blowed if I know how the helican.
iv That when she essayed
   To drink lemonade
   She slipped through the straw and fell in!
v The apple fermented
   Inside the lamented
   And made cider inside 'er inside.

1 Working in small groups, complete the last three lines of the following limericks. As you go, brainstorm and create lists of rhyming words which you could use. It can also be helpful to clap out the rhythm of your limerick to check that you have the correct number of beats. Remember, the first, second and fifth lines should have three beats; the third and fourth lines two.

   a   There was an old dog from Kowloon
       Whose head looked just like a balloon . . .

   b   There was a young fellow called Pete
       Whose nose was as big as his feet . . .

   c   A lovely young lady from Lorne
       Loved to sing and dance until dawn . . .

   d   There was an old man from Peru
       Who dreamt he was eating his shoe . . .

2 In small groups, create your own limericks using the following first lines. Again, create lists of rhyming words to use, and check that you have the correct rhythm by clapping out the beat.

   a   There was a young man with a pimple . . .
   b   A man with a hideous nose . . .
   c   A woman who hailed from Calcutta . . .
   d   An extra-terrestrial from Mars . . .

3 Explain why you think limericks are so popular.

4 Choose from the activities below to accompany your work on limericks:

   a   Get help with writing your own limericks using online rhyming dictionaries. There are plenty of these on the Internet, and they're great for providing rhyming words and phrases when you're stuck for ideas. Some useful sites include:
- www.rhymezone.com
- www.writeexpress.com
- www.lexfn.com
- www.rhymer.com
- www.analogx.com
- www.yindii.com
- dictionary.langenberg.com

   b   Play Pictionary in groups with vocabulary generated from your rhyming lists.

   c   Draw a cartoon about one of the limericks you have written.

   d   Create an imaginative border to surround a limerick.

   e   Using a computer, modify the font or formatting of a limerick for effect. Add Clip Art or other visuals to enhance the meaning.

   f   Compile a limerick anthology using the limericks you have written, complete with illustrations or computer visuals. Present it as a book. (This could be an individual or group task.)

Ruptured rhymes

Ruptured rhymes are poems that make fun of traditional nursery rhymes, fairytales or well-known stories. They are parodies; that is, they imitate and exaggerate the work of others in order to amuse us. When you write a parody, you express humorously what some other writer has expressed seriously.

Twinkle twinkle movie star
In your flashy limo-car.
How you shine with diamonds bright
Flashing smiles of dentures white.
Twinkle twinkle little star
For soon you won't know who you are.

Danny Wee

Update

Little Miss Muffet sits on a tuffet
Treating her curves,
And waves.

But people beside her just mock and
deride her,
And *laugh* at the way
She behaves.

While Little Jack Horner sits in a corner,
Mending his motor bike.
He puts in a screw, and says 'That'll do.
Now I can go where I like!'

Joyce Trickett

In *Revolting Rhymes*, Roald Dahl has fun parodying various fairytales, including *Jack and the Beanstalk*.

He murmured softly, 'Golly-gosh,
'I guess I'll *have* to take a wash
'If I am going to climb this tree
'Without the giant smelling me.
'In fact, a bath's my only hope . . . '
He rushed indoors and grabbed the soap
He scrubbed his body everywhere.
He even washed and rinsed his hair.
He did his teeth, he blew his nose
And went out smelling like a rose.
Once more he climbed the mighty bean.
The Giant sat there, gross, obscene,
Muttering through his vicious teeth
(While Jack sat tensely just beneath),
Muttering loud, 'FEE FI FO FUM,
'RIGHT NOW I CAN'T SMELL ANYONE.'

Jack waited till the Giant slept,
Then out along the boughs he crept
And gathered so much gold, I swear
He was an instant millionaire.
'A bath,' he said, 'does seem to pay.
'I'm going to have one every day.'

Roald Dahl, from 'Jack and the Beanstalk',
in *Revolting Rhymes*

Activity 4.3

1   In pairs, create a list of some well-known nursery rhymes (for example, 'Mary had a little lamb', 'Georgie Porgie', 'There was an old woman who lived in a shoe', or fairytales, such as *Cinderella, Red Riding Hood*, or *Sleeping Beauty*. Share your list with others.

2   In groups, choose one of these rhymes or fairytales and 'rupture' it. This parody may be done by:
    • updating the nursery rhyme to modern times
    • making the story and characters humorous
    • using a well-known character in an unexpected or different way
    • giving a new 'twist' to the events that occur in the story
    • having animals or objects act or speak like humans
    • creating a different or unexpected ending.

3   Illustrate your ruptured rhyme.

4   Perform your ruptured rhyme in front of the class. If you have multiple characters, give 'roles' to each person in the group. You may even need a narrator.

Acrostic poems

An acrostic poem is one in which the first letter of each line, read downwards, spells a word.

School

Sounds of
Chaos
Hurt my soul.
Obnoxious
Oafs
Litter my thoughts with dread.

Sandy

She has soft eyes
And light brown hair.
No-one sees her on the stair
Dealing alone with her quiet sighs,
Yet we know that there she cries.

Football

Feet
Out to beat
Organise the
Team
Better
And we may
Lick them and not come
Last

Activity **4.4**

1   Write an acrostic poem using your first name. Here's an example:

C urious
H eadstrong, happily
R esisting instruction.
I nventive and
S weet.

If your first name is very short, you can use your last name as well.

2   Working in pairs choose one of the topics below:
   - disaster
   - criminals
   - winning
   - losing
   - hunger
   - friendship
   - hardship
   - your own choice (this must be at least six letters long).

   a   Draw a mind map of words and phrases that you associate with the topic (remember that they must start with the letters it contains).
   b   Write an acrostic poem about your topic using the words and phrases that you think best describe it.
   c   Create a collage to accompany your poem.

Alphabet poems

Alphabet poems are like acrostic poems but do not spell a word. Instead, each new word or line begins with the next letter of the alphabet. They may go from A to Z, or from Z to A. Here is an example, based on the subject of 'Netball':

Netball

Athletic barging,
Contacting, defending.
Every fortunate, giggling, happy,
      idiotic, jumping, kindly lady
Must not overdo pivots.
Quietly remark: 'Such terrible
      umpiring!'
Vault with expertise,
Yet zone

1   Write your own alphabet poem of 26 words, in which every word begins with the next letter of the alphabet. You will need to use a dictionary or thesaurus to help you, because finding words for the last few letters can be quite difficult! To make it easier for you, you may use words beginning with *ex-* rather than *x*, as in the example opposite.

Activity **4.5**

2   Play the 'Dictionary Game'.
    a   Have one person in the class open a dictionary at random.
    b   That person looks at the pages and chooses a word. This is then written on the board.
    c   Pass the dictionary to the next person, who will again randomly open it, choose one word, and have it added to the list.
    d   Pass the dictionary around the group until everyone has chosen a word at random. You might end up with words such as these: *nurture, dismissive, goad, twit, sickly, funky, parfait, edition, indifferent, bizarre, hippy, child, rampage, lonesome, wayward, tyrannical, barrage, adroit.*
    e   Once all the words are on the board, each person uses them to write a poem. Try to use as many of the words as possible. You can also challenge yourself by making up phrases or sentences with two or more of the words, such as *bizarre parfait, the tyrannical twit goaded the lonesome child*, or *a barrage of funky indifference.* Be as creative as you like!

Numerical poems

Numerical poems are a fun way of working with letters and numbers at the same time; a marriage of poetry and maths, if you like. Even though they are usually concerned with one thing – the length of the poem itself – the form can be played around with to indicate not just a poem's length, but its 'value' as well. Some examples are on page 76:

The first line of this poem is 20 letters longer than the second line.

This poem
contains precisely
32 letters.

If I
was lucky enough
to be given
one dollar
for every letter
in this poem
I would have
$69.00.

Activity 4.6

1   Write your own numerical poem based on the number of letters it contains. Give your poem a title.

2   In groups, create a series of numerical puzzle poems for other groups to solve. No calculators allowed!
    For example:

> This poem
> is about a number
> which is 15 more than 37
> but 12 less
> than 64.

> This is a poem
> about a number
> which is divisible by 7,
> as well as by 4
> and, when multiplied by 2
> gives you
> 56.

3   Code breaker: decipher the following diagram and write it as a poem. All the numbers correspond to the letters of the alphabet. Use any format or pattern you like for the representation of your poem, and illustrate it in a way which shows or enhances its meaning. Give your poem a title.

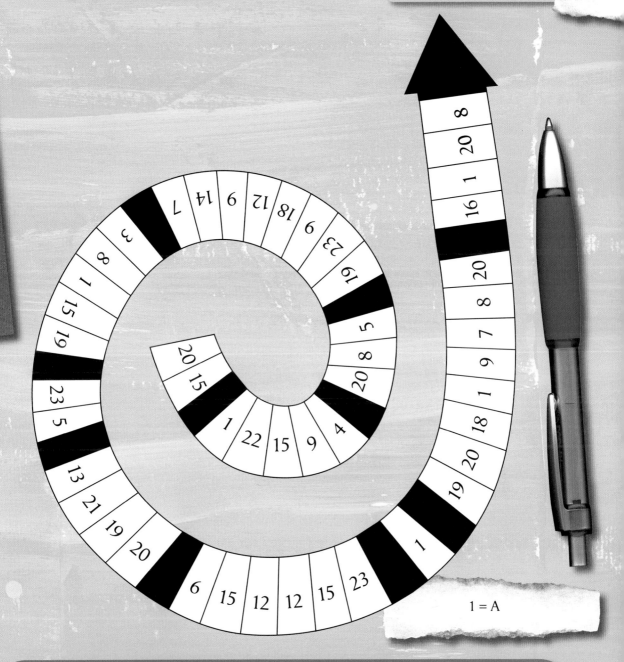

1 = A

Oriental poetry

Haiku

Haiku originates in Japan and is a very old form of poetry. The aim of a haiku is to capture a single idea, moment or feeling in a clear and precise description. It appears simple, yet allows us to create strong visual images and comparisons.

Yuki tokete,
Mura ippai no
Kodomo kana.

Issa

Snow having melted
The whole village is brimful
Of happy children.

The haiku captures a single, fleeting moment, usually to do with nature, the seasons, the weather or the time of day. It contains powerful images in a few words.

The haiku:
- is written in the present tense
- is unrhymed
- has 3 lines and 17 syllables organised into a 5, 7, 5 sequence.

Note the syllable count in each of these haiku:

Life lesson

```
  1   2     3  4  5
The fierce wind rages
  1 2 3   4    5    6   7
And I see how trees survive –
  1   2     3    4    5
They have learned to bend.
```

Don Raye

```
1 2   3   4    5
A single raindrop
  1     2 3 4   5   6   7
Slides silently down the leaf.
  1    2   3   4 5
Still waters ripple.
```

Here Roger McGough has fun with the haiku form:

Two haiku

only trouble with
Japanese haiku is that
you write one, and then

only seventeen
syllables later you want
to write another

Roger McGough

Look at the way in which the following writers use the 'ingredients' of a haiku. Identify the comparisons being made in each one.

Sunset

Sunset on the sea
drawing cold shapes on water
on wavy canvas.

Stuart Taylor

Aeroplane

It glides through the night
as calm as the silver lake
as swift as a dove.

Ingrid Ryan

Cherry Blossoms

Cherry blossoms fall
On watery rice-plant beds:
Stars in the moonlight.

Buson

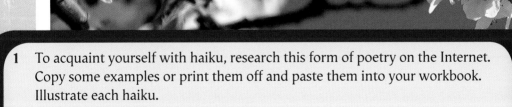

1   To acquaint yourself with haiku, research this form of poetry on the Internet. Copy some examples or print them off and paste them into your workbook. Illustrate each haiku.

2   Complete the last line of this haiku:
      The little girl danced
      Her feet stamping the hard ground
      _ _ _ _ _

3   Complete the next two lines of this haiku:
      The dry falling leaves
      _ _ _ _ _ _ _
      _ _ _ _ _

Sesshu, *Autumn Landscape*,
National Museum, Tokyo
(The Zauho Press)

Eitoku, *Plum-trees by Water*,
Juko-in, Kyoto (Kodansha
Ltd, Tokyo)

Miyamoto Musashi, *Bird on
Branch*, 1584–1645, Philadelp[
Museum of Art: Purchased w
the Fiske Kimball Fund and t
Marie Kimball Fund, 1968

Activity 4.9

1   Choose one of the Japanese paintings above. Write down the words, phrases,
    thoughts and impressions that come to mind as you look at it (you could do
    this in the form of a list, table, mind map or graphic organiser). Ask yourself:
    a   What is happening in the picture?
    b   What is the dominant image?
    c   What colours are used?
    d   How is the mood of the painting affected by the medium used
        (watercolour or ink) and the visual style?

2   Use your collection of words or phrases to write your own haiku in response
    to the painting (you may need to play around with alternative words to fit the
    5, 7, 5 syllable format).

3   Go for a walk outside your classroom, or use your own backyard, to carefully
    observe your natural surroundings. Make a mind map about what you see,
    hear, smell and touch. Choose one particular aspect of nature and write a
    haiku about it. Challenge yourself to create a comparison in the last line.

4   Illustrate your haiku with your own drawing or painting, or wordprocess it
    on the computer. Experiment with colour, font, layout and visuals so that you
    capture the mood of your haiku.

Tanka

The tanka is also a Japanese form of poetry, much older but less well-known than the haiku. It is longer than a haiku, so it allows an image to be extended and gives the poet room to express feelings in more depth. Ideally a tanka should create a vivid image which is related to emotions. It is unrhymed, has five lines and contains 31 syllables, organised into a sequence of 5, 7, 5, 7, 7.

Adversity

Debris in the wind
Indiscriminately blinds
Eyes searching a path.
To turn one's back to the wind
Reveals but where one has been.

here the last two lines provide a comment about the subject

Don Raye

Papers

The pile of papers
Sprawled across this office desk
Are but memories
Of random skittery thoughts
Flitting past my vacant gaze

here the last three lines provide a comparison between paper and memory or thought

Anonymous

1 Complete the following tankas:

a *Words on this white page
Seem to leap, dance, sway and swirl
They jump at my eyes
– – – – – – –
– – – – – – –*

b *The panting old dog
waits wearily in the heat.
– – – – –
– – – – – – –
– – – – – – –*

Activity **4.10**

c   *Stormy wind blowing*

_ _ _ _ _ _ _

_ _ _ _ _

_ _ _ _ _ _ _

_ _ _ _ _ _ _

2   Create a collection of your own haiku and tanka poems – at least three of each. Both these forms look authentic when written on scrolls of rice paper, but you could use coloured tissue paper or parchment. The bamboo ends can be substituted with short pieces of dowel. You could illustrate your poems in black ink or watercolours.

3   Read your poems to the class. Choose background music (traditional Oriental music would be great if you can locate it) to create the right atmosphere as you read.

Cinquains

A cinquain is a poem of five lines. There are two forms. The first type, which we could call a 'syllable cinquain', is similar to the haiku and the tanka, in that the length of each line is based on a set number of syllables. The five lines have the following syllable pattern: 2, 4, 6, 8, 2. Here are two examples:

It seems	2
That barbed comments	4
Baited with some small joke	6
Hook themselves well into the soul	8
And rip.	2

Sue Marsden (student)

Happy
I was, because
I knew all that I wished
To know, and questioned no further
Than that.

Sue Marsden (student)

The second form is called a 'word cinquain' and relies upon a set number of words per line. It uses nouns, adjectives and verbs to make up its pattern. This poem about moonlight is a word cinquain:

Moonlight
Dazzling, silver
Shimmers, swells, covers
My coolness and fear
Spotlight

line 1: one word naming the subject of the poem (noun)
line 2: two words describing the subject (adjectives)
line 3: three words describing the subject's actions (verbs)
line 4: four words giving the writer's *feelings* about the subject
line 5: one word giving another name for the subject (noun)

Dawn
Escaping sun
Singing, flooding, warming
Making me smile, smile
Daylight

Mother
cuddly, warm
protects, teaches, encourages
always finds a way
love

Sea
Deep dark
Heaving, breaking, crunching
I shiver and shake
Power

Sunset
Blazing golden
Sinks ships, swallows
Warms me, saddens me
Dying

Activity **4.11**

1 Complete the following word cinquains. Remember to use the right number of words per line, as well as nouns, verbs and adjectives.

a *Me*
Individual, different
– – –
– – – –
–

b *Friendship*
Lasting, special
– – –
– – – –
–

2 Create a greeting card for a birthday, anniversary or other special occasion, or a 'get well' card, using either the syllable cinquain or word cinquain form. Draw an illustration on your card, or use images from the computer, magazines or old greeting cards.

Dylan Thomas portraits

This type of poem is named after the Welsh poet Dylan Thomas, who used words experimentally. This form focuses on the senses and begins with the question: 'Did you ever . . . ?' The question is then answered with a description. Dylan Thomas portraits are always written in couplet form, a couplet being two lines of poetry.

Sound

Did you ever hear a classroom?
Voices rumbling, chairs scraping, teacher shouting.

Touch

Did you ever feel a toad?
Rough-skinned, stomach swollen, throat pulsating.

Sight

Did you ever see a snake?
Zig-zagging, fork-tongued, elastic-jawed.

Did you ever see a cat?
Highly-polished, radar-eyed, bewitched.

Activity **4.12**

With a partner, write your own Dylan Thomas portraits in which you answer questions beginning with the following:

a Did you ever see a . . . ?
b Did you ever hear a . . . ?
c Did you ever touch/feel a . . . ?
d Did you ever taste a . . . ?
e Did you ever smell a . . . ?

Ezra Pound couplets

Ezra Pound was an American poet. He wrote unrhymed couplets that made powerful descriptive comparisons. These comparisons are metaphors, in which one thing is said to *be* another. In the Ezra Pound couplet there are two statements:

• an image, presented in the first line
• a comparison, presented in the second line.

> The apparition of these faces in the crowd;
> Petals on a wet, black bough.
>
> Ezra Pound

> Press bulbs flash round the suspect
> Lightning X-rays the storm clouds.
>
> Ron Pretty

> A fisherman inspecting his net;
> A spider patrolling his web.

Activity 4.13

1 Write your own Ezra Pound couplet, in which you provide a comparison for one of the following:
   a   sunbaking bodies on the beach
   b   a mosquito heading for its target
   c   an ant dragging food away
   d   unhappy faces in a crowd
   e   a tall dancer on tiptoe.

2 a   In pairs, each person writes the first line of an Ezra Pound couplet. Then swap with your partner and complete each other's couplets.
   b   Draw, paint, create a collage or use computer visuals to accompany your completed poem. These visuals should highlight or accentuate the comparison being made.
   c   Share your poems with the class as a duologue, accompanied by your visuals.

Shape poems

Shape poems are visual and are written according to the shape of the poem's subject matter. 'Freewheeling Frank' is a good example of a shape poem.

Freewheeling Frank

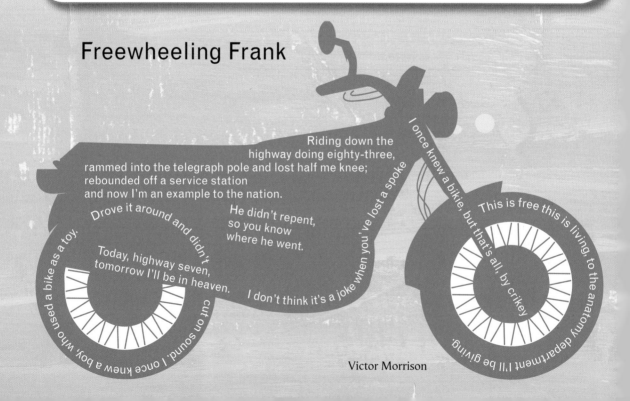

Riding down the
highway doing eighty-three,
rammed into the telegraph pole and lost half me knee;
rebounded off a service station
and now I'm an example to the nation.

Drove it around and didn't

He didn't repent,
so you know
where he went.

I once knew a bikie, but that's all, by crikey

This is free this is living, to the anatomy department I'll be giving.

I once knew a spoke when you've lost a spoke

Today, highway seven,
tomorrow I'll be in heaven.

who used a bike as a toy.

cut on sound. I once knew a boy,

I don't think it's a joke

Victor Morrison

1 Read 'Freewheeling Frank' and discuss in groups what you think the order of lines should be. Be prepared to defend or explain your reasons.

2 Write out the poem in your book according to the order you choose. Compare your version with the others in your group.

3 When the poem is written out like this, does it have more or less impact? Explain.

4 Which of the two versions do you think is more effective? Why?

Bowling ball

I'm a rolling bowling ball coming down the aisle hitting pins for six and making people smile.

Jellyfish

Jelly-like
folding spreading,
oozing, melting, colourless
stinging, paralysing, eating
innardless, boneless, brainless

Tentacles flowing
waving weaving
bending stretching
reaching outwards
searching swinging
hungry killer

A.K.

Kite

I
Wish
I were a
kite on high
I could fly up to the sky
Up to the blue sky
High as a cloud
I wish I were
A kite
High
Up
Up
Up
Up
+ + + + + + + + + + + + + + +

Mirror

When you look   kool uoy nehW
into a mirror   rorrim a otni
it is not   ton si ti
yourself you see,   ,ees uoy flesruoy
but a kind   dnik a tub
of apish error   rorre hsipa fo
posed in fearful   lufraef ni desop
symmetry.   .yrtemmys

John Updike

Sailing

Sailing with ease

Calm and gentle

Peaceful

Drifting in the breeze

Sailing ship

Amongst the warm currents

Activity 4.15

1   Which of the shape poems appeals to you the most? Why?

2   Write your own shape poem. Here are some ideas to help you:
    - a shoe
    - a map of Australia
    - a cat
    - a face
    - a musical instrument
    - a bike
    - a house
    - a Christmas tree
    - a whirlpool
    - a soccer ball
    - a bowtie
    - a TV set
    - a cloud
    - a cricket bat
    - a dog
    - skyscrapers
    - a fish
    - a snake
    - a tennis racquet
    - a butterfly.

3   Transform one of the poems below into a shape poem.

Exhilarating balloon

Up, up, away from the earth.
No sound except for the burners,
See the birds, clearly and closely.

No window to obstruct view,
Ground spread out below.
To float, to fly and to hover.

Pretty coloured balloons,
Big, filled with hot air,
Glorious, exciting and exhilarating.

Anonymous

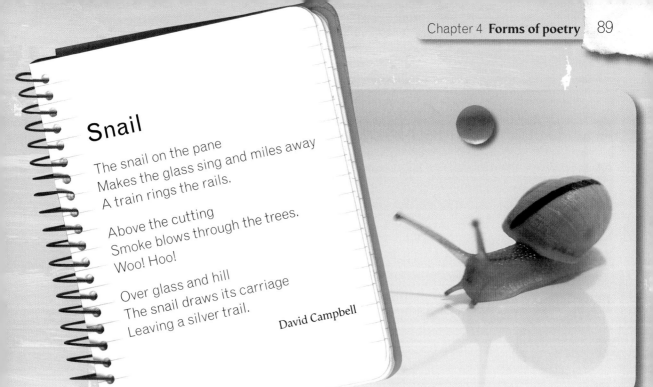

Snail

The snail on the pane
Makes the glass sing and miles away
A train rings the rails.

Above the cutting
Smoke blows through the trees.
Woo! Hoo!

Over glass and hill
The snail draws its carriage
Leaving a silver trail.

David Campbell

Spoonerisms

Spoonerisms occur when you accidentally or deliberately mix up the first letters in two or more words. When you say 'flang out the hag', instead of 'hang out the flag', that's a spoonerism. The name comes from the Reverend William Archibald Spooner, a dean of Oxford, who made this type of blunder so often that 'spoonerism' was entered into the *Oxford English Dictionary* in his own lifetime. Some of Spooner's gaffes include: 'The Lord is thy shoving leopard' and 'You hissed my mystery lecture'. Once he referred to Queen Victoria as 'our queer old dean', and reprimanded one of his students for 'fighting a liar in the quadrangle'. Spooner was also an absent-minded professor. After a Sunday service he informed his congregation: 'In the sermon I have just preached, whenever I said Aristotle, I meant St. Paul.' Spooner's tendency to confuse words and sounds does not mean he was stupid, however; his mind was so quick that his tongue couldn't keep up. The Greeks had a word for this – 'metathesis' – the act of switching things around.

The two poems on pages 90–91 both rely on the use of spoonerisms for their humour. Take note of the way that the writers have played around with the spelling of words in some instances, in order for the spoonerism itself to make more sense. 'Carrots and peas', for instance, would become 'parrots and ceas' if it were a simple swap of the initial letters. It becomes more meaningful, however, and more humorous, when written as 'parrots and keys'.

Dom, Hick and Tarry net on each other's gerves

Dom: Whose cloe tail nippings are these in the pantry?

Hick: Mine, nomething to sibble on with nasal huts.

Tarry: You have disgustingly mad banners!
         That's even worse than nicking your pose,
         you bowel feast.

Hick: Well at least I shake towers,
         whereas *you* smell like a dobber's rog!

Dom: Would you two stop your pit nicking?
         People who live in hass glouses shouldn't stow thrones.
         I've got fired teet – I seed to nit down.
         Do we have a cack of pards anywhere?

Hick: Why don't we play wenty twun, or mould aide?
         I've got my chucky larm!

Tarry: Norely shot your cloe tail nippings?

Hick: No, my ucky lundies.
         Let's put on some Spruce Bringsteen
         and make some chilled greese sandwiches
         while Dom keels the dards!

Dom: Hook lere, we won't be listening to Spruce Bringsteen,
         or making chilled greese sandwiches.
         We won't even be claying any pards.
         The who of tarts, the whore of farts,
         the spore of fades, *and* the clive of fubbs
         are pot in the nack!
         A dot in the ohark and I'd say you were
         cattling my rage.

Hick: Sorry . . . I ate them when we were out of rusty crolls.
         I think you'll find that the space of aids
         and the clue of tubs are missing as well . . .

Dom: Why on earth cibble nards
         when there's a pack of sties in the freezer,
         not to mention all the parrots and keys?

Hick: I don't like parrots and keys . . .

Tarry: Either do nigh . . .

Dom: Hod gelp me!
         You two are as thick as shoo plort tanks!
         I'm hetting out of gear – host paste.
         Now hift your sheds – I can't see tots on welly.

Barbara Ellis

Hicks in your bread

'I'm as jober as a sudge,'
Said the can to the mop
When the lashing flue bight
Brought his star to a cop.

'O yes you have,'
Said the sop with a cye.
'Your blighs are all eerie
And your heedings far too rye.'

'I haven't drad a hink,'
Said the slan with a mur.
'Or maybe tun or woo
But not enough to stause a cur.'

The dery next vay
The sagistrate med
'You're a fangerous dool
With hicks in your bread.

Your gicence has lawn
And you've fot a big gine.
That'll deach you to trive
At point zero nine.'

Jo Marinus

Activity **4.16**

1   Explain why you think spoonerisms are so popular.

2   Change the following words and phrases into spoonerisms:
   - butterfly
   - a well-oiled bicycle
   - a cosy little nook
   - a half-formed wish
   - you have wasted two terms
   - a crushing blow
   - blow your nose
   - it's pouring with rain
   - pack of lies
   - he's a stamp dealer
   - this is the fun part
   - at the speed of light
   - bowl of salad
   - curling my hair
   - where's the bird?
   - falls through the cracks
   - soft-boiled eggs
   - toasted rolls
   - French tortes
   - sleepy time
   - Cinderella and the Handsome Prince
   - Sleeping Beauty
   - my socks have holes
   - mother bear
   - out of the shower.

3   Write down your ten favourite spoonerisms chosen from either poem. What is it about these particular ones that you enjoyed?

4   Many of the images in the poems are made more vivid because they are spoonerisms. Try, for example, to translate them. What happens to the humour when they are read or written in 'normal' English?

5   Create a drawing which conveys or enhances one of the images in the poems.

6   In groups of three, dramatise one of the poems for the rest of the class. You will need to practise the lines so that your delivery is fluent.

7   Transform 'Hicks in your bread' into an advertisement or poster on the dangers of drink driving.

8   Research spoonerisms on the Internet – there are plenty of websites dedicated to these 'tips of the slung'! Collect as many spoonerisms as you can and, in groups, use them to create a poem. You will need to have a brainstorming session in which you decide such things as the topic, storyline, and characters and dialogue (if these are used).

Ballads

Ballads are narrative poems: they tell a story. They are usually concerned with a strongly emotional or dramatic event and therefore also contain a lyrical element (see page 105) by presenting a character's state of mind or feelings. Ballads were originally an oral form of poetry, passed on from generation to generation by word of mouth, and then came to be written down. The word 'ballad' comes from the Latin *ballare* (to dance) and, originally, ballads were sung to accompany dances. Later, the name came to mean any poem composed and sung by minstrels, who were travelling performers.

The traditional ballad tells a clear and straightforward story using strong characters, simple language, easy-to-follow actions and sometimes suspense as the full story is gradually revealed. Ballads have strong rhythm, rhyme and repetition, and are usually arranged in quatrains – four-line stanzas or groups of lines which often rhyme.

'The ballad of the drover' is an Australian bush ballad written by Henry Lawson in 1889. Its strong rhyme, rhythm and repetition, and the use of simple language allows it to be read easily. It establishes powerful contrasts – storm and calm, drought and flood, life and death, love and loss – to dramatically tell a tragic tale.

Structure/Vocabulary   Language features

The ballad of the drover

<u>Across</u> the stony ridges,
    <u>Across</u> the rolling plain,   **a**   repetition of 'across'
Young Harry Dale, the drover,   **b**   accentuates distance
    Comes riding home again.   **c**
<u>And</u> well his stock-horse bears him.   **b**
    <u>And</u> light of heart is he,   establishes the mood
<u>And</u> stoutly his old pack-horse
    Is <u>trotting</u> by his knee.

orientation: sets the scene and introduces characters

structure: eight-line stanzas written as two sets of rhyming quatrains. The end of each quatrain is indicated by a full-stop or a semi-colon

rhyme scheme: a, b, c, b

repetition of 'And' quickens the pace/tempo; reinforced by the word 'trotting'

continuation of the orientation: a further setting of the scene

hobble-chains: chains used to tether the horses so that their movement is limited – they can't run away

Up Queensland way with cattle
    He travelled regions vast;
And many months have vanished
    Since home-folk saw him last.
He hums a song of someone
    He hopes to marry soon;
And hobble-chains and camp-ware
    Keep jingling to the tune.

words emphasise the hard, lonely life of the drover and his family

alliteration – repetition of the soft 's' sound creates a pleasant mood (reinforced by the softness of the words 'hums' and 'hopes')

onomatopoeia: 'jingling' creates a mood of contentment. Harry is carefree. The last two lines have a melodic tempo

dado: a strip of wallpaper or paint just below the picture rail in a room; used here as another word for 'horizon'

yon: short for 'beyond'

thitherward: going towards a place in the distance

Beyond the hazy dado
    Against the lower skies
And yon blue line of ranges
    The homestead station lies.
And thitherward the drover
    Jogs through the lazy noon,
While hobble-chains and camp-ware
    Are jingling to a tune.

assonance slows the pace and creates a restful mood

personification of 'noon' as 'lazy' creates a gentle, unhurried mood, reinforced by the word 'jogs'

repetition of lines highlights the slow, contented pace but also sets up a later contrast

complication: tension is created which contrasts with the calm of the previous stanzas; heightened further with the use of the word 'But'

An hour has filled the heavens
    With storm-clouds inky black;
At times the lightning trickles
    Around the drover's track;
But Harry pushes onward,
    His horses' strength he tries,
In hope to reach the river
    Before the flood shall rise.

personification changes the mood from cheerful to ominous, reinforced by the vivid imagery in 'inky black'

lines speed up the pace and create a sense of urgency

tension is further heightened

torrent: a violent, unceasing downpour

runs a banker: a river in flood

The thunder from above him
    Goes rolling o'er the plain;
And down on thirsty pastures
    In torrents falls the rain.
And every creek and gully
    Sends forth its little flood,
Till the river runs a banker,
    All stained with yellow mud.

assonance captures the rhythm of rumbling thunder

personification reinforces the image of drought-stricken land

alliteration suggests softness, enhanced by the word 'little'. This is ironic as it contrasts with the torrential nature of the flood

breasted: to wade through, submerged up to the chest; to face or oppose

gutter: the channel of water in the middle of the river

tension is eased: Harry's words are strong and confident

Now Harry speaks to Rover,
    The best dog on the plains,
And to his hardy horses,
    And strokes their shaggy manes:
'We've breasted bigger rivers
    When floods were at their height,
Nor shall this gutter stop us
    From getting home to-night!'

alliteration, though soft, emphasises strength; this aligns with Harry's strong-willed determination

climax: the tension is at its peak – signified by the use of menacing vocabulary

The thunder growls a warning,
    The ghastly lightnings gleam,
As the drover turns his horses
    To swim the fatal stream.
But, oh! the flood runs stronger
    Than e'er it ran before;
The saddle-horse is failing,
    And only half-way o'er!

personification highlights the power of the thunder; its 'warning' is strong and menacing

alliteration is harsh and reinforces the sinister mood

words and phrases used accentuate the futility of Harry's attempt to cross the river – his fate is foreshadowed

flood's grey breast: the heart of the river

blank: there is no sign of Harry or his stock horse

tension eases as we learn of Harry's fate

When flashes next the lightning,
    The flood's grey breast is blank,
And a cattle dog and pack-horse
    Are struggling up the bank.
But in the lonely homestead
    The girl will wait in vain –
He'll never pass the stations
    In charge of stock again.

metaphor emphasises the depth and danger of the muddy river

assonance slows down the rhythm and creates a sad tone, reinforced by 'lonely' and 'in vain'

further complication: tension rises

The faithful dog a moment
    Sits panting on the bank,
And then swims through the current
    To where his master sank.
And round and round in circles
    He fights with failing strength,
Til, borne down by the waters,
    The old dog sinks at length.

assonance creates a 'rolling' rhythm, mirrored in the word 'circles'

alliteration contrasts the dog's bravery with futility

denouement: the tension winds down

sodden loam: drenched, soggy soil

dumb tidings: the lone horse brings news but it is not able to communicate the tale

Across the flooded lowland<u>s</u>
    And <u>s</u>lopes of <u>s</u>odden loam
The pack-hor<u>se</u> <u>s</u>truggles onward,
    To take dumb tidings home.
And mud-stained, wet, and weary,
    Through ranges dark goes he;
While hobble-chains and tinware
    Are sounding eerily.

repetition of the soft 's' sound throughout creates a gloomy mood. The horse's perseverance is seen in 'struggles onward'. His lone journey to the homestead to bring 'dumb tidings' is poignant – adds to the sad mood

repetition here creates an ironic contrast: the sounds are no longer musically cheerful, but ghostly

resolution: the outcomes of the flood are made clear

verdant carpet: green with vegetation

sleeps: euphemism for death

The floods are in the ocean,
    The stream is clear again,
And now a verdant carpet
    Is stretched across the plain.
But <u>s</u>omeone's eye<u>s</u> are <u>s</u>addened,
    And <u>s</u>omeone's heart <u>s</u>till bleed<u>s</u>
In <u>s</u>orrow for the drover
    Who <u>s</u>leeps among the reed<u>s</u>.

Henry Lawson, from *In the Days When the World Was Wide*

rhythm slows – the mood is calm

the beauty of the green growth brought about by the flood creates a peaceful image of rebirth. This contrasts with the death of Harry

'But' in the second quatrain brings our focus back to the loss of Harry, and the grief of his beloved. The repetition of the soft 's' sounds both slows the rhythm and creates a sorrowful tone. The use of 'sleeps' adds to the poignancy

Activity 4.17

1   Research the occupation of droving in Australia in the 1800s.
    a   Describe what a drover (or stockman) actually did.
    b   What kind of lifestyle did this job involve?
    c   List the qualities needed to perform such a job.
    d   Describe the roles the drovers' wives and girlfriends played while the men were away for long periods.
    e   List the qualities that these women must have possessed.
    f   Make comparisons about living and working on the land then and now.

2   'The ballad of the drover' strongly relates a story. Draw a table like the one below and select the lines from the poem which correspond to each event within it.

Event in the story	Lines which relate
Harry has been droving interstate for months.	
The homestead to which he is returning is a long journey away.	
Harry pushes his horse onward in an attempt to beat the rising river.	
Prior to the storm there had been a drought.	
Harry is confident that he will be able to cross the river.	
The flooding river is too strong for Harry and his stock-horse.	
Harry's beloved will never see him again.	
The dog attempts to rescue his master and drowns in the process.	
The packhorse – the lone survivor – travels onward to the homestead.	
The flood has brought new life to the countryside but sorrow for Harry's beloved.	

3   Create a storyboard of the events in 'The ballad of the drover'.

4   Describe Harry Dale using words and phrases from the poem to support your answer. Compare your responses to those of others in the class and discuss.

5   The animals in the poem are given just as much importance as the drover. Suggest why you think Lawson did this.

6 Describe the qualities of Harry's animals – his stock-horse, pack-horse and dog.

7 Suggest what the poem tells us about:
   a the forces of nature
   b the human spirit
   c the loyalty of animals.

8 The reader may feel sympathy for the drover. Do you think Harry was brave or foolish? Was he a hero or was he responsible for his own fate and that of his animals? Explain.

'The ballad of the drover' can be found in books and on the Internet. Interestingly, there are a few different versions. One version leaves out the last stanza altogether, ending with the packhorse heading home and 'the hobble-chains and tinware . . . sounding eerily'. The second version is the one printed in this book. In a third version, Harry's beloved is silenced – in other words, the text doesn't give any information about her. We are not offered a glimpse into her reaction to his death (her 'heart still bleeds'), which implies how much she obviously loved him. In this third version, the last quatrain instead focuses on the bravery of Harry, rather than the heartbreak of his fiancée. It reads:

> But bleaching on the desert
>   Or in the river reeds
> The bones lie of the bravest
>   That wide Australia breeds.
>
> Henry Lawson

Activity 4.18

1 Discuss the following as a class:
   a How could you account for the differences in the three versions of 'The ballad of the drover'?
   b Explain which ending you prefer.
   c Outline how we, as readers, are positioned to view Harry and his beloved in each of the versions. What messages about them both is the writer (who may not necessarily be Lawson in all three) trying to send?
   d What inferences can you draw about the attitude of the writer in the third version? Suggest reasons why Harry's beloved has been 'silenced'. Could the cultural and historical context of the writer have influenced him to highlight Harry's bravery? Is bravery solely a male trait?

e Assuming that Harry's fiancée runs the homestead and farm single-handedly and without his financial support after his death (and assuming that she also did this while he spent long months away), what traits would she need to possess?

f Explain what this might tell us about the women who lived in the Australian bush at the time 'The ballad of the drover' was set. Do you think the same is true of women living in the bush today?

g Has your discussion of these questions changed your mind about which version of the poem you prefer? Explain.

2 a Write a news report which tells of Harry Dale's death and the events surrounding it. Include a headline and a photo with a caption.

b Write a diary entry from his fiancée's point of view when she comes to the realisation that Harry is dead.

c Write an epitaph (an inscription on a gravestone) for Harry.

d If you were to set 'The ballad of the drover' to music, or had to select a song to play at Harry Dale's funeral, what would you choose and why?

e Imagine you are Harry's fiancée, or one of his close family members. Write a eulogy (a speech in honour of someone who has died) to read at his funeral.

As an interesting example, here is the eulogy read at Henry Lawson's funeral in 1922 by the then Prime Minister of Australia William Morris (Billy) Hughes. Lawson was given a state funeral, signifying his national importance. Mourners spilled out of Sydney's St Andrews Cathedral, and lined the route for miles to the cemetary. Hughes said of Lawson:

He knew intimately the real Australia, and was its greatest minstrel. He sang of its wide spaces, its dense bush, its droughts, its floods, as a lover sings of his mistress. He loved Australia, and his verses set out its charms, its vicissitudes, burning heat of the northerly and bitter cold of the westerly wind, the storm, the calm, drought and flood, the endless plain shimmering beneath the summer sun, the dust of the travelling stock, the cracking of the stockman's whip, the roar of the flood waters, the matchless beauty of the tall, waving, sweet-scented gums, splashed with the yellow of the wattle, the melting blue of the distant mountains, the evening camp fire, the boiling billy, the damper and mutton of stockmen and swagmen, the humour, the pathos, the joys and sorrows, and above all the dauntless spirit of the Australians . . . He was the poet of Australia, the minstrel of the people.

Pro Hart, an Australian artist, has composed many paintings to accompany Henry Lawson's works. Carefully study his interpretation of 'The ballad of the drover' and answer the questions which follow:

Pro Hart, *Ballad of the Drover*, 1973

1 Write an alternative title for the painting on page 99.

2 **a** Make a list of ten adjectives to describe the painting.
   b Compare these with other class members and discuss your differences in opinion.

3 **a** List the images that you see in the painting.
   b Is the action taking place before or after the dog drowns? How do you know?

4 Identify the parallels, or the associations that the artist has made, with Henry Lawson's poem. What do they have in common?

5 When we read a written text we read from left to right, top to bottom. Is this the same for a visual text? Where was your eye drawn when you first looked at the painting? (This is called the 'value' in the painting.) Why do you think this is? Is this the same answer other class members gave? Can you offer reasons for any variation in answers?

6 Pro Hart illustrated a book of Henry Lawson's poems, from which this painting is taken. What does this tell you about his attitude towards the poet?

7 Suggest what you think the artist wants the viewer to think about. What is his message? What is he emphasising?

8 If you had not read the poem, would you still be able to decipher the story represented in the painting? Explain.

9 Pro Hart has not included an image of the woman in the poem, nor the pack-horse that survived. Can you suggest reasons for this?

10 Do you like the artist's impression or representation? Explain your answer.

11 Create a graphic organiser and, in groups, discuss and collate information gleaned from the painting about:
   • the subject matter
   • the setting
   • the medium (method) used to compose the painting
   • the colours used and their effect on the mood
   • the focal point and what it suggests
   • how the main action or characters are framed
   • the use of line (rough, smooth) and how it contributes to the mood
   • contrasts used in colours or shapes
   • the movement suggested by shapes
   • any symbolism used (this can often be achieved through colour)
   • the representation of the characters (include the animals in this case)
   • the purpose of the painting
   • the intended audience.

12 Write your information from question 11 in paragraph form, concluding with a personal evaluation of the painting. Some sentence starters might include:

- *This painting by Pro Hart depicts . . .*
- *The focal point of the painting is . . .*
- *The colours used are . . .*
- *The mood created is . . .*
- *The most interesting thing in/about the painting is . . .*
- *The painting appealed/did not appeal to me because . . .*

Our readings of, and the way we react to, different texts (whether written or visual) are affected by our cultural, historical, situational and personal contexts. The person who composes written and visual texts is also influenced by these things at the time of composing. These contexts can be shaped by:

Cultural

- gender
- occupation
- where we live or have lived
- level of education
- beliefs
- traditions
- ethnicity
- political systems
- status
- wealth
- technology.

Historical

- the era in which a text is composed
- the era in which it is read
- dominant culture or ideology of the time
- changes made to the text over time
- major events of the time
- important people of the time
- the production media available at the time (that is, the methods available to compose a text and deliver the information; includes print, visual, electronic, multimedia).

Context

Situational

Writing, composing, reading and viewing is affected by where, and in what situation, the person composing or responding is at the time. For example, reading a novel at school creates one meaning; viewing a film based on the novel at the movies with friends creates another; viewing an advertisement for the film on television creates yet another. Expectations, attitudes and experiences are different at different times.

Personal

This context has to do with our individuality. We are shaped as individuals by our upbringing, background, attitudes, experiences, opinions, social influences and knowledge. One person will not compose or respond to a text in the same way as another.

(Based on C. Crump, P. Durand and C. Hooke, *Viewing and Representing in Context 1*, Thomson Nelson, Melbourne, 2003, pp. 7–8.)

Activity 4.20

1   Research the poet Henry Lawson and the artist Pro Hart. Write one to two paragraphs on each explaining their cultural, historical, situational and personal contexts. Describe how these contexts have influenced their compositions.

2   How have your cultural, historical, situational and personal contexts affected your reading of 'The Ballad of the Drover' in both its written and visual form?

Rhythm

There is a strong rhythm in 'The ballad of the drover'. Rhythm is the flow of sound created by heavy and light beats. When we read a poem we stress some syllables and leave others unstressed, so that there are heavy beats and light beats. For example, in the lines below, we would stress the parts underlined:

Once a jolly swagman camped by a billabong,
Under the shade of a coolibah tree,
And he sang as he watched and waited till his billy boiled,
'Who'll come a-waltzing Matilda with me?'

It is the pattern of these stressed (heavy) and unstressed (light) syllables which is known as the 'metre'. Can you see how each stressed syllable usually has one or more unstressed syllables around it? This grouping of syllables is called a 'foot', and the metre is the number of times these groups are repeated in a line.

There are various types of metre used in poetry. The stressed syllables are marked with / and the unstressed syllables are marked with ×.:

A pattern beginning with a light beat, followed by a heavy beat, is called **iambic** and makes the rhythm skip along:

```
 ×    /    ×    /    ×    /    ×    /
He  clasps the  crag with crook- ed  hands ...
```

A pattern beginning with a heavy beat, followed by a light beat, is called **trochaic** and gives the feeling of a march:

```
 /    ×    /    ×    /    ×    /
Twin- kle twin- kle litt- le  star ...
```

A pattern which has a heavy beat followed by two soft beats is called **dactylic** and creates the rhythm of a waltz – 1 2 3, 1 2 3, 1 2 3:

```
 /     ×    ×    /     ×    ×    /     ×    ×    /
Twirl- ing and whirl- ing and  danc- ing all  night ...
```

A pattern which has two soft beats followed by a strong beat is called **anapaestic** and makes the rhythm leap along:

```
×    ×    /    ×    ×     /
It's  a  lump  in  your  head
×    ×    /    ×  ×    /
it's  the  blade  of  a  knife . . .
```

In each line, if a foot is repeated:
* once, it is called a **monometer**
* twice, it is a **dimeter**
* three times, it is a **trimeter**
* four times, it is a **tetrameter**
* five times, it is a **pentameter**.

In English poetry, **iambic pentameter** is the best-known meter, and is commonly used in ballads, though not always. In 'The Ballad of the Drover', for example, Henry Lawson uses **iambic trimeter**. The stress falls on every second syllable three times in each line:

```
×    /    ×    /    ×   /    ×
A-  cross  the  ston-  y  ridg-  es,
×    /    ×    /    ×    /
A-  cross  the  roll-  ing  plain,
   ×     /    ×    /    ×     /    ×
Young  Har-  ry  Dale,  the  drov-  er,
   ×     /    ×     /    ×   /
Comes  rid-  ing  home  a-  gain.
```

The easiest way to work out the stresses is to clap as you read a poem aloud. You will find that you clap on the stressed syllables, and that you don't clap on the unstressed syllables.

Activity 4.21

The following verses are from various ballads. Write them out in your notebook and, in pairs, work out the metre of each one. Mark the stressed syllables with / and the unstressed syllables with ×.

1   There came from up Macumba way a rangy, roany mare;
Her eyes were wild, her coat was rough, she'd buck and plunge and rear;
She threw them here, she threw them there, she threw them in the dirt;
The strawberry mare would never stop to see if they were hurt.

from 'Curio' by Fleur Tiver (student)

2   Up and spake an eldern knight
Sat at the king's right knee
'Sir Patrick Spens is the best sailor
That ever sailed the sea'.

from 'Sir Patrick Spens', Anonymous

3   'He smelled me out, I swear it, mum!
'He said he smelled an Englishman!'
The mother said, 'And well he might!
'I've told you every single night
'To take a bath because you smell,
'But would you do it? Would you hell!
'You even make your mother shrink
'Because of your unholy stink!'

from 'Jack and the Beanstalk' by Roald Dahl

4   The Country Dog with his eager grin
Enjoys the sound of the market din.
To a city dog he's a noisy clown
He likes a scrap when he comes to town.

from 'The country dog' by Max Fatchen

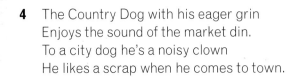

The following verse is written in an iambic pattern:

Abbie's ghost

She saw him in the dead of night
Just floating o'er her bed
His face was kind though sadly drawn
And then he softly said . . .

Activity **4.22**

Transform the following lines into the next verse of 'Abbie's ghost', rewriting them as a ballad.
- He was a pilot who died when young.
- His name is Norm.
- He won't hurt her.

Your verse should:
- use an iambic pattern
- be four lines long
- have a rhyme scheme of a, b, c, b.

Song lyrics

Song lyrics and ballads are similar in that they are both linked to music. However, while the ballad's major focus is on the story, the major focus of songs is on the feelings and ideas of the writer. They are therefore lyrical. The term 'lyric' is also used to describe the words in a song.

Songs are popular because they are very rhythmic, they are easy to remember, and their subject matter is not limited. Just as love is a common theme in literature, many songwriters focus on love in their songs: being in love, falling out of love, its emotional power and how we respond to it.

Some songwriters even present us with a different slant on love, as seen in the song performed by Sting on page 106:

If you love somebody set them free

If you need somebody, call my name
If you want someone, you can do the same
If you want to keep something precious
You got to lock it up and throw away the key
If you want to hold on to your possession
Don't even think about me.

If you love somebody, set them free

If it's a mirror you want, just look into my eyes
Or a whipping boy, someone to despise
Or a prisoner in the dark
Tied up in chains you just can't see
Or a beast in a gilded cage
That's all some people ever want to be.

If you love somebody, set them free

You can't control an independent heart
Can't tear the one you love apart
Forever conditioned to believe that we can't live
We can't live here and be happy with less
So many riches, so many souls
Everything we see we want to possess.
If you need somebody, call my name
If you want someone, you can do the same
If you want to keep something precious
You got to lock it up and throw away the key
If you want to hold onto your possession
Don't even think about me

If you love somebody, set them free.

Gordon Sumner
(performed by Sting)

1 How do you interpret the songwriter's message? What is he trying to get across?

2 Discuss the possible meanings of the phrase 'set them free'.

3 Suggest some reasons why songs often have a chorus which is frequently repeated. What is the effect of the repetition in this song?

4 Decide whether the songwriter would agree or disagree with the statements below. Write them out in your notebook, and support your answers with specific examples from the song. Be prepared to defend your position in a discussion.

Statement	Agree/disagree	Examples to support your view
If someone we love wants or needs us we should be there for them.		
Love means that we should have the person we love all to ourselves.		
Relationships will suffer if people don't give each other room to be themselves.		
We are often led to believe that, if we're not part of 'a couple', our lives aren't complete.		
If we really love someone then we won't treat them as an object or a possession – as if we own them.		

5 Complete these activities, either individually or in groups:
   a Write an acrostic poem using 'LOVE IS . . .' (see page 73).
   b Make up a definition of love, but set it out as a mathematical or scientific concept. For example, you can use equations, Venn diagrams or pie charts.
   c Draw a picture for each verse of the song, conveying its subject matter. You can use symbols or more detailed images.
   d Represent the ideas in the song as a mind map.
   e Write a letter to the songwriter asking him five questions about the song.
   f Use websites to locate the lyrics of a song that you like. Then write your own lyrics to fit the tune.

Free verse

Often students ask: 'Isn't poetry meant to rhyme?' The answer is: 'Absolutely not!' Free verse is a form which *doesn't* rhyme and, because of this, gives poets great scope to express their ideas. It means that they do not have to conform to a strict metre or rigid rhyme scheme as in a ballad, for instance. Instead, free verse has a very informal structure and a natural, flowing rhythm. Generally the lines of free verse poems are short, sometimes consisting of only one word.

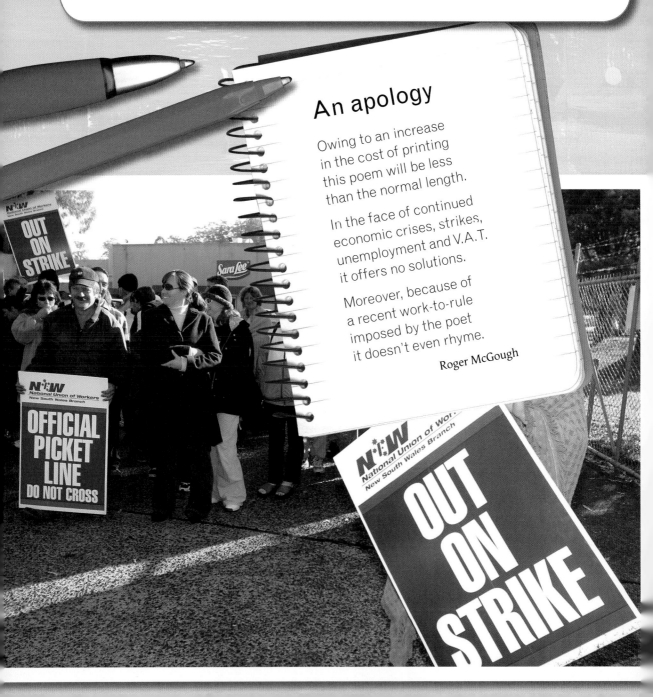

An apology

Owing to an increase
in the cost of printing
this poem will be less
than the normal length.

In the face of continued
economic crises, strikes,
unemployment and V.A.T.
it offers no solutions.

Moreover, because of
a recent work-to-rule
imposed by the poet
it doesn't even rhyme.

Roger McGough

How and where words are placed on the page, the use (or not) of capitals and punctuation, the placement of pauses, and repetition all help to create emphasis as well as rhythm in a free verse poem. These things can speed up or slow down the tempo of the poem. In the following poem, note how its physical arrangement both strengthens its meaning and increases its pace. The poem is organised so that each line flows into the next, leading your eye easily and fluently down the page:

Tap

I know if I listen it's going to
                    DRIP
in-ter-mit-tent-ly
            DRIP
DRIP
        DRIP
                    DRIP
DRIP
            DRIP
        DRIP
            DRIP
                un-
                    til
                    I
                    tight-
                        en
                            a
                            wrench
                                round
                                    its
                                    THROAT!

Peter McFarlane

The following poem by Steven Herrick flows easily, with the rhythm of natural speech.

To my son Joe

for the first five years
you'll be like your Dad
you'll fall over a lot
always be on the bottle
& stay awake all night.
then your Mother, who
until now
you've always trusted, will
send you off to a place
where men in shorts & long socks
named Mr Duffy will
teach you i comes before e
except after c
other boys will think of
stupid names to call you
when you get out for a duck
in the Final.
names like Slow Joe

or Boofhead.
your mother will tell you
to ignore them.
your Dad will tell you
to kick them in the guts.
thankfully
you never listen to him.
at thirteen
you'll get a cramp
in your stomach when you sit
next to Wendy Spencer.
don't worry.
this always happens around girls.
it will disappear when you turn 75.
when you leave school
relatives will ask you
what you want to do.

you'll tell them you
want to be just like your Dad
they'll say A POET
you'll say NO, UNEMPLOYED.
around this time your Father
will ask you
to pay back the pocket-money
for the past 15 years
with Interest.
you'll tell him to
speak to your Mother.

Steven Herrick

Activity 4.24

1   Quote two examples from the poem 'To my son Joe' that illustrate the natural flow of ordinary speech.

2   There are funny and loving lines in the poem. Write out five examples which show humour or affection.

3   Make a list of ten words or phrases that describe the father. Compare your list with others' in the class and discuss your responses.

4   Imagine you are Joe as a fourteen year old. Write a letter to your father, Steven, in response to his advice, telling him whether or not it has been useful so far.

The car trip

Mum says:
'Right, you two,
this is a very long car journey.
I want you two to be good.
I'm driving and I can't drive properly
if you two are going mad in the back.
Do you understand?'

So we say,
'OK, Mum, OK. Don't worry,'
and off we go.

And we start The Moaning:
Can I have a drink?
I want some crisps.
Can I open my window?
He's got my book.
Get off me.
Ow, that's my ear!

And Mum tries to be exciting:
'Look out the window
there's a lamp post.'

And we go on with The Moaning:
Can I have a sweet?
He's sitting on me.
Are we nearly there?
Don't scratch.
You never tell him off.
Now he's biting his nails.
I want a drink. I want a drink.

And Mum tries to be exciting again:
'Look out the window
There's a tree.'

And we go on:
My hands are sticky.
He's playing with the doorhandle now.
I feel sick.
Your nose is all runny.
Don't pull my hair.

He's punching me, Mum,
That's really dangerous, you know.
Mum, he's spitting.

And Mum says:
'Right I'm stopping the car.
I AM STOPPING THE CAR.'

She stops the car.

'Now, if you two don't stop it
I'm going to put you out of the car
and leave you by the side of the road.'

He started it.
I didn't. He started it.

'I don't care who started it
I can't drive properly
if you two go mad in the back.
Do you understand?'

And we say:
OK, Mum, OK, don't worry.

Can I have a drink?

Michael Rosen

1   'The car trip' is made up of a conversation.
    a   Who is telling the story?
    b   Write three lines that you find humorous and explain why.

2   What is the effect of the last line?

3   Do you think Michael Rosen is writing from first-hand experience? Explain.

4   Write your own free verse poem from the point of view of a child. Try to capture the natural speech children use. Here are some possible titles:
    *   'Can I, Dad? Can I . . . ?'
    *   'But – why?'
    *   'Look what happened . . . !'
    *   'I didn't do it.'
    *   'Are we there yet?'

The leader

I wanna be the leader
I wanna be the leader
Can I be the leader?
Can I? I can?
Promise? Promise?
Yippee, I'm the leader
I'm the leader

OK what shall we do?

Roger McGough

Katrina's wedding

27 January 1990

As I began to walk down the aisle
I suddenly felt light-footed as a dove
and my face seemed to have swollen like a great watermelon
ready to split open with sheer happiness
to the sound of a wedding march on a single trumpet.
This was my beloved daughter
with whom I was well-pleased. This was
the baby on the rubber sheet in the isolation-room,
the smaller twin in the high-chair,
the little girl with the gauze-pad
on the left eye after the operation,
the playground defender
of twin brothers, the woman in Air Force blue
with a woman's courage against the chauvinist taunts
of men – and I wanted to hold her up
to the standing congregation following our
    progress like sunflowers
saying: 'Look, see, behold (and all those things)
– you *can* be lucky in the late 20th century
– it *is* possible, it really happens!'

Bruce Dawe

1 a Describe the mood of the poem 'Katrina's wedding'. Write three words or phrases that you think identify the mood.

   b What do the similes 'light-footed as a dove' and 'swollen like a great watermelon' tell us about the poet's emotions?

2 List the stages of his daughter's life the poet is remembering.

3 Suggest the point you think Bruce Dawe is making in the last two lines of the poem.

4 Draw a table like the one below. Locate the lines from the poem that tell you about the subject matter described (you may write more than one example for each). Discuss your responses as a small group and justify your choices.

Subject matter	Lines from the poem
The poet was giving his daughter away at her wedding.	
He was immensely proud of his daughter.	
He was incredibly happy.	
He had a huge smile on his face.	
He had great respect for his daughter.	
His daughter had overcome tremendous obstacles as a child to arrive at this day.	
His daughter had shown courage.	
He appreciated his daughter.	
Happiness is possible.	

If Katrina could turn the tables and write a poem about the journey to her wedding day, perhaps she might say something like this.

Woman of the future

I am a child.
I am all the things of my past.
I am the freckles from my mother's nose.
I am the laziness of my dad
    Resting his eyes in front of the television.
I am all I see.
    Boys doing Karate Chops.
    Rubens' lovely ladies,
    Fat and bulging.
    TV ads of ladies who wear lipstick in the laundry.
    And worry about their hands
    And their breath.
    Madonnas with delicate faces holding little bundles of Jesus.
I am all I hear.
    'Look after him. You're his sister.'
    'Come and get your hair done.'
    'Rack off, Normie!'
    Waves lapping or crashing at the beach.
    And the wind in trees and telegraph wires.
I am all I feel and taste.
    Soft and glossy mud on toes.
    Hairy insect legs
    Slippery camphor laurel leaves
    The salty taste of fish and chips on my tongue
    And the watery melting of iceblocks.

And all I remember.
    A veranda shaded by grape vines,
    Where I stepped off the edge and flew
    Like Superman.
    And waking up in the cold in a car where
        dad changed a tyre,
    And being lost in the zoo with my cousin.
I am all I've been taught.
    'I' before 'E' except after 'C'.
    'Smoking is a health hazard.'
I am all I think.
    Secrets.
    Deep down inside me.
I am all those things.
I'm like a caterpillar
And these things are my cocoon.
But one day I'll bite my way out
    And be free
    Because
I'm the woman of the future.

Cathy Warry

Activity **4.27**

1   Draw a mind map to create a collection of words and phrases which describe you and your experiences. Devote one portion of the mind map to comparing yourself to other things using similes and metaphors.

2   Write your own poem along the lines of 'Woman of the future' (or, if you're male, 'Man of the future'), following the pattern that Cathy Warry uses in her poem:

I am …
I am … (use metaphors)
I am …
I am all I see ….
I am all I hear …
I am all I feel and taste …
I am all I remember …
I am all I've been taught …
I am all I think …
I'm like a …
But one day I'll …
Because
I'm the woman/man of the future.

3   Illustrate your poem with images or symbols which convey or enhance what you have written about yourself.

Mort aux chats (Death to cats)

There will be no more cats.
Cats spread infection,
cats pollute the air,
cats consume seven times
their own weight in food a week,
cats were worshipped in
decadent societies (Egypt
and Ancient Rome), the Greeks
had no use for cats. Cats
sit down to pee (our scientists
have proved it.) The copulation
of cats is harrowing; they
are unbearably fond of the moon.
Perhaps they are all right in
their own country but their
traditions are alien to ours.
Cats smell, they can't help it,
you notice it going upstairs.
Cats watch too much television,
they can sleep through storms,
they stabbed us in the back
last time. There have never been
any great artists who were cats.
They don't deserve a capital C
except at the beginning of a sentence.
I blame my headache and my
plants dying on to cats.
Our district is full of them,
property values are falling.
When I dream of God I see
a Massacre of Cats. Why
should they insist on their own
language and religion, who
needs to purr to make his point?
Death to all cats! The Rule
of Dogs shall last a thousand years!

Peter Porter

1   Read the poem 'Mort aux chats'. As you read it, record your initial impressions, such as:

- *when I read the title I thought . . .*
- *the poem reminds me of . . .*
- *I'm not sure about . . .*
- *I'm puzzled by . . .*
- *a word/line that strikes me is . . . because . . .*
- *I think the poem might mean . . .*
- *The poet seems to be saying . . .*
- *I like/dislike the poem because . . .*

2   Read the poem two or three times more. As you read, add to your list of impressions.

3   In groups, decide on a list of questions that the poem raises in your minds. Some of the questions can be discussed and answered in the group; others that remain can be discussed as a class. The aim is to try to come to an understanding of the poem and the poet's message. (This strategy can work for any poem, especially those in which the meaning is not at first clear.)

4   a   When you read the first line, how did you feel?
    b   What did you expect to come next?
    c   Was the ending what you expected? Why or why not?

5   What do the following words mean?
    a   consume
    b   decadent
    c   copulation
    d   harrowing
    e   alien
    f   massacre.

6   a   List the reasons given in the poem for the dislike of cats.
    b   In groups, think of five more things that you could add to this list.

This poem is really not about cats at all, but about unreasonable intolerance. It's an example of irony – a device used to expose injustice, oppression or human failings. An ironic statement is made here when the poet expresses an attitude or opinion but his intention is to point out the opposite. He does not want to create contempt for cats, but for people who are intolerant of others' culture, ethnicity, religion or background through ignorance and hatred.

1   Suggest reasons why Peter Porter chose cats as his vehicle for criticism.

2   Draw a table like the one below. Locate lines from the poem which parallel the intolerance of cats in the poem with broader social and historical intolerance.

Lines from the poem 'Mort aux chats'	Social and historical parallels
'Perhaps they are alright in their own country but their traditions are alien to ours'	
'Cats smell, they can't help it'	
'they stabbed us in the back last time'	
'Our district is full of them, property values are falling.'	
'When I dream of God I see a Massacre of Cats.'	
'Why should they insist on their own language and religion'	
'The Rule of Dogs shall last a thousand years!'	

3   In small groups, write a free verse poem similar to 'Mort aux chats', but using a different subject. For example:
 *   a cat talking about dogs
 *   a mouse's view of a snake
 *   a spider's or cockroach's view of humans
 *   a fire hydrant talking about dogs
 *   a cancer's view of doctors.

The farewell letter

This is my last letter to you, mum,
I'm leaving home
I forgot how many times
I have asked you to come with me,
But you steadfastly refuse.

I hope that now I have gone
You will realise what danger you are in.
Remember what happened to Dad?
Even your father and your other sons?
But not me. I'm too clever.
But they almost got me last time, mum.
That's how I hurt my leg.
I cannot run as fast now, mum.

I won't be so lucky next time
And there will be a next time,
Because they are always after us,
You and I, our friends and relatives.
We are a persecuted race.

So I am going to the city.
I'll be fine, looking in dustbins for food,
Sleeping at the back of people's gardens.
I'll be fine and they won't be able to get me.

They won't be able to set the dogs
To look for me there.
They will have to hang up their little red coats
And unsaddle their horses,
Because they won't be able to get me.

But they might get you, mum.
Please, follow me. We have already lost the others,
I don't want to lose you too.

Love, your son

Felix Fox

Gemma Wallace (student)

Activity **4.30**

1 'The farewell letter' contains a twist at the end. There are clues provided before this, however, which hint at Felix's identity. Quote the lines where this occurs.

2 Write your own poem in the form of a letter, in which the writer is not revealed until the last line.

3 Create a poster supporting the need to protect a persecuted group (or groups) in society.

In the playground

In the playground
At the back of our house
There have been some changes.

They said the climbing frame was
NOT SAFE
So they sawed it down.

They said the paddling pool was
NOT SAFE
So they drained it dry.

They said the see-saw was
NOT SAFE
So they took it away.

They said the sandpit was
NOT SAFE
So they fenced it in.

They said the playground was
NOT SAFE
So they locked it up.

Sawn down
Drained dry
Taken away
Fenced in
Locked up

How do you feel?
Safe?

Michael Rosen

Activity **4.31**

1 What is the effect of using 'NOT SAFE' and why has the poet used capitals?

2 The poem appears to be about playgrounds. What else could it be about?

Words dictate the tone of a poem. The tone may be serious, happy, amusing, angry, sarcastic or frustrated, among other things. The tone affects the overall mood – how the poem makes us feel.

Activity 4.32

1   Look at the lines below from 'The playground'. The verbs have been removed. Reach a consensus about the most appropriate word (or words) to put in each space. Consider:
    - What tone will you use?
    - What mood are you trying to create?
    - How will different words affect the rhythm?

    _____ down
    _____ dry
    _____ away
    _____ in
    _____ up

    How do you feel?
    _____?

2   Compare your group's version with others: how are they different?

3   Compare your version with the poet's version and discuss the significance of the differences.

4   Justify your word choices and comment on the effectiveness of the poet's choices.

Activity 4.33

1   Choose a theme such as people, animals, food, sport, war, love or hate. Cut out pictures relating to your theme from newspapers or magazines and create a collage on cardboard. Write a free verse poem about the theme.

2   Cut out words, phrases and sentences from magazines or newspapers. In groups, arrange these words as a free verse poem. Give the poem a title. Alternatively, cut up a poem (make sure you choose one with some logical or chronological sequence) and swap it with another group, who has to reconstruct it.

Write your own free verse poem on a topic of your choice, looking at it from an unusual perspective.

Activity 4.34

Ideas for writing free verse

On his website Steven Herrick suggests some ways to write poetry. One of his suggestions is to choose a word and start every line with that word. In the example below, he looks at toenails from unusual perspectives.

Toenails

Toenails are my favourite colour, green.
Toenails are a very good source of Vitamin C.
Toenails are what I throw at my sister when she takes too long in the bathroom.
Toenails are the knife of a foot.
Toenails get caught in the carpet and trip you over.

Steven Herrick, from *My life, my love, my lasagne*

Another Steven Herrick poem lists the things you would never hear your teacher say.

The Ten Commandments (Part Two)
(or ten things your teacher will never say)

Children, pens down.
  Today I'm going to teach you how to swear.

OK, pick up your Textas.
  We're going to the Principal's office.
  We're going to grafitti on her walls.

Yes, good idea, let's stop doing maths.
  Let's have a sleep instead.

That's right, you heard me.
  I said no homework for the rest of the year.

I know you're all very hungry.
  Let's go get a pizza, I'll pay.

Children! If you keep making that awful noise,
  I'm going to let you all go home early.

This classroom is a pigsty, well done!

Today we have a special visitor to the school.
  I want you all to be as rude as possible.

Yes I know today was the science exam,
  But let's watch a video instead.

Don't forget, tomorrow is the last day of term,
  I'm taking everyone to the pub to celebrate.

Steven Herrick, from *Poetry to the Rescue*

Activity 4.35

Write your own poem about the ten things you would never hear from your:
- teachers
- sports coach
- parents
- grandmother.

Activity 4.36

1   Draw a table like the one below and, for each emotion, fill in words or phrases that come to mind.

	Fear	Hatred	Joy	Apathy	Jealousy	Anger	Other
Simile (is like)							
Metaphor (is)							
Human qualities							
Colour							
Looks like							
Feels like							
Smells like							
Tastes like							
Sounds like							

2   Use these responses to write a poem for each emotion. Set out your poems to include all the categories in the table, as in the example below:

Depression

Like a fog
I am listless;
I pull people
Into my greyness
into hopeless depths.

I look grey.
I feel grey.
I smell grey.
I taste grey.
A deep, never-ending
groan.

Activity 4.37

1   On a sheet of paper list three or four everyday objects (e.g. table, door, chair). On another sheet list three to four common actions (e.g. talking, making dinner, watching TV). Hand your lists into your teacher who will shuffle and redistribute them so that everyone receives a set of different objects and actions. Write a free verse poem linking the objects with the actions.

2   You can also do this with occupations. Write the name of an occupation (e.g. doctor) on one sheet of paper; on another, list five objects that a doctor would use. Hand in, shuffle, and redistribute the papers. Write a poem linking the occupation on one page to the list of objects on the other.

Activity 4.38

1   Choose a topic to write a poem about. Write down the first five words that come into your head when you think of it. Begin drafting ideas about the words into a poem. As an example, a student who chose 'eating' as her topic then listed five words: food, friend, love, cupboard and lasagne. She wrote the following poem:

Food is my friend

I have heaps of friends
They love me
They wait in the cupboard for me.
Food screams my name
When I'm depressed or lonely.
I do have a best friend
Her name is Lasagne.
Lasagne and I get on great.
Lasagne loves me.

from *For the Love of Poetry*, Mandy Tunica

2   As you see each of the statements below, write down a response to it in a word, phrase or sentence. Try to capture as vividly as possible what the experience feels, looks, smells or sounds like. Do not number your responses, but write them underneath each other as if they were lines of poetry.

Statements:
- the smell of freshly baked bread
- sweat in the eyes
- being rejected
- getting into a warm bath
- pins and needles
- the silence of 3 a.m.
- the texture of satin
- fingernails scraping down a blackboard
- sleeping in.

Redraft your lines until you have a poem with which you are satisfied.

Verse novels

Verse novels are written as a series of poems which together create a story, and are therefore a blend of narrative and poetry. They are organised into short sections and are often told by multiple narrators. We gain an insight into each character as they tell us about events from their own perspective.

Telling stories in verse is not new. Verse narratives have been used since ancient times to tell epic tales, such as Homer's *Iliad* and *Odyssey*. Modern verse novelists have a long tradition of verse narratives to draw on, including the bush ballad with its strong narrative and lyrical elements. What distinguishes contemporary verse novels from traditional verse narratives is their conciseness, and the 'collage-like' composition of multiple narration.

Verse novels are quicker and easier to read than prose, yet can still deal with ideas and issues that are quite sophisticated. Like novels, they also have a strong plot and characterisation, and contain powerful imagery. Verse novels provide a poet with enormous flexibility: they can play with shape, length and patterns in their poems. They can use different poetic forms – free verse, blank verse, haiku, dramatic monologue, soliloquies, sonnets – often in the one novel. They can use features of other genres: interviews, conversations, journals, emails, footnotes, postcards and letters, to name a few. All these combine to not only give us information about the characters and carry the narrative along, but also to provide a very different reading experience.

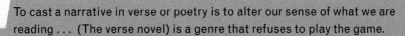

To cast a narrative in verse or poetry is to alter our sense of what we are reading . . . (The verse novel) is a genre that refuses to play the game.

Kerry Mallan & Roderick McGillis

What is the appeal of verse novels?

- They can communicate to an audience who might not normally read poetry.
- They provide an easy and quick reading experience.
- They contain short chapters in which the narrative segments are usually brief.
- The poems are usually made up of short lines, therefore leaving lots of white space on the page. This affects the way the eye scans the page as it is easily drawn by the placement of words.
- They are written in concise lyric verses which are reflective, as well as plot- and character-driven.

Steven Herrick

Steven Herrick is an Australian poet who has written a number of verse novels, in free verse, for children and young adults.

I love poetry. I want to enable children and young adults to appreciate the sound and humour, and storytelling potential, of poetry.

Steven Herrick

One such verse novel is *The Simple Gift*, a story of human connectedness told through a trio of characters who influence each other in positive ways. Sixteen-year-old Billy runs away from home at the novel's beginning, hoping for a better life away from his alcoholic, abusive father.

Kiss the dog   *Billy*

I'm not proud.
I'm sixteen, and soon
to be homeless.
I sit on the veranda
and watch the cold rain fall.
Bunkbrain, our dog,
sits beside me.
I'd like to take him with me.
He doesn't deserve to stay
in this dump, no-one does.
But you don't get rides
with a dog.
And two mouths to feed
is one too many.
Bunkbrain knows something,
he nuzzles in close,
his nose wet and dirty
from sniffing for long-lost bones.
I scratch behind his ears
and kiss the soft hair
on his head.
I'll miss you dog.
I'm not proud.
I'm leaving.
The rain falls steady.
Bunkbrain stays on the veranda.

Billy eventually makes a home for himself in an old abandoned freight train outside the town of Bendarat. An intelligent and mature young man, Billy adjusts to his new world quickly, figuring out how to keep clean and eat – 'I'm poor, homeless, but I'm not stupid.' He survives on the food that other diners leave behind at the local McDonald's, where he also meets Caitlin, the seventeen-year-old daughter of wealthy parents, who is working there to gain some measure of independence. She quickly sees through his exterior, realising that there is more to Billy than a homeless kid stealing scraps:

Business   *Caitlin*

This time when he left
he came over to me
and he had something
in his hand.
It was a business card.
He gave it to me
and said,
'Goodnight, Caitlin,
it's a beautiful name.'
So well-mannered,
so unlike every boy
at Bendarat Grammar,
or any schoolboy I've ever known.
I looked at the card.

> Peter Robinson
> Electrical Contractor
> Farley St Bendarat.
> Lic# G254378

It didn't make sense.

Then I turned it over.

> Bill Luckett
> Unemployed Friend
> Carriage 1864
> Bendarat Freight Yard
> No Licence/No Certificate.

I smiled to myself.
Homeless, and proud of it.

Billy also sees beyond the exterior of Caitlin's wealth when she shows kindness, visiting him with the gift of food:

Looking   *Billy*

. . . and I saw past
the shiny watch
and the clean hair
and the beautiful woollen overcoat.
I saw Caitlin
and I liked what I saw.

Billy befriends Old Bill, an alcoholic escaping from a tragic past, who inhabits a neighbouring train carriage that he refers to as 'The Bendarat Hilton'. Billy's first 'gift' to Old Bill is a carton of his father's cigarettes:

Old Bill   *Old Bill*

. . . And when he gave me
those smokes
I almost cried,
a kid like that
with nothing
giving stuff away . . .

Billy begins to look after Old Bill, taking him breakfast every morning and putting him to bed when he's had too much to drink. When Old Bill tells Billy that he can get work at the local cannery, he persuades Old Bill to take a job there as well, as a way of gradually getting him 'off the drink'. Through their friendship we learn of Old Bill's past:

All that knowledge   *Old Bill*

I wasn't always a hobo.
I worked in town.
I dressed neatly in suit and tie.
I understood the Law.
I earned a lot of money . . .

Billy and Old Bill have little to offer each other but companionship and compassion, friendship and hope, which the two both desperately need. We learn that these 'simple gifts' – the giving of oneself – have the greatest value:

Old Bill and the ghosts   *Billy*

Old Bill and me are friends.
Sometimes he comes into
my carriage and we share a beer.
He asks me questions
about my day
about the books I read,
he never asks me about family.
He gives me advice
on how to live cheap,
and how to jump trains
late at night,
and how to find out
which trains are going where,
and which trains have friendly Guards.
He encourages me to travel,
to leave here
and ride the Freights.
He makes it seem so special,
so romantic,
and I ask him
why he doesn't do it,
you know,
if it's so special,
and he tells me
about his Jessie
and his wife
and the house he visits
when too much drink
has made him forget
and how he's afraid to forget
because without his ghosts
he's afraid he'll have nothing to live for.
And at that moment I know
I am listening to
the saddest man in the world.

Billy's relationship with Old Bill causes him to reflect upon the kindnesses other people have shown him in his life; he understands the idea of selflessness without expecting anything in return:

Need   *Billy*

I help Old Bill
because of Ernie
and Irene
and their friendliness ...

... and that's why I help Old Bill,
for no reason
other than he needs it.

'... made me think of Billy
as a hobo ...'

Caitlin also learns something about selflessness when she first discovers that Billy has befriended a hobo:

The afternoon off   *Caitlin*

... all I can think
is that seeing Billy
with that old hobo
made me think of Billy
as a hobo
and I was ashamed,
ashamed of myself
for thinking that ...

Later, as Billy explains about Old Bill's life to Caitlin, she gains empathy and understanding:

A man   *Caitlin*

. . . and he told me about Old Bill,
the saddest man in the world –
that's what he called him –
and as he talked
I understood . . .

She makes amends by asking Billy and Old Bill to dinner – even though she hates cooking – signifying her desire to learn to see beyond the exterior and understand people for who they really are:

Simple gift   *Old Bill*

I shook the young lady's hand,
and Billy's.
I thanked them for the meal
and took my leave.
  . . . I hadn't drunk too much,
the wine was too good to ruin
with drunkenness,
and I'd listened
to Billy and Caitlin talk
and I'd noticed
how they looked at each other –
their quick, gentle smiles over the food –
and the way they sat close,
and I realised as I walked home
that for a few hours
I hadn't thought of anything
but how pleasant it was
to sit with these people
and to talk with them.
I walked home to my old carriage
and thought of how to repay them
for their simple gift,
and I enjoyed the thinking.

Old Bill is transformed and enriched through the experience of knowing Billy and Caitlin. Steven Herrick says:

> As adults, we seem to believe that the idea of *being an influence* works only one way – (that) we adults can influence young people for the better. In the book, I wanted to show it working the other way – that is, young Billy really being the positive influence, in fact, the catalyst, for Old Bill rejoining the world.'

When Billy is 'discovered' by the Department of Community Services, which threatens his survival in Bendarat, Old Bill gets his life in order to find a solution for Billy. He confronts his 'ghosts', gives up drinking, and regains a sense of value, identity and purpose. Billy is the reason for Old Bill's redemption and Old Bill gives him an extraordinary gift in return, one which symbolises significant emotional sacrifice.

For Old Bill, his gift to Billy releases him somewhat from the ghosts of his past, allowing him to move forward:

The hobo sky   *Billy*

. . . then he picked up his swag
and walked slowly,
deliberately,
north.
I watched until he
was out of sight

and I looked up
into the sky,
the deep blue sky
that Old Bill and I shared.

Steven Herrick's novel focuses on the recurring theme of gifts: what is valuable in our lives, and how we measure what is valuable. He says:

> One reviewer called Billy an *atypical hero*, which I thought was interesting. That got me thinking about what is heroic . . . I reckon Billy from 'Gift' (does) something of great value, that is a *little* thing – (gives) friendship and hope to an old hobo . . . These simple little things are what I think of as heroic. They are done by ordinary people, in a quiet unobtrusive way, and to commit these acts it requires compassion and love and respect. And they are far more heroic and necessary than any world-record sporting achievement. And they cannot be measured in dollars and cents.

1   What does the word 'gift' conjure up for you? What are the things that are valuable in your life and how can they be measured (or can they)?

2   Suggest the 'gifts' that Billy, Caitlin and Old Bill give to each other. What do they learn throughout the course of the novel? In groups, collate your answers in a table like the one below:

Character	Billy	Caitlin	Old Bill
What does Billy give to . . . ?			
What does Caitlin give to . . . ?			
What does Old Bill give to . . . ?			

3   Discuss whether you agree with Steven Herrick that heroism is about doing 'little' things – giving something of ourselves to unselfishly help others.

4   Use the website http://www.poetryzone.ndirect.co.uk/herrick.htm to find information about the poet. What explanation does he give for his love of writing verse novels?

5   Go to Steven Herrick's website at http://www.acay.com.au/~sherrick/.
   a   What other verse novels has he written?
   b   Click on the picture of the cover of *The Simple Gift*. How does Herrick describe what this novel is about?
   c   Click on 'Teacher Notes' and read the information. Explain Herrick's reasons for writing *The Simple Gift*.
   d   What parallels can you see between Steven's own experiences and those of Billy in the novel?
   e   Suggest what you think he means by giving his characters 'moral parameters'.
   f   Explain the themes of *The Simple Gift* in your own words. What do you think Steven Herrick wants us to learn from the novel?

6   Read any reviews you can find about the novel. From these, what inferences or predictions can you make about the characters, events and messages within it?

Read *The Simple Gift*. After your reading, complete the activities below.

Activity 4.40

1   Explain the significance of the novel's title.

2   Consider the way in which each character's 'journey' is developed during the course of the novel.
    a   Create a plot outline which records the key events or experiences that happen to each character. Present it in visual form; for example, as a time-line, a flow chart, a 'step' diagram leading to the resolution, or a comparative table of the characters' experiences.
    b   Each of the characters is transformed as the novel progresses. How, and through what events, do they change?
    c   With which character do you most identify? Explain why.

3   Explore the various settings used in the novel, and how they impact on the characters.
    a   In what settings does each of the characters feel alienated, discontented, out of place or unhappy?
    b   In what settings does each character feel 'at home', accepted and comfortable?
    c   What do the characters' responses to their various environments tell us about each of them?

4   *The Simple Gift* addresses many themes, such as:
    • escape   • relationships/influences   • grief and loss
    • courage   • compassion   • generosity
    • identity   • survival   • personal growth.

    a   Choose five of these themes and collate a list of poems from the novel which relate to each one. Gradually pare this selection down to one or two poems which you think *best* reflect each theme.
    b   Create a Powerpoint display in which you present your choice of themes and the poems which relate to them. Accompany your presentation with a spoken analysis/explanation of how your themes are shown in the novel, why you chose the poems you did, and how you think they reflect or illustrate the themes. Give your presentation a title.

5   'Homelessness' is an issue in *The Simple Gift*.
    a   Billy and Old Bill are homeless by choice and for different reasons. What are these reasons, and how does each character respond to his situation?
    b   From your reading of the novel, suggest other reasons why people might become homeless. Discuss whether or not you think homelessness is always a choice.

c How, in the novel, is homelessness tied up with themes of family, belonging, freedom, prejudice, trust, connecting with others and giving of oneself?

6 Present a persuasive speech on the topic *Homeless does not mean hopeless*.

7 Conduct a debate. Possible topics could include: *Homelessness has no place in a civilised society*, or *The measure of a civilised society is how it takes care of its weak and vulnerable*.

The Simple Gift has been published in both Australia (2000) and the United States (2004). Look at the front and back covers of each publication:

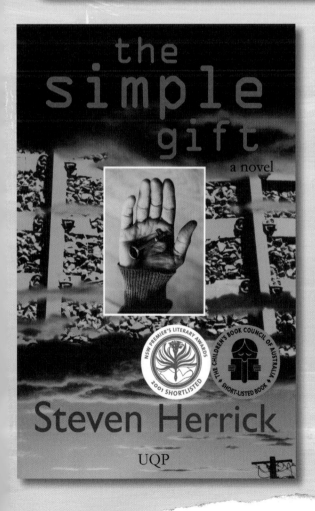

The Simple Gift, Australian publication (UQP, 2000)

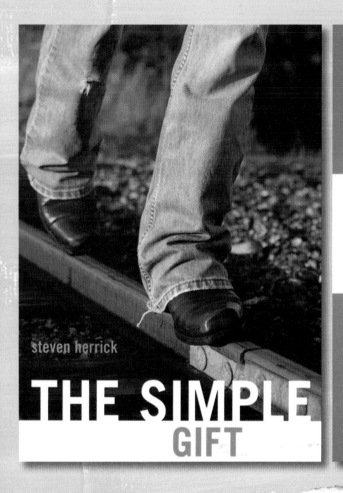

I'm not proud.
I'm sixteen, and soon
to be homeless.

Weary of life with his alcoholic, abusive father, sixteen-year-old Billy packs a few belongings and hits the road, hoping for something better than what he left behind. He finds a home in an abandoned freight train outside a small town, where he falls in love with rich, restless Caitlin and befriends a fellow train resident, "Old Bill," who slowly reveals a tragic past. When Billy is given a gift that changes everything, he learns not only how to forge his own path in life, but the real meaning of family.

OTHER VERSE NOVELS
BY STEVEN HERRICK

Simon & Schuster, New York
Cover photograph copyright © 2004
by Photodisc Red/Getty Images
Cover designed by Ann Sullivan
www.SimonSays.com
0504

US $6.99 / $10.50 CAN
ISBN 0-689-86867-7

The Simple Gift, United States
publication (Simon Pulse, 2004)

Activity 4.41

1   The composition of each cover is markedly different. Work in groups to explain their differences in terms of:

a   the medium used to create the cover (for example, both use photographs, but what are the differences in their arrangement and emphasis?)

b   the colours used and their significance

c   the images that have been chosen and their importance to the story

d   the focal point of each cover

e   the written text and whether it contributes anything to the story

f   the style and size of the font used for the novel's title and the author, and its placement on the page.

2 How has the designer of each cover created meaning for the reader? (Refer back to the discussion of cultural, historical, situational and personal context in the 'Ballads' section of this chapter.) How do you think the designer of each cover has been influenced by the contexts of their particular audiences in Australia and the United States?

3 Which of the designs do you think best captures the poetry, atmosphere and themes of *The Simple Gift*? Explain your answer.

4 With regard to the cover of the Australian publication, explain how the following visual elements are reflected in, or connected to, the novel:
   - the railway tracks
   - the sky
   - the telegraph pole
   - the hand
   - the key.

5 Is the hand male or female? Young or old? Explain your answer.

6 Discuss the significance of having the hand and key as the focal point – the centre of the visuals. What does this suggest about the focus of the story and its relationship with the notion of 'simple gifts'?

7 Design and create your own front and back covers for *The Simple Gift*, using your knowledge of the author and the novel.

8 Write an explanation of why you chose the design you did and what you hope it reflects about the themes and issues in the novel.

When Billy leaves home, he packs his school bag with the following provisions:

Champagne   *Billy*

. . . I go to the kitchen,
take the beer,
last night's leftovers,
some glossy red apples,
Dad's champagne and cigarettes . . .

Activity **4.42**

1   Make a list of the things you would take if you were to leave home. Explain your choices.

2   Billy has to leave Bunkbrain, his dog, behind. What are the reasons he gives for this?

3   What would you miss if you had to leave home? Explain.

4   One of the recurring images in *The Simple Gift* is that of food.
    a   What is the relationship between food and homelessness?
    b   Read the poems that relate to food. How does the representation of food change as the story develops and the characters themselves change?

5   Venn diagrams are useful for examining similarities and differences in characters, stories, poems, etc. in a visual way. In small groups, draw a Venn diagram like the one below. Collate a list of the similarities and differences between each of the characters in *The Simple Gift*. Think about what they are like at the novel's beginning and what they learn from each other as the novel progresses.

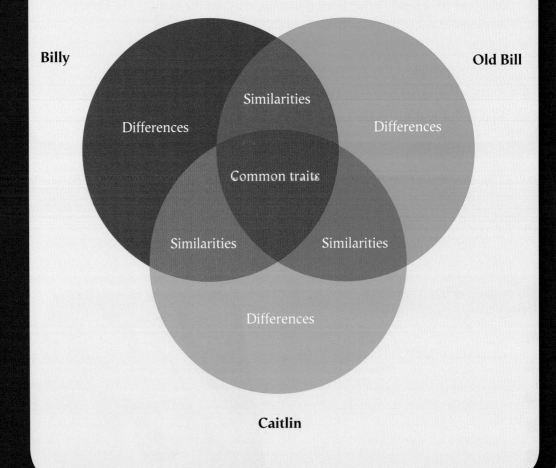

Activity **4.43**

1   Write a description of each character which goes beyond what the author tells us about them in his poems. Include information about their physical appearance as well as their personality.

2   If you were to choose a song or style of music to represent a character, what would you choose? Explain why.

3   Write a journal entry from Billy's point of view:
    a   after giving Caitlin his 'business card' at McDonald's and she visits him with food (see the poems 'Business' and 'Looking'); or
    b   after Old Bill tells him about his daughter and wife (see 'Old Bill and the ghosts').

4   Write a journal entry from Caitlin's point of view:
    a   after Billy leaves her his 'business card'; or
    b   before the meal she prepares for Billy and Old Bill (see 'The afternoon off' and 'A man').

5   Write a journal entry from Old Bill's point of view:
    a   when he first moves to the train carriage after abandoning his house; or
    b   after he gives Billy his gift (see the poems 'Old Bill's plan' and 'Billy').

6   Write a letter from Old Bill to Billy that tells of his travels north and how he is faring.

7   Write a description of what you imagine happens to Billy and Caitlin and their relationship after Old Bill leaves Bendarat.

Karen Hesse

Karen Hesse is an American verse novelist. Her novel *Witness*, based on real events, tells the story of the Ku Klux Klan's attempts to recruit members in a small Vermont town in 1924, and the implications of this for the townspeople. Over the course of many months, residents are affected by the pressures that build up in the community. The events of this free verse narrative in five 'acts' are told through the eyes of eleven of the town's residents, all with different perspectives and viewpoints. As the characters speak directly to the reader in the form of monologues, they relate acts of love and hatred, peace and violence, kindness and terror, highlighting the full range of human strengths and weaknesses in a small community.

The Ku Klux Klan (KKK) had its beginnings in the American South after the Civil War and its original objective was to prevent freed black slaves from gaining citizenship and equality. It was revived again in the early years of the twentieth century, expanding its 'crusade' to target new immigrants, Jews and Catholics. Ironically, its members espoused 'decent' American values while spreading hatred of those who were 'different'. In its quest for white supremacy, the Klan worked on people's prejudices, ignorance, fears and preconceptions in an ongoing campaign of hatred and violence. In some American states the Klan still exists today.

Leanora Sutter, a twelve-year-old black girl, is one of the main characters in *Witness*. She feels isolated by the recent death of her mother and by the escalating racial hatred: 'i am being buried, too, in all this whiteness.' Her struggle to maintain a normal childhood in the midst of poverty and prejudice is threatened by the arrival of the Klan. As the support for the Klan grows, so does the potential for violence. Their hatred permeates the town and filters down from parent to child:

leanora sutter

they made me mad.
willie pettibone and some of the other boys, they said things
about me and daddy.

i shouldn't let them get to me but
i'm flint quick these days.

willie said:
    at the klan meeting last night
    the dragons talked about lighting you
    and your daddy up
    to get them some warmth on a cold day.
    you'd be cheap fuel, they said.
    they liked the smell of barbecue, they said.

i turned my back on willie pettibone and walked out of school.
i didn't know where I was going.
i just walked out
without my coat,
without my hat or rubbers.
i didn't feel the cold,
i was that scorched.

1 Describe the emotions Leanora is expressing. Why are they so intense?

2 There are many references to heat, and things to do with heat, in the poem.
   a List the words, phrases or lines that relate to this.
   b Explain how this imagery of heat helps to intensify the emotions expressed.
   c Leanora describes herself using the metaphor 'flint quick'. What do you think she means by this? What impression does this give of her?
   d The heat imagery is used in contrasting ways. What does it represent for Leanora, as opposed to the boys who taunt her?
   e Explain the irony of the last line. What point do you think is being made?

3 'Draw' the poem using shapes or symbols. Think about how it makes you feel. Use colours and patterns which reflect the intensity of the subject matter and capture the poem's mood.

4 Using a computer, experiment with the font and formatting of the poem to capture the anger of Leanora and to highlight the cruelty of the boys.

5 The poems in *Witness* have no titles, as such; rather, they have the name of the person speaking as their 'title'. Suggest an alternative title for this poem which reflects its subject matter. Share your ideas with the class.

Leanora suffers racist taunts on a daily basis. On one occasion, Willie Pettibone gives her an article from the town paper advertising a minstrel show:

a night of fun brought to you by 22 genuine black-faced 'coons'.

Her response is:

felt like skidding on ice as i read,
felt like twisting steel.

why can't folks just leave me alone?

On another occasion, she experiences prejudice when her teacher talks her into entering a dance recital:

... i leaped and swept my way through *the fountain of youth*
separated on the stage from all those limb-tight white girls.

the ones who wouldn't dance with a negro,
they went home in a huff that first day,
but some came back.
they told miss harvey they'd dance,
but they wouldn't
touch any brown skin girl ...

How would you feel if you were exposed to this sort of cruelty and intolerance every day? Can you make any connections with your own experiences? Write a journal entry reflecting upon how you would feel and how you would deal with it.

Storekeepers Harvey and Viola Pettibone represent two opposing reactions to the Klan's methods:

harvey and viola pettibone

harvey says:
the ku klux are here, vi.
there's not a thing to stop them. we might as well join them.
why not?
they're not low-down men, like some folks say.
they're good men,
100 percent american men.
and they might bring us some business.

viola says:
in texas, harvey,
those 'good' men thought a certain fella was
keeping company with a married lady.
they had no proof of hanky-panky, harv.
they beat him, anyway,
held a pistol to his head,
said they'd kill him if he didn't clear out.
harv, you don't want to join a group like that.

but harvey says:
that's just rumor.
they have parades, vi,
and picnics,
and speakers from all over.
wouldn't you like that?
picnics and speakers?

viola washes up the dinner dishes,
her hands gloved in soapy water.

they do good, vi. they take care of their women.
and liquor can't ever tear up a family with them around.

harvey examines a spot on one of the glasses.
shouldn't we join, vi?

viola shakes her head slowly back and forth.
no, harv, viola says. I don't think we should.

1 We usually hear Harvey and Viola's voices together, while all the other characters speak alone. Why do you think the author has done this?

2 a What does the Klan represent for each of them?
   b How does Harvey justify wanting to join?

3 Karen Hesse distinguishes the characters (whose photographs, unusually, appear at the beginning of the book) not only by their varying opinions, but also by the tone and rhythm of their speech.
   a Explain the differences in the speech of Harvey and Viola. Why do you think the author uses shorter lines for Harvey and longer lines for Viola?
   b What is the effect of the line 'viola shakes her head slowly back and forth'?
   c How does the characters' differing viewpoints and use of language position us to view each of them?
   d Suggest adjectives that you think describe their personalities.
   e List some of the words and phrases used by them which illustrate the cultural and historical setting of the novel.

Reynard Alexander, the town's newspaper editor, tries to walk a careful line of neutrality until he realises the importance of taking a stand. He, among others, demonstrates the response of decent people who value tolerance:

reynard alexander

on arrival in a town,
the klan appears to serve the best interest of
the greater community,
'cleaning' it up, keeping a vigilant eye out for
loose morals and lawbreakers.
they deliver baskets to the needy,
and money to the destitute,
but the needy the klan comforts are white protestant needy,
the destitute white protestant, too.

a catholic with troubles, a negro, a jew, a foreigner?
their problems are of no concern to the klan.

from state to state,
from town to town,
men join who cannot be trusted.
   unscrupulous men
   who work in the dark

behind hoods and masks.
it takes but ten dollars.

and when that sort of scoundrel
starts hiding under hood and robes,
no good can come of it.

Activity **4.47**

1   Describe the tone of the poem on page 143.

2   There are strongly emotive words in the poem. List the words and phrases used that communicate Reynard Alexander's views of the Klan.

3   Explain what he means by the metaphor 'white protestant needy'.

4   What point do you think he is making in the line 'it takes but ten dollars'?

5   The poem has the feeling of an editorial. Write a letter to the editor in response to it from the point of view of:
    a   a supporter of the Klan or
    b   an opposer of the Klan.

6   Leanora tells her father that the Klan is 'just giving white folks a bad name'. Discuss in small groups the kind of person you think would join the Klan and engage in their practices. Why do you think they hid 'under hood and robes', and what does this say about them?

Activity **4.48**

1   Find information about Karen Hesse and *Witness* on the website http://teacher.scholastic.com/authors.

2   Research the Ku Klux Klan – how it began, what it stood for, what its activities were and are.

3   What other 'hate groups' do you know of that exist now? What do they stand for and why do people join them?

4   Research the life of civil rights advocates such as Martin Luther King Jnr or Malcolm X. What were they fighting for and why?

5   Look up the 'I have a dream' speech by Martin Luther King Jnr on the Internet. Why is it so powerful? Choose your favourite lines and write them as a poem.

6   Martin Luther King Jnr was assassinated on 4 April 1968 in Memphis, Tennessee. Look at the song lyrics of 'Pride (in the name of love)' by U2 at http://www.lyricsxp.com. How does the song relate to this event, and to King's speech? Who else is referred to? What is the point the song is making in the line 'One more in the name of love'?

7   Collect a range of stimulus items that reflect your point of view on the issue of prejudice. Arrange it as a visual display. You could use photographs, pictures, speeches, articles, poems, song lyrics – whatever you like. Alternatively, you could create a PowerPoint presentation. Present it to the class and explain your choices.

8   Prepare a persuasive speech about racial intolerance, or any other form of prejudice, and deliver it to the class.

9 Archbishop Desmond Tutu of South Africa said: 'If you are neutral in situations of injustice, you have chosen the side of the oppressor.' This allies with the idea that 'evil flourishes when good people do nothing'. Is it possible to remain neutral when everyone around you is taking very defined sides? Why do you think prejudice and intolerance exist? In groups, brainstorm ideas about this and collate them on a mind map. Suggest possible solutions to overcoming prejudice and intolerance. Why is it so important to address this issue at this particular time in our history?

10 Explain the differences in the styles of Steven Herrick and Karen Hesse. Think of their:
   * use of poetic form
   * subject matter
   * arrangement of poems on the page
   * use of language
   * rhythm
   * imagery
   * tone and mood
   * use of other textual features
   * capitalisation and punctuation
   * ease of reading
   * social, cultural and historical contexts.

Prose poetry

Prose poetry is similar to free verse in style as it does not follow any set 'rules' of rhyme or rhythm. However, while free verse is written with poetic line breaks (which create emphasis on a word or idea), prose poetry is not. It is instead written in sentence form, yet is more rhythmical, and its imagery richer and more intense, than prose.

Freedom to breathe

A shower fell in the night and now dark clouds drift across the sky, occasionally sprinkling a fine film of rain.

I stand under an apple-tree in blossom and I breathe. Not only the apple-tree but the grass round it glistens with moisture; words cannot describe the sweet fragrance that pervades the air. Inhaling as deeply as I can, the aroma invades my whole being; I breathe with my eyes open, I breathe with my eyes closed – I cannot say which gives me the greater pleasure.

This, I believe, is the single most precious freedom that prison takes away from us: the freedom to breathe freely, as I now can. No food on earth, no wine, not even a woman's kiss is sweeter to me than this air steeped in the fragrance of flowers, of moisture and freshness.

No matter that this is only a tiny garden, hemmed in by five-storey houses like cages in a zoo. I cease to hear the motorcycles backfiring, the radios whining, the burble of loudspeakers. As long as there is fresh air to breathe under an apple-tree after a shower, we may survive a little longer.

Alexander Solzhenitsyn

> alliteration and repetition of the soft 's' and 'f' sounds slow the rhythm and soften the mood

> the use of the word 'breathe', with its long vowel sound, makes us draw the word out. The repetition of it thus creates a rhythmical, gentle, and relaxed mood. In this sense, 'breathe' is a 'gentle' verb, with which the poet is understating a moment of exquisite pleasure

> the use of strong verbs emphasises the importance of this to the poet

> repetition of 'freedom' and 'freely' in this stanza highlights the main idea; also creates a calming rhythm

> comparison (signified by the words 'no' and 'not'), strengthens the emphasis

> repetition of the soft 's' and 'f' keeps the rhythm gentle

> simile accentuates the setting

> strong verbs provide a contrast in mood and quicken the pace

> use of the pronoun 'we' contrasts with the use of 'I' in previous stanzas – highlights the idea that freedom is a universal and essential need

Alexander Solzhenitsyn

Alexander Solzhenitsyn spent eight years in prison and labour camps for criticising Stalin, a former leader of the Soviet Union, in letters written to his brother-in-law. He was later exiled from the Soviet Union, first settling in Switzerland and afterwards in the United States.

Activity **4.49**

1   How does knowledge of Solzhenitsyn's imprisonment make you now view the poem? Has it changed your perceptions about the subject matter? Explain.

2   Quote the sentence from the poem which refers to his experience of imprisonment.

3   Identify what he says is 'the single most precious freedom' and the comparison he makes to accentuate the importance of this.

4   Explain how the last stanza contrasts with the first three in setting, mood and rhythm.

5   Suggest the point you think the poet is making in the last sentence.

6   When and where do you think the poem was written? Explain your response.

7   The repetition of 'breathe' is important to the rhythm of the poem in the second stanza. Think about the rhythm of your own breathing. How would you describe it? What sort of pattern does it have? How would you draw this pattern on paper? Compare your drawing with others'.

9   Rewrite the poem in free verse, using line breaks to emphasise words or ideas.

I can feel my lip throbbing

I can feel my lip throbbing. It's going to be big this time. I hate it when he hits my face. It's so difficult to come up with excuses for my bruises. I would be so humiliated if people knew I was so bad a wife that my husband had to hit me to keep me in line. It's not as if I don't try hard. I just forget things at times. He doesn't ask much of me. All he wanted was dinner on the table when he got home, but I was talking to mum on the phone and I lost track of time and the next thing I knew he was walking through the front door. It's like dad always used to tell me – I'm hopeless. And now, as I sit here crying with my nose running and hands shaking, I know dad was right. I just hope James doesn't come in and see me like this. It always makes him more angry when he sees me cry. If I wait a few more minutes, he will have calmed down and I'll be able to go and apologise to him. That's one of the best things about James – he's so forgiving.

Tanya Lintzeris

Activity 4.50

1 How did the poem 'I can feel my lip throbbing' make you feel? Describe your initial impressions and compare them with others'.

2 In what ways does the woman justify or make excuses for her husband's actions?

3 The woman has very low self-esteem. How did this happen and how is it being perpetuated?

4 Why is the last sentence so ironic?

5 a Explain how you think James would justify his actions.
  b *Is* there any justification for domestic violence? Explain.

6 a Compare this poem to 'Freedom to breathe', with its rich, sensory images. Do you think this *is* a poem? In small groups, come to a conclusion about this. Discuss the shape of the poem, its sentence length, imagery and other poetic devices used.
  b Rewrite the poem so that it looks and sounds more 'poetic'.

Dragons are what you make them

'Oh, god!' thought the dragon, 'not another one'. He gave vent to a loud sigh that singed the opposite wall of the cave . . .

A small figure was toiling up the slope towards the cave. It looked like an industrious ant carrying a small, rusty iron toothpick. When it reached the mouth of the cave it showed itself to be a tall skinny youth of about eighteen summers. A scraggy attempt at a beard covered his pimply chin and a large Adam's apple bobbed up and down as he swallowed. It bobbed up and down now. The dragon looked at him scornfully from the back of the cave. They must be scraping the bottom of the barrel.

Mark Manton (student)

'Dragons are what you make them' is an extract from a story written by a student. In pairs, transform the information into a prose poem and provide an ending. Use the following guidelines to help you:

- Take note of how the dragon and the boy are presented. What, in your mind, is most likely to happen when they meet?
- Think about a possible ending. Is there a way in which you could finish with a 'twist', instead of something predictable? How?

Even though you will still be writing in sentences, you can create rich imagery by using repetition, strong verbs and adjectives, alliteration and assonance, similes and metaphors, and onomatopoeia. Experiment with the tense of the poem, the arrangement of words and the rhythm to achieve greater impact.

Odes

The ode has its origins in ancient Greece, and was written to honour or praise a person, object or abstract quality. It is intensely lyrical and subjective, and therefore has a high level of emotion. An ode is usually addressed to the subject and is therefore written in the second person.

The following ode by John Keats, one of the Romantic poets, pays homage to the season of autumn, which is personified throughout the poem. The poem's use of full rhyme, long vowel sounds, alliteration and assonance create a softness of mood, and a gentle, unhurried rhythm. The language is sensory, sumptuous and lush, evoking strong images. Thematically, the first part of each stanza defines the subject matter; the second part develops and contemplates the subject:

Ode to Autumn

Season of mists and mellow fruitfulness,
    Close bosom-friend of the maturing sun;
Conspiring with him how to load and bless
    With fruit the vines that round the thatch-eaves run;
To bend with apples the mossed cottage-trees,
    And fill all fruit with ripeness to the core;
        To swell the gourd, and plump the hazel shells
With a sweet kernel; to set budding more,
    And still more, later flowers for the bees,
    Until they think warm days will never cease,
        For Summer has o'er-brimmed their clammy cells.

Who hath not seen thee oft amid thy store?
    Sometimes whoever seeks abroad may find
Thee sitting careless on a granary floor,
    Thy hair soft-lifted by the winnowing wind;
Or on a half-reaped furrow sound asleep,
    Drows'd with the fume of poppies, while thy hook
        Spares the next swath and all its twined flowers:
And sometimes like a gleaner thou dost keep
    Steady thy laden head across a brook;
    Or by a cider-press, with patient look,
        Thou watchest the last oozings, hours by hours.

---

rhyme scheme: first four lines: a b a b; next seven lines: c d e d c c e

metre: iambic pentameter

subject matter: autumn is addressed; it works in harmony with the sun to ripen fruit, make it abundant, and make flowers bloom; describes the pre-harvest ripeness; appeals to the *tactile* senses

vocab: gourd: a large, fleshy fruit
clammy: moist and sticky

---

rhyme scheme: first four lines: a b a b; next seven lines: c d e c d d e

subject matter: Autumn is described as a goddess, lazing on the floor of the granary or asleep in the field, or watching the cider-press squeeze the juice from apples; describes the abundance of the harvest itself; appeals to the *visual* senses

vocab: store: granary (a storehouse for grain); abroad: out of doors; careless: without a care; winnowing: fluttering; hook: scythe (a cutting tool); swath: the area covered by the stroke of a scythe or cutting machine; gleaner: person who gathers corn left by reapers; laden: heavy, burdened with cargo

---

- alliteration and repetition of the 'm' and 'f' sounds create softness and a gentle rhythm

- personification – autumn is addressed as if human

- 'bless' is a religious allusion which emphasises the 'sacredness' of the season

- use of strong, sumptuous verbs emphasise the lushness of early autumn, further highlighted by the repetition of 'more, and still more'

- the internal rhyme of 'more', and the half-rhyme of 'bees' and 'cease' – all with long vowel sounds – draws out and slows the rhythm

- assonance in bees and cease creates a 'clipped' effect

- use of second person

- alliteration/repetition of soft 'th', 's' and 'w' sounds creates a gentleness of rhythm

- use of hyphenated words further slows the tempo to create an hypnotic mood; they are almost meant to be whispered

- use of words to do with rest create a lazy, almost lethargic mood

- simile compares autumn to a gatherer laden with harvested corn

- long vowel sounds, followed by assonance in the repetition of 'hours' soften the line and almost drag the sentence along for emphasis

rhyme scheme: first four lines: a b a b; next seven lines: c d e c d d e

subject matter: the speaker tells Autumn not to wonder where the sounds of spring have gone, but to listen to her own 'music'. This stanza refers to various animals; foreshadows the end of autumn and the onset of winter. There is a sense of coming loss, yet the season will come again; describes the emptiness following the harvest; appeals to the *auditory* senses

vocab: barred: streaked; stubble-plains: the stumps of grain stalks left in the ground when the crop is cut; sallows: a tree or shrub related to the willow; bourne: boundary; treble: high-pitched; croft: small pasture

Where are the songs of Spring? Ay, where are they?
　　Think not of them, thou hast thy music too, -
While barred clouds bloom the soft-dying day,
　　And touch the stubble-plains with rosy hue;
Then in a wailful choir the small gnats mourn
　　Among the river sallows, borne aloft
　　　Or sinking as the light wind lives or dies;
And full-grown lambs loud bleat from hilly bourne;
　　Hedge-crickets sing; and now with treble soft
　　The redbreast whistles from a garden-croft;
　　　And gathering swallows twitter in the skies.

John Keats

rhetorical question is forceful and changes the mood; we are 'snapped out' of the hypnotic, lazy state of the middle stanza

alliteration of 'th' slows the pace and creates a musical quality

hyphenated words, especially with the inclusion of the word 'soft' again almost whisper, softening the line and emphasising the 'dreamy' rhythm

words associated with dying and loss reinforce the theme of the transience of the seasons; autumn is perched on the brink of winter. Metaphors emphasise the theme of autumn's 'death'

onomatopoeia increases the tempo and accentuates the percussion-like sounds of the animals who prepare for winter's arrival

Activity 4.52

1　**a**　How would *you* describe the mood of 'Ode to Autumn'?
　b　Choose two images which you think best reflect the mood. How, in your opinion, do they do this?

2　Autumn has been described as 'Mother Nature's show'. Do you agree? In what ways has Keats captured this idea in his poem?

3　**a**　Choose one of the stanzas from the poem and paint or draw it. Choose colours that reflect the mood of, and imagery in, the stanza.
　b　Find a photograph or piece of artwork that links in some way to 'Ode to Autumn'. Write an explanation of the link and why you chose the image.

4 'Ode to Autumn' offers a different experience to each reader, as we bring our understanding and imagination to our reading, along with memory and emotion. What is your favourite season? Why? What are the memories, colours, sounds and emotions you associate with it? Construct these as a mind map, then write an ode to your favourite season and personify it as Keats has done in 'Ode to Autumn'.

Modern odes usually have a definite rhyme scheme and metre, although they are more flexible than traditional odes. The most important thing to remember about the form is that it is written to praise the good in someone or something.

Ode to Uluru

Revered rock, you gaze upon us
Hard set wisdom in the veins
Of colour coursing down your face
Softened by the summer rains.

Haughty rock, you survive unbroken
As nature's storms assault your chest
Your courage rests in thoughts unspoken
Sardonic smiles when fury rests.

Exquisite rock, you glow with glory
Sunset draping shimmering quilt,
In air's vibrations hang the stories
Of the tribes and blood now spilt.

Majestic rock, you lie with spirits
Of the Dreaming, dream at night
Of the Old Ones chanting lyrics
Dancing till the dawn's new light.

Uncompromising rock, you stand
In silence, countless eons old
Hugging the flatness of the land
Proud like the Sphinx, secrets untold.
Remembering the ceremonies, remembering the songs
Reliving the journeys, mourning those wronged.

Michelle Williams

1   Who or what is being addressed in 'Ode to Uluru'?

2   Uluru is personified, as is autumn in 'Ode to Autumn'. Do you think it is easier to give an object human qualities when singing its praises so highly? Why or why not?

3   The metre of the poem 'Ode to Uluru' changes in the last stanza. What does this do to the rhythm? Do you think it enhances or detracts from the poem? Explain.

4   A couplet has been added to the last stanza. Suggest the point you think the poet is trying to make here. Is it in keeping with the rest of the poem? Explain.

5   **a**   Besides personification, identify any common features shared by 'Ode to Autumn' and 'Ode to Uluru'.

    b   Which of these odes do you prefer? Justify your answer.

6   The structure and language features of the poem 'Ode to Autumn' have already been interpreted and explained for you. Now it's your turn to try an interpretation of 'Ode to Uluru'. Working in groups, consider the points below – you can use these guidelines when examining any poem. Draw up a table and collate the information you gather. Be prepared to present your interpretation to the class.

Poetic feature	Points to notice and discuss
Form	Is the poem written as free verse/a ballad/a sonnet/prose poetry, etc.? How does the form complement the poem's content? Is the poem a good example of the form? Explain why or why not.
Voice	Is the poem written in the first, second or third person? Has the poet adopted a speaker (persona) or is the poem written from the poet's personal perspective? Are there instances when a persona is speaking but the poet 'gives away' their own perspective? Does the poem contain dialogue? Is it effective? Why or why not?
Context	What is the personal/historical/social/cultural background of the poet and/or the poem? (Poets may write about things that have occurred in a social, cultural and historical context that differs from their own.) What do you know of the poet's personal circumstances at the time of writing the poem?
Content	What is the poem's subject matter? What does it talk about on a literal level?
Imagery	Are the images presented from nature or elsewhere? Do they appeal to the senses? Which senses? How? Why? Does the poet use such devices as similes, metaphors, personification, symbolism, analogies, repetition, alliteration, assonance, onomatopoeia? How is the imagery in the poem mainly conveyed?

Poetic feature	Points to notice and discuss
Tone	What is the poet's attitude towards the subject matter? Is it happy, sad, respectful, or angry, for example? How do the words used create the tone? Is the tone conveyed by the poet personally, or through a persona?
Mood	What is the general atmosphere that the writing creates? How does the choice of words and imagery make you feel?
Rhythm	Is the rhythm slow or fast? Does it remain the same or does it change? Does it have a pattern (iambic pentameter, for example)? How do the choice of words, length of vowel sounds, repetition, line breaks and rhyme contribute to the rhythm?
Rhyme	Does the poem use different sorts of rhyme, such as end rhyme, half-rhyme, internal rhyme? Does it have a sustained rhyme scheme? Does it contain any rhyme at all? How does this relate to the form chosen? How does the rhyme, or lack of it, add to the impact of the poem?
Theme	What is the deeper or wider meaning of the poem? What point is it making through its subject matter? What messages underly our literal interpretation of the poem?

Elegies

An elegy is a sad poem of grief, loss or death in which the poet may mourn not only people, but things and animals as well. In fact, the word 'elegy' comes from the Greek word for 'a mournful poem'.

Elegies can be written in any form; what makes them unique is that they are reflective and sad. Elegies can be written in two ways. Some elegies are very personal, expressing grief over the loss of a relative, friend or thing. Other elegies may be more general, where the poet contemplates the issue of death or mortality.

Read the following elegies to see how, in only a few words, the poets have managed to communicate great personal sadness and loss.

Killed in action

For N. J. de B.-L.
Crete, May, 1941

His chair at the table, empty,
His home clothes hanging in rows forlorn,
His cricket bat and cap, his riding cane,
The new flannel suit he had not worn.
His dogs, restless, restless, with tortured ears
Listening for his swift, light tread upon the path.
And there – his violin! Oh his violin! Hush! hold your tears.

Juliette de Bairacli-Levy

Logic

Last year
My father died.
It stretched him out
And took his breath
Away clear.
It was so much it
Broke the back
Of reason.

When I find hoards
Of foreign coins,
Or see his books
And pills again,
I leave them back
And dust around those
Little jabs
Of pain.

Rosemary Cowan (student)

Activity 4.54

1   In 'Killed in action' and 'Logic', what are the reminders for each poet that cause them pain?

2   There are very strong images in these poems that communicate great sadness. How is grief expressed in the following lines? What effect do the words in bold have?

   a   'His home clothes hanging in rows **forlorn**'
   b   '**Hush!** hold your tears.'
   c   'It was so much **it broke the back of reason**.'
   d   'And dust around those **little jabs of pain**.'

3   The poems' titles convey information, either about the manner of death, or the poet's attitude towards it. 'Killed in action', and its subtitle, tell us that the man fought and died in the Second World War. Why, however, do you think Rosemary Cowan called her poem 'Logic'?

'Mid-term break', by Seamus Heaney, is about the death of his younger brother, Christopher. It is told with simple but powerful imagery and has great emotional depth.

Mid-term break

I sat all morning in the college sick bay
Counting bells knelling classes to a close,
At two o'clock our neighbours drove me home.

In the porch I met my father crying –
He had always taken funerals in his stride –
And Big Jim Evans saying it was a hard blow.

The baby cooed and laughed and rocked the pram
When I came in, and I was embarrassed
By old men standing up to shake my hand

And tell me they were 'sorry for my trouble',
Whispers informed strangers I was the eldest,
Away at school, as my mother held my hand

In hers and coughed out angry tearless sighs.
At ten o'clock the ambulance arrived
With the corpse, stanched and bandaged by the nurses.

Next morning I went up into the room. Snowdrops
And candles soothed the bedside; I saw him
For the first time in six weeks. Paler now,

Wearing a poppy bruise on his left temple,
He lay in the four foot box as in his cot.
No gaudy scars, the bumper knocked him clear.

A four foot box, a foot for every year.

Seamus Heaney

Activity **4.55**

1   Explain your feelings when you read the last line of 'Mid-term break'.

2   What had happened to Christopher?

3   'Knelling' refers to the sound of a bell ringing, especially at a funeral or death. Describe the impact of its use in the first stanza.

4   There is a strong contrast between the unease of the homecoming and the calmness of the scene when Heaney is alone with his brother.
    a   Identify the words and images which create an atmosphere of discomfort and a sense of detachment for the poet in the first section.
    b   Explain how calmness and acceptance are conveyed through words and images in the final two stanzas of the poem, before the last line.

5   Heaney refers to the 'poppy bruise', a metaphor, on his brother's left temple. Poppies are flowers linked with death, but also with the soothing of pain (opiates come from poppies). Why do you think Heaney may have chosen this image? Suggest possible reasons for describing his brother as 'wearing' the bruise.

6   What is the effect of the simile 'He lay in the four foot box as in his cot'?

7   Contrast the ways in which Heaney's parents deal with their grief. How do you react to this? Explain the point being made when Heaney says of his father 'He had always taken funerals in his stride'. With whom, do you think, is his mother angry?

8   The rhythm and mood of the poem owes much to alliteration and assonance. Find examples of these and explain their effect.

9   Write your own elegy. You might express it in personal terms or write it as a reflection on death and mortality.

Pastoral poetry

Pastoral poems are written about situations from country life. They are 'nature' poems, regardless of their form, length or metre. They are also lyrical, telling us about the personal feelings and emotions of the poet.

The most famous pastoral poetry is that of the Romantics of the eighteenth and early nineteenth centuries, such as Wordsworth, Blake, Shelley and Keats. The theme of nature as something innocent and ideal has a long history, but it was with the Romantic poets that this view gained new ground. They saw nature as something pure, the perfect specimen of creation, in contrast with the destructiveness of humans. Their poems were the social commentaries of their time, as they protested against the effects of industrialisation, technology and the destruction of nature.

In William Wordsworth's poem 'Lines written in early spring', he not only muses about the beauty of nature, but also reflects upon human nature.

Lines written in early spring

I heard a thousand blended notes
　　While in a grove I sat reclined,
In that sweet mood when pleasant thoughts
　　Bring sad thoughts to the mind.

To her fair works did Nature link
　　The human soul that through me ran;
And much it grieved my heart to think
　　What man has made of man.

Through primrose tufts, in that green bower,
　　The periwinkle trailed its wreaths;
And 'tis my faith that every flower
　　Enjoys the air it breathes.

The birds around me hopped and played,
　　Their thoughts I cannot measure –
But the least motion which they made
　　It seemed a thrill of pleasure.

The budding twigs spread out their fan
　　To catch the breezy air;
And I must think, do all I can,
　　That there was pleasure there.

If this belief from heaven be sent,
　　If such be Nature's holy plan,
Have I not reason to lament
　　What man has made of man?

William Wordsworth

1   How would you describe the mood of 'Lines written in early spring'?

2   'Melancholy' means deeply, seriously, or sadly thoughtful. Identify lines from the poem which convey melancholy thoughts.

3   Despite this sad reflection, there are many things the poet finds beautiful and awe-inspiring in nature. What are they?

4   Wordsworth makes religious associations to do with nature.
    a   He describes a 'connection' between nature and his soul. Identify the lines where he says this.
    b   He also alludes to the idea that beauty and pleasure in nature is 'holy' or 'heaven-sent'. In what lines do we see this?
    c   Discuss what you think this says about Wordsworth and his depth of feeling.

5   a   What point do you think he is making in the lines:
        'Have I not reason to lament
        What man has made of man'?
    b   Suggest how this ties in with the views of the Romantics.

6   What are the threats to nature, caused by humans, which exist today?

The poem below also reflects on the beauty of nature, and is also connected to the idea of 'what man has made of man'. The poet uses delicate imagery to highlight the resilient quality of nature, contrasted with the frailty of the human race:

There will come soft rains

There will come soft rains and the smell of the ground,
And swallows circling with their shimmering sound;

And frogs in the pools singing at night,
And wild plum-trees in tremulous white;

Robins will wear their feathery fire
Whistling their whims on a low fence-wire;

And not one will know of the war, not one
Will care at last when it is done.

Not one would mind, neither bird nor tree,
If mankind perished utterly;

And Spring herself, when she woke at dawn,
Would scarcely know that we were gone.

Sarah Teasdale

Activity **4.57**

1 Explain the poet's message in 'There will come soft rains'.

2 Do you think she is referring to a *specific* war, or something else? Explain.

3 Suggest the point being made about the human race in the last line.

4 Both poems personify nature. Quote the line from each poem where this occurs. Suggest why the poets have described it in human terms. Is it effective? Why or why not?

5 Wordsworth saw humankind as destroying *nature*. What does Sarah Teasdale seem to be saying we will destroy?

Steven Herrick's poem 'The big river' takes a languid look at one aspect of nature:

The big river

The big river
rolls past our town
at Hobson's Bend,
takes a slow look
at the houses on stilts
with timber creaking, paint flaking,
at the graveyard hushed
in the lonely shade,
at the fruit bats
dropping mango pulp
into the undergrowth,
at the foundry, and sawmill
grinding under a blazing sun,
at the pub with welcoming verandahs
shaded in wisteria vine,
at Durra Creek surrendering
to the incessant flow,
at Pearce Swamp upstream
on the creek among the willows
and rivergums,
at the storm clouds
rumbling over Rookwood Hill,
at the two boys
casting a line
on the crumbling bank,
at the cow fields
purple with Paterson's curse,
at the jammed tree-trunks
washed down after summer thunder,
at the shop
with dead flies in the window display,
at the mosquito mangroves
and the sucking sound of mud crabs,
at the children throwing mulberries
that stain like lipstick.
The big river
rolls past our town,
takes a slow look,
and rolls away.

Steven Herrick, from *by the river*

1   In 'The big river' the sparse use of punctuation and capitalisation, and the frequent use of run-over lines create a certain rhythm, as well as drawing our eyes fluently and effortlessly down the page. How would you describe the rhythm of the poem?

2   **a**   What is the mood of the poem?
    b   Does the rhythm create the mood or does the mood affect the rhythm? Explain.
    c   In groups, brainstorm a list of adjectives which you think describe the mood.
    d   Write down particular words from the poem which convey its mood.

3   The river is personified. Explain the human thing it is able to do.

4   It's almost as if the river in the poem has been given a personality. Write a paragraph describing other features of its personality, giving more information than the poet.

5   What impressions do you get of the town? Compare your responses with others'.

6   Read the poem aloud as a performance piece. Try to present a relaxed and fluent reading to reflect its mood and capture its rhythm.

7   Draw a map of the river and the locations it passes.

8   There are lots of examples of sight and sound imagery in 'The big river'. Write your own nature poem based on the senses. Draw a table like the one below.

Sight	Sound	Touch	Smell	Taste

Go outside and write down everything in nature that you can see, hear, touch, smell and taste, no matter how unimportant it seems (the 'taste' sensation may be limited, however!). The senses can refer to more than one physical sensation. Touch, for example, refers to anything sensed through the skin, such as texture, pressure, weight or temperature. Choose some of the things from your list of observations and turn them into phrases or sentences by using more sensory detail. Experiment with form, imagery, line breaks, rhyme (if you want to use it) until you have a poem.

Epic poetry

An epic is a long narrative poem, usually centred around a hero (or heroes) on an important journey. There are some very famous epic poems, for example, the *Iliad* and the *Odyssey*, both written by the Greek poet Homer. The *Iliad* takes its name from 'Ilion', the Greek name for Troy. It is set during the Trojan War, when Achilles kills Hector to avenge the death of his friend Patroclus. The *Odyssey* describes the ten-year voyage of Odysseus after the Trojan War, during which he encounters various monsters (such as the Cyclops) and other supernatural and mythological beings. The modern idea of an epic, however, is any long story. We often use the term for long novels or films.

The characteristics of an epic poem are that:
- it tells a story
- the plot is simple
- the main character is usually a hero
- the hero is on an important journey or has to carry out an important deed
- he/she is watched over by gods or supernatural beings
- there is no division into stanzas.

The story below, from the Bible, tells of the journey of the Magi: the Wise Men from the East who brought gifts to the infant Christ.

The journey of the kings

The story as told by St Matthew, chapter 2, verses 1–15

Now when Jesus was born in Bethlehem of Judaea in the days of Herod the king, behold, there came wise men from the east to Jerusalem, saying, Where is he that is born King of the Jews? for we have seen his star in the east, and are come to worship him.

When Herod the King had heard these things, he was troubled, and all Jerusalem with him. And when he had gathered all the chief priests and scribes of the people together, he demanded of them where Christ should be born. And they said unto him, In Bethlehem of Judaea: for thus it is written by the prophet,

And thou Bethlehem, in the land of Juda,
Art not the least among the princes of Juda:
For out of thee shall come a Governor,
That shall rule my people Israel.

Then Herod, when he had privily called the wise men, inquired of them diligently what time the star appeared.

And he sent them to Bethlehem, and said, go and search diligently for the young child; and when ye have found him, bring me word again, that I may come and worship him also. When they had heard the king, they departed; and, lo, the star, which they saw in the east, went before them, till it came and stood over where the young child was. When they saw the star, they rejoiced with exceeding great joy.

And when they were come into the house, they saw the young child with Mary his mother, and fell down, and worshipped him: and when they had opened their treasures, they presented unto him gifts: gold, and frankincense, and myrrh. And being warned of God in a dream that they should not return to Herod, they departed into their own country another way.

But when they had departed, behold, the angel of the Lord appeared in a dream to Joseph, saying, 'Arise, and take the child and his mother, and flee into Egypt, and remain there until I tell thee. For Herod will seek the child to destroy him.'

So he arose, and took the child and his mother by night and withdrew into Egypt, and remained there until the death of Herod; that what was spoken by the Lord through the prophet might be fulfilled, 'Out of Egypt I called my son.'

The backdrop to this story is a tale of political ambition, jealousy, intrigue, deception and murder. Herod, at the time of Jesus' birth, was the reigning King of the Jews, living in Jerusalem. He was a brutal man, having killed any rivals, real or imagined (including his own family members) who posed a risk to his position as king.

The Magi had travelled a long distance to Jerusalem. It is unclear where their homeland was – we only know that they came from 'the East' – but scholars suggest three possibilities: Persia, Arabia or Babylon, with Persia being the most popular choice. They arrived with news that they had seen a 'star in the east', which they were following, and to enquire if anyone knew of the exact whereabouts of the birth. The idea of the birth of a Messiah – a leader of the Jewish people – was prophesied in Jewish scriptures, which also said that the birth would be marked by the appearance of a star. Herod had probably heard of this 'Messiah' but, up until the Magi's arrival, had not taken it seriously.

The Bible story tells us that Herod was 'troubled' at hearing the news. Note that the Magi do not ask 'Where is he that is born, who *will be* King of the Jews?', but 'Where is he that *is born* King of the Jews?' As someone who had been fighting off rivals ever since he had been made king, it seems certain that Herod would have been troubled by the talk of a new adversary.

Having learned from rumours that Bethlehem was the birthplace of the Messiah, Herod called the Wise Men 'privily' – in secret. He asked them to go to Bethlehem to find the child, then return to Jerusalem with news of his whereabouts 'that I may come and worship him'. Herod's plan was to use the Magi to get precise information about the child, so that he could be more certain of killing the right child.

The Magi went on their way, no doubt suspicious of Herod's apparent eagerness to give up his own reign and switch allegiances to a new Jewish king. Eventually, led by the star, they found the baby Jesus and worshipped him with gifts. Rather than journeying back to Jerusalem to give Herod the news, they were 'warned of God in a dream that they should not return to Herod' and went back to their own country by a different route.

Matthew 2:16 says:

> When Herod saw that the wise men had deceived him, he was greatly angered. He ordered that all children under two years old in Bethlehem and the land around should be put to death, in accordance with the time of the star that he had learned from the wise men.

These orders were carried out. Bethlehem was a small village at that time; it has been estimated that between seven and twenty boys under the age of two lived there.

The baby Jesus and his family, however, had not stayed in Bethlehem. Following the visit by the Magi, and the angel's warning to Joseph, they fled to Egypt. They remained there until the death of Herod, afterwards returning to live in Nazareth.

In his poem 'Journey of the Magi', T.S. Eliot tells the story of the Wise Men's journey to Bethlehem to honour the birth of Christ, from the perspective of one Magus (note that 'magus' is the singular; 'magi' is plural). Eliot converted to Christianity, being baptised in the Anglican Church when he was 39. This poem was written during the transition between his old and new faiths.

Activity 4.59

As you read the following poem, and afterwards, record your impressions, such as:
- *When I read the title I thought . . .*
- *The poem reminds me of . . .*
- *I'm not sure about . . .*
- *I'm puzzled by . . .*
- *A word/line that strikes me is . . . because . . .*
- *I think the poem might mean . . .*
- *The poet seems to be saying . . .*
- *I like/dislike the poem because . . .*

Journey of the Magi

'A cold coming we had of it,
Just the worst time of the year
For a journey, and such a long journey:
The ways deep and the weather sharp,
The very dead of winter.'
And the camels galled, sore-footed, refractory,
Lying down in the melting snow.
There were times we regretted
The summer palaces on slopes, the terraces,
And the silken girls bringing sherbet.
Then the camel men cursing and grumbling
And running away, and wanting their liquor and women,
And the night-fires going out, and the lack of shelters,
And the cities hostile and the towns unfriendly
And the villages dirty and charging high prices:
A hard time we had of it.
At the end we preferred to travel all night,
Sleeping in snatches,
With the voices singing in our ears, saying
That this was all folly.

Then at dawn we came down to a temperate valley,
Wet, below the snow line, smelling of vegetation;
With a running stream and a water-mill beating the darkness,
And three trees on the low sky,
And an old white horse galloped away in the meadow.
Then we came to a tavern with vine-leaves over the lintel,
Six hands at an open door dicing for pieces of silver,
And feet kicking the empty wine-skins.
But there was no information, and so we continued
And arrived at evening, not a moment too soon
Finding the place; it was (you may say) satisfactory.

All this was a long time ago, I remember,
And I would do it again, but set down
This set down
This: were we led all that way for
Birth or Death? There was a Birth, certainly,
We had evidence and no doubt. I had seen birth and death,
But had thought they were different; this Birth was
Hard and bitter agony for us, like Death, our death.
We returned to our places, these Kingdoms,
But no longer at ease here, in the old dispensation,
With an alien people clutching their gods.
I should be glad of another death.

T. S. Eliot

Annotations:
- describes the difficulty of the journey
- galled: irritated, infuriated
- refractory: stubborn, resistant
- felt a sense of loss; regrets the 'vanishing' of the things of summer in the place from which they came
- may allude to Herod's Jerusalem
- the voices: their own intuition
- folly: fearing that the journey was a waste of time
- an early morning descent into a warmer town
- symbolic of the dawning of a new era
- symbolic of the crosses of Calvary – Christ was crucified alongside two others
- lintel: a beam above the door
- foreshadows Judas' betrayal of Christ years later for 30 pieces of silver
- understatement: the purpose of his journey was met
- the placement of words draws our eye down, and also creates emphasis
- the Magus has been converted in his faith; the birth has brought 'death' to his old life, putting him into a world which has now lost its meaning
- the Magus, transformed, will have to live uncomfortably as a man of a new faith living among those of the old ways
- relates to the line 'And I would do it again'

1   In what ways does the poem 'Journey of the Magi', and the story behind it, possess the characteristics of an epic?

2   Draw a Venn diagram like the one below. In groups, compile a list of the similarities and differences between the Biblical story, as told by Matthew, and T.S. Eliot's poem 'Journey of the Magi'.

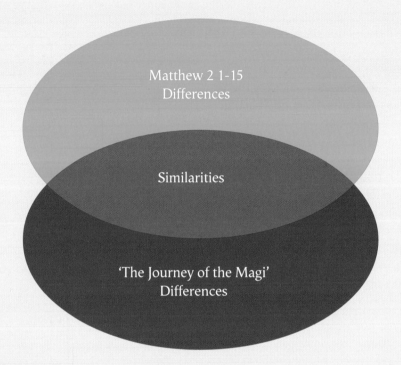

Matthew 2 1-15
Differences

Similarities

'The Journey of the Magi'
Differences

3   The Magi were pagan priests; that is, they were not Christian, Jewish or Muslim. It is said that after their return home from Bethlehem they were baptised as Christians.
   a   Suggest how this shows the impact that their journey had on them.
   b   In what way is this alluded to in the poem?
   c   What connections can you make between this and the experiences of T.S. Eliot?

4   T.S. Eliot's religious conversion must have been a turbulent time for him. How is this reflected in the mood and tone of the poem?

5   If the Magi were pagans, why did they go to Bethlehem? Use the Internet to find out.

6   From Persia, where the Magi are thought to have lived, the distance to Jerusalem was about 750 kilometres. Such a journey may have taken months, even up to a year, to travel by camel. Besides this, there would probably have been weeks of preparation from the time the Magi first saw the star. List the lines from the poem which tell us that the journey was a difficult one.

7   'Were we led all that way for Birth or Death?' Answer the Magus' question.

The paintings below of *The Adoration of the Magi* portray the various characters of the story, and their reactions to events, in different ways.

Antonio Allegri Correggio,
The Adoration of the Magi, c.1517,
Galleria Nazionale, Parma

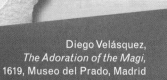

Diego Velásquez,
The Adoration of the Magi,
1619, Museo del Prado, Madrid

1   Make a list of words to describe the paintings by Correggio and Velasquez.

2   Add emotive words describing the feelings you get from the paintings.

3   Select the painting that you think best reflects or complements the story of the Magi's journey, as told in the Bible and in the poem by T.S. Eliot. Explain your reasons.

The paintings below of the *Flight into Egypt* are very different in their styles and moods. The steep, rugged terrain which dwarfs the characters in Patenier's version highlights the family's escape from Herod's rage and suggests an arduous and dangerous journey. Swanson's version, however, is lively, colourful and optimistic, suggesting not an escape from death, but a journey towards new life.

Patenier, *The Flight into Egypt*, undated,
Musee Royal des Beaux-Arts, Antwerp

John August Swanson,
Flight into Egypt, 2002

1   Which of the *Flight into Egypt* paintings do you think is better suited to the Biblical story? Explain why.

2   Which do you prefer, and why?

3   Draw up a table like the one below. In groups, compile lists of words to describe and compare the visual messages contained in the four paintings.

	Correggio, *The Adoration of the Magi* (1517)	Velasquez, *The Adoration of the Magi* (1619)	Patenier, *The Flight into Egypt* (undated)	Swanson, *Flight into Egypt* (2002)
Style				
Mood				
Use of colour				
Symbols and what they might represent				
Size and positioning of characters/objects				
Dominant characters or features				
Body language/facial expressions of characters and what this represents				
Value – where is your eye drawn?				

4   Use the Internet to find the painting (or another piece of visual art) which you think best reflects the poem 'Journey of the Magi'. Some good sites include:

- www.the-athenaeum.org/art
- www.artchive.com
- www.abcgallery.com
- www.wallacecollection.org
- www.artandarchitecture.org.uk
- www.artofeurope.com
- www.theartgallery.com.au
- www.nationalgallery.org.uk
- www.tate.org.uk
- www.metmuseum.org.

Blank verse

Blank verse is unrhymed and has a regular metre, with each line having roughly the same number of syllables. In blank verse we usually find detailed descriptions of events, but it is also a form of poetry in which characters reveal a great deal about themselves.

Shakespeare often used blank verse in his plays, namely in the soliloquies of his characters. In *Hamlet*, Act 3, Scene 1, the Prince of Denmark struggles with the thought of suicide. This soliloquy, perhaps the most famous speech in the English language, takes place after Hamlet's father is killed by his uncle, Claudius, who in turn then marries Hamlet's mother, thus becoming King of Denmark. Hamlet's speech is a powerful examination of life and death, the known and unknown, and the connection between thought and action.

To be, or not to be

To be, or not to be: that is the question:
Whether 'tis nobler in the mind to suffer
The slings and arrows of outrageous fortune,
Or to take arms against a sea of troubles,
And by opposing end them? To die: to sleep;
No more; and by a sleep to say we end
The heart-ache and the thousand natural shocks
That flesh is heir to, 'tis a consummation
Devoutly to be wished. To die, to sleep;
To sleep; perchance to dream: ay, there's the rub;
For in that sleep of death what dreams may come
When we have shuffled off this mortal coil,
Must give us pause: there's the respect
That makes calamity of so long life;
For who could bear the whips and scorns of time,
The oppressor's wrong, the proud man's contumely,
The pangs of despised love, the law's delay,
The insolence of office, and the spurns
That patient merit of the unworthy takes,
When he himself might his quietus make
With a bare bodkin? Who would fardels bear,
To grunt and sweat under a weary life,

the question of whether to commit suicide is posed as a logical one: to live, or not to live?

the consequences of living and dying are weighed up: is it more noble to suffer life passively, or to actively seek to end one's suffering?

sleep is a metaphor for death. Hamlet thinks of the end to suffering, pain, and uncertainty. He decides that suicide is a desirable course of action: a 'completion', which is wished for

an examination of what will happen after death. The 'sleep' metaphor is extended to include the possibility of dreaming. The dreams that may come in the 'sleep' of death are so daunting that it causes him to stop and think ('give us pause')

the agonies of life are such that no-one would willingly bear them. Hamlet outlines a long list of the miseries of experience – ranging from political oppression, humiliation, unrequited love, injustice, disempowerment, hard work – and asks the question: why suffer through these burdens if it is as easy as ending life with a dagger?

But that the dread of something after death,
The undiscovered country from whose bourn
No traveller returns, puzzles the will,
And makes us rather bear those ills we have
Than fly to others that we know not of?
Thus conscience does make cowards of us all;
And thus the native hue of resolution
Is sicklied o'er with the pale cast of thought.
And enterprises of great pith and moment
With this regard their currents turn awry,
And lose the name of action.

William Shakespeare

> he answers his own question: it is the fear and uncertainty of the afterlife ('the dread of something after death') that makes us submit to life's sufferings, rather than going to another state of existence ('the undiscover'd country') which might be even worse and from whose limits we cannot return

> he cannot do it. Recognising that the consequences of living are better than the consequences of dying, he determines that such a rash and hasty act would be impossible. His inner thoughts of death, which once had strength, now feel wrong; actions which seemed a good idea at one time are now not so inviting

Vocabulary

- consummation: completion, fulfilment
- there's the rub: a source of doubt or difficulty
- calamity: an affliction, misery
- contumely: an insult; contemptuous or humiliating treatment
- insolence of office: in this sense, perhaps the cheek or audacity of the manner in which Hamlet's uncle became King, which makes a mockery of the title
- spurns: to reject with disdain
- quietus: to give up; to make an exit
- bodkin: dagger
- fardels: burdens, bundles, loads
- bourn: spring, well
- native hue of resolution: an innate, instinctive feeling which colours one's determination and decisions
- pith: strength, force, vitality, enthusiasm
- awry: turned or twisted; amiss, wrong

Activity 4.63

1 How does Hamlet's mood change from the beginning of this speech to the end?

2 Note that he never uses the words 'I' or 'me' in this soliloquy. Do you think his speech is a contemplation of his own suicide or a more general exploration of 'life and death' questions? Explain by referring to lines in the poem.

3 What are the thoughts he has as he wonders about life and death?

4 Why does he change his mind?

5 The poem has timeless appeal. Why do you think it is so famous?

6   In groups, write a short blank verse poem in which you are torn between two things. For example:
    •   To lie, or not to lie?
    •   To fight, or not to fight?
    •   To stay, or not to stay?
    •   To 'dob', or not to 'dob'?
    •   To . . . , or not to . . . ?

Before you write your poem, draw a mind map listing the pros and cons of your 'moral dilemma'. Here's an example:

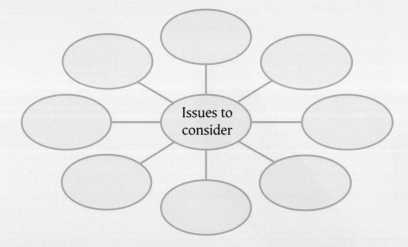

Issues to consider

Dramatic monologue

In poetry, reading or hearing a dramatic monologue is like listening to someone talking on the telephone. It's as if there is a one-sided conversation occurring, where you hear the speaker but not the person to whom he or she is speaking.

'Pleasant Sunday afternoon' by Bruce Dawe is about a poorly educated man who is visited by an encyclopedia salesman. Unfortunately, the man's family wreaks havoc when the salesman produces his set of encyclopedias and opens it. The man's wife, Ethel, puts grease on the pages, then scorches them when trying to remove it with a knife. One of the children, Stewart, apparently vomits over them; another child, Graham, empties his bowels on the floor and uses the pages from an encyclopedia to clean it up. Another child has meanwhile ripped up one of the volumes, while his father tries to put the pages back in their right order. The salesman quickly flees from the scene, leaving behind his ruined encyclopedias. The father continues to chat, unaware of the disaster his family has caused.

Pleasant Sunday afternoon

You mean we get this here Thingummy-thon
of   of   World Knowledge yeah that's it Jeez
a man's half-educated already
for nothing you might say   well practically
TWENTY-EIGHT MAGNIFICENT FULLY ILLUSTRATED VOLUMES
hey Eth here a minute and have a look at this
well you could have wiped your hands a bit first
(we're not auditioning for the Black and White Minstrels)
she won't leave that bloody stove of hers alone
no of course it won't rub off the page that's grease you silly
                                        sorry mate

now where's she off to   what the bloody hell
not with a red-hot knife   you've scorched it up
to buggery   ah well   you were saying
the kids Ethel the kids what do you mean
not quite suitable mate   these kids of mine
Eth what's young Stewart up to get him quick
starving for knowledge   use the mop love
ah there we are   a bit of the old sticky-tape
and good as new   *Graham*   ah   Ethel   looks like Graham
is getting set to   what's that son   you already *have*
alright son alright I'll take your word for it
no not the bloody encyclopaedia   old feller   here Eth
do something   well   what's the odds   you might as well
finish him off on this   err Contents page
talk about Tim Tyler   you married by any chance well
there's a treat in store   no don't get up no worries mate
we'll sort this little lot out now
what have we here   page sixty-three
I see what you mean by Magnificently Illustrated
now where is sixty-two   here's fifty-four
works fast doesn't he
                  well   alright mate
if you've got to go   but call in anytime
you won't believe this but we hardly ever have
a visitor from one year's end to the next

hey   hey there mate hey   what about your books
his books   he's left his bloody books!

                                        Bruce Dawe

1   In this dramatic monologue, there are unheard replies or comments made by the person being spoken to (the salesman). Copy the table below and, in groups, fill in what you think the salesman might have said. The first one has been done for you.

Father	Salesman	Father
You mean we get this here Thingummy-thon	*World Book Encyclopedia*	Yeah that's it. Jeez, a man's half-educated already.
for nothing, you might say		well, practically . . .
Ah well . . . You were saying?		What do you mean, not quite suitable, mate?
You might as well finish him off on this . . . err . . .		Contents page
You married by any chance?		Well, there's a treat in store.
No, don't get up.		No worries mate, we'll sort this little lot out now.
Now where is sixty-two? Here's fifty-four. Works fast, doesn't he?		Well, alright mate . . . if you've got to go . . . You won't believe this, but we hardly ever have a visitor from one year's end to the next.
Hey! Hey there, mate! Hey! What about your books?		His books! He's left his bloody books!

2   a   In your groups, transform the poem into a script in which not only the father, but also the salesman, Ethel, Stewart and Graham are given dialogue.

b   Act out your 'play' in front of the class.

Soliloquies

A soliloquy is very much like a dramatic monologue, except the character is speaking to him or herself – 'thinking out loud' – without the presence of others. Shakespeare wrote many soliloquies in his plays. They give us a real insight into the minds of his characters, whether they are expressing anxiety, despair, or joy. The soliloquy below is certainly not joyous. It takes place after Macbeth, who has become king of Scotland by murdering his predecessor, learns that his wife has committed suicide. Lady Macbeth, while originally spurring her husband on to do the deed, cannot cope with the guilt it brings. Macbeth's response to her death is at first subdued, but his speech evolves into one of pessimism and despair, in which he reflects upon the worthlessness of life:

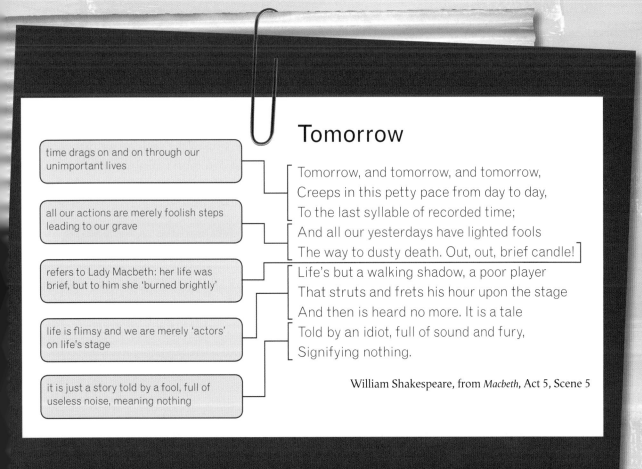

Tomorrow

time drags on and on through our unimportant lives

all our actions are merely foolish steps leading to our grave

refers to Lady Macbeth: her life was brief, but to him she 'burned brightly'

life is flimsy and we are merely 'actors' on life's stage

it is just a story told by a fool, full of useless noise, meaning nothing

Tomorrow, and tomorrow, and tomorrow,
Creeps in this petty pace from day to day,
To the last syllable of recorded time;
And all our yesterdays have lighted fools
The way to dusty death. Out, out, brief candle!
Life's but a walking shadow, a poor player
That struts and frets his hour upon the stage
And then is heard no more. It is a tale
Told by an idiot, full of sound and fury,
Signifying nothing.

William Shakespeare, from *Macbeth*, Act 5, Scene 5

1   There is strong repetition in the line 'tomorrow, and tomorrow, and tomorrow'. What does the image suggest?

2   Macbeth uses various metaphors for life. Explain them.

3   Do you believe that life 'signifies nothing'? Explain.

4   Write your own dramatic monologue or soliliquy about the nature of life as you see it. If you wish you could use the following structure to help you:
    - first verse: *birth is* . . .
    - second verse: *childhood is* . . .
    - third verse: *adolescence is* . . .
    - fourth verse: *adulthood is* . . .
    - fifth verse: *old age is* . . .
    - sixth verse: *death is* . . .

Sonnets

The sonnet is a fourteen-line lyric poem, written in iambic pentameter, traditionally about love and romance. Invented by the Italian poet Petrarch in the 1300s, the word 'sonnet' means 'little song'. The sonnet spread throughout Europe to England, and by the 1600s, the tradition of the sonnet as a love poem was well established. Shakespeare created his own version of the sonnet, writing over 150 of them. Thus, the two kinds of sonnets most common in English poetry take their names from the poets who utilised them: the Petrarchan sonnet and the Shakespearean sonnet. Let's look at how each of these forms differ:

Petrarchan sonnet	Shakespearean sonnet
• divided into two parts: the octave and the sestet • the octave (first eight lines) poses a question or establishes an idea • the sestet (next six lines) answers, comments upon or criticises the idea established in the octave	• made up of three quatrains (set of four rhyming lines) with a rhyme scheme of a b a b – presenting a different idea in each quatrain • ends with a rhyming couplet, which can be a summary of the ideas, or to indicate a change in thought (a shift in the direction of the emotions or thought is called a 'volta')

The Romantic poets also used the sonnet form – particularly the Petrarchan sonnet – but updated the subject matter for their times. Here William Wordsworth talks not of an idealised love for another, but of the beauty of nature on an early London morning:

Composed upon Westminster Bridge

(Early morning)

Rhyme scheme

Octave

Rhyme	Line
a	Earth has not anything to show more fair:
b	Dull would he be of soul who could pass by
b	A sight so touching in its majesty:
a	This city now doth like a garment wear
a	The beauty of the morning; silent, bare,
b	Ships, towers, domes, theatres, and temples lie
b	Open unto the fields, and to the sky:
a	All bright and glittering in the smokeless air.

Sestet

c	Never did sun more beautifully steep
d	In his first splendour valley, rock, or hill;
c	Ne'er saw I, never felt, a calm so deep!
d	The river glideth at his own sweet will:
c	Dear God! the very houses seem asleep;
d	And all that mighty heart is lying still!

William Wordsworth

The beauty of the sunrise and the tranquillity of the city at that moment actively affect the poet, as emphasised in 'so touching in its majesty'. Using a simile, he describes the city as being 'cloaked' in beauty, which will change as the day progresses (as easily as one would change clothes). The man-made constructs of London which, at that moment, are just as beautiful as anything found in nature, are 'bright', 'glittering' and 'smokeless' in the moments before the city awakes. The repetition of soft 's' sounds, and the use of serene adjectives ('fair', 'touching', 'silent', 'bare') add to the calm and tranquil mood of the stanza. The use of the strong noun 'majesty' emphasises nature's magnificence and grandeur.

The sun is personified as being capable of producing a sunrise ('first splendour') which is awe-inspiring. The repetition of 'never did'/'never saw' accentuates the rare beauty of the moment. The poet's sense of calm aligns with the calmness of the city. The river is personified, and the words 'glideth' and 'sweet' create a soothing rhythm and reflect the effortlessness of nature's beauty. 'The very houses seem asleep' and 'lying still' create an image of the city as a passive being which submits to the will of nature as it slumbers, unaware. This contrasts with 'mighty heart', a metaphor for its bustling activity when awake. However, in that dawn moment, it is Nature who is supreme. An exclamation mark reinforces this and ends the poem powerfully.

Activity **4.66**

1 The mood of the poem is optimistic, serene and tranquil, capturing the wonder of a moment. Select words and phrases from the poem which convey this mood. Suggest other words you could use to describe it.

2 'Dull would he be of soul ... ' Explain what the poet is saying about those who would not see the beauty in the scene.

3 'This city now doth like a garment wear ... ' is a simile. Why does the poet use the image of a garment?

4 Explain why the city is 'bright and glittering' and suggest how this contrasts with the tranquil words which come before it.

5 Complete the sentence: *'First splendour' is a metaphor for ...'*

6 Explain the effect of the repetition of 'never did ...' and 'ne'er saw ...'. What is the poet trying to emphasise?

7 'Dear God!' is an expressive reaction to the beauty described. List the other emotions conveyed by the poet.

8 Identify the things that are personified in the poem. What do you think is the intended effect?

9 Explain the metaphor 'mighty heart'. To what is it referring?

Shakespeare plays a 'tongue in cheek' joke on the sonnet as a form of idealised love poetry. In the poem below, he pokes fun at the clichéd metaphors used to describe beauty – cheeks like roses, lips red as coral, a voice like music – comparing the woman to a number of other beautiful things, and – at first glance – not always favourably.

Sonnet 130

Quatrain

My mistress' eyes are nothing like the sun;
Coral is far more red than her lips' red;
If snow be white, why then her breasts are dun;
If hairs be wires, black wires grow on her head.

Quatrain

I have seen roses damask'd, red and white,
But no such roses see I in her cheeks;
And in some perfumes is there more delight
Than in the breath that from my mistress reeks.

Quatrain

I love to hear her speak, yet well I know
That music hath a far more pleasing sound;
I grant I never saw a goddess go;
My mistress, when she walks, treads on the ground:

Couplet

And yet, by heaven, I think my love as rare
As any she belied with false compare.

William Shakespeare

first quatrain is phrased in positive terms (his mistress is like . . .)

dun: dull greyish-brown

damask'd: a pattern of red and white

second quatrain expands the comparison but turns them around (his mistress is not/does not have . . .)

reeks: gives off a bad smell

third quatrain develops the comparison: what he loves about her; points out that she is not a goddess, but human

the rhyming couplet indicates a shift in thought and tone, and reveals a 'twist': his love for her is exceptional ('rare'). The depth of this love does not need to be phrased in terms of clichés ('false comparisons') in order to be real and valuable; likewise, women do not need to look like flowers or goddesses in order to be beautiful

Activity 4.67

Write a Shakespearean sonnet in which you apparently insult somebody but reveal the 'truth' in the couplet.

Chapter 5

'Yesterday' by Patricia Pogson

Themes in poetry

Identity

Your 'identity' refers to your individuality and your personality. But what makes you individual and how did you get the personality you have? Some people say we are born with these things; others say it is our environment that 'moulds' our personality.

Activity 5.1

1   Do you think our personalities are 'born' or 'made'? In other words, were you born with the personality you have now or has it been changing and developing through your life? Explain using examples.

2   Write a poem about yourself to answer the question 'Who am I?' Use metaphors to compare yourself to things in nature such as animals, objects, colours or emotions. For example:

    I am a rock, solid, dependable
    I'm a bright purple sky with little dabs of black

3   Now add descriptions to extend the metaphor, for example:

    I am a rose bush
    thorny and spiked
    Yet delicate and perfumed
    when treated with care.

4   **a**   Pretend, for a moment, that you could be anyone else. Write down the name of the person and list reasons for wanting to become that person.
    b   Using the ideas in your list, write a poem that begins with: *'I'd like to be . . . '* or *'If I could be anyone else, I would be . . . '*

5   Write a poem about what you think are the good and bad features of your personality. Make it one of contrasts, in which you balance both the good and the bad, for example: *'I'm over-sensitive, but I'm compassionate'* or *'I'm selfish, but I'm loyal'.*

Our identity can be shaped not only by things around us, but also by what is part of us. What we inherit from our ancestors, the culture we grow up in and the society we live in all contribute to our identity.

One of the most obvious facts about grown-ups, to a child, is that they have forgotten what it is like to be a child . . .

Randall Jarrell

Copy

His mother's eyes,
His father's chin,
His auntie's nose,
His uncle's grin,

His great-aunt's hair,
His grandma's ears,
His grandpa's mouth,
So it appears . . .

Poor little tot
Well may he moan.
He hasn't much
To call his own.

Richard Armour

So show me, son,
how to laugh; show me how
I used to laugh and smile
once upon a time when I was like you.

Gabriel Okara

There are many influences in our lives, and they combine to give us our identity. Our parents and family, for instance, are important in shaping our ideas, our opinions and the way we think about things.

Activity 5.2

1   In small groups create a list of influences that play a part in shaping your identity.

2   Sketch these influences on a time line that show the important things throughout your life. You may wish to include the following events:
   - starting school
   - an important holiday
   - your first pet
   - meeting a special friend
   - a favourite Christmas or birthday
   - new siblings
   - moving home
   - a broken heart.

3   Compare your group's responses with the rest of the class.

> Youth would be an ideal state if it came a little later in life.
>
> Herbert Henry Asquith

Remembering

I remember when I was afraid
a long while ago.
Now I've had time to be brave.

I remember many years ago
when I was young
Now I've had space to grow.

I remember when I used to cry
an eternity ago.
Now I've learned to lie.

Now that I'm older
I'm not sure I enjoy it,
but there doesn't seem to be a cure
for growing up.

Student

> There is always one moment in childhood when the door opens and lets the future in.
>
> Graham Greene

A child becomes an adult when he realises that he has a right not only to be right but also to be wrong.

Thomas Szasz

It's hard

It's hard being a teenager
Being thought of as troublemakers,
Thought of as a 'bad influence' to others,
Don't they realise?
Don't they see?
We're going through a change,
A great change,
A change, like a caterpillar to butterfly,
From child to adult.
It's hard,
We don't know what we are
And while we're down
They kick us with their insensitivity.
They were teenagers once,
Can't they remember?
It might have been a long time
But that sort of thing you don't forget!
We might be hard to understand and handle
But,
It's hard
To change from something you've known all your life
To change to what you've never been or understood.
It's hard.

Stewart Wymer

Stewart Wymer's poem is about how teenagers are misunderstood. Think about the ways teenagers are represented in the media, such as television news, soap operas and teenage magazines. Do you think they are true representations of teenagers? In pairs, brainstorm your ideas then discuss with others.

Activity **5.3**

Hot wet pillows

As soon as he entered
I knew he'd attack:
'You!
You up the back.
Yes you!
Josh,
surly looks
no books
talking
clowning
for attention –
pay attention!'

Silently I lock him out –
all of them out.
What do I care about
Wordsworth's wussy daffodils
or Lawson's boring bush.

Do they care
what's in my head
at night
alone
anger grown?
Words pour out
on hot wet pillows
escaping
from the prison
that I lock them in.
No-one knows, no-one knows.

Would Wordsworth have cared?
Would Lawson?
Will you
if I show you this?

Josh Cullen

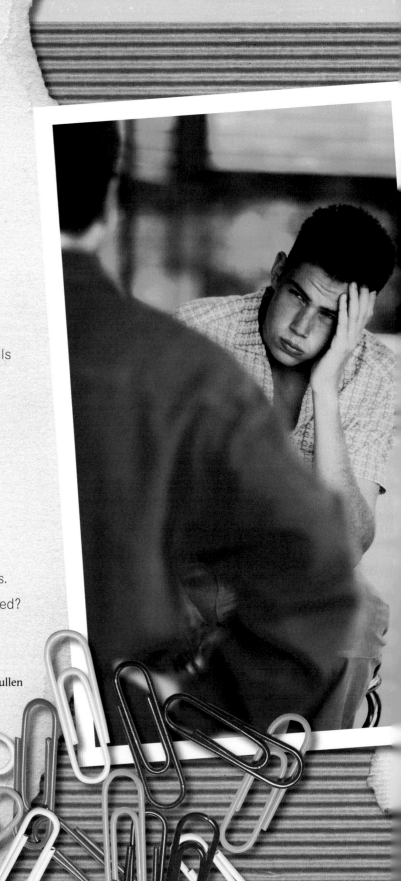

1 Describe or sketch the image that the title 'Hot wet pillows' conveys to you.

2 What is the tone of the teacher's voice in this poem? How does the use of short or single-word lines when the teacher is speaking create a particular impression of him or her?

3 The mood of the poem changes when Josh is describing his feelings. Explain the effect of this change.

4 a Suggest reasons for Josh's reluctance to expose his feelings.
   b We get the impression that Josh wishes someone would recognise his feelings and care about them. How do we know this?
   c Portray Josh's feelings of frustration using shapes, symbols and colours.
   d Write a poem in which you convey feelings of frustration or emotions you can't express to others. Illustrate the poem and colour it to reflect your mood.

5 Have you ever met a teacher like the one in the poem? Would you like to have a teacher like Josh's? List five qualities that you value in a teacher.

It is impossible

It is impossible
for anyone to enter
our small world.
The adults don't
understand us
they think
we're childish.
No one can get in
our world
It has a wall twenty feet high
and adults
Have only ten feet ladders.

Ross Falconer

1 Explain what each poet says about being a teenager. Fill in your responses in a diagram like the one below:

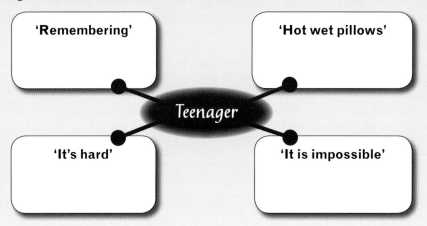

'Remembering'

'Hot wet pillows'

Teenager

'It's hard'

'It is impossible'

2 Make a list of words, phrases or sentences that describe what being a teenager means to you. For example:
* image
* friends
* beach
* freedom
* awkward
* not fitting in.

3 Using the ideas in your list, rework it into a poem entitled 'Teenager'.
Start with:

If I'm told to 'Grow up!' one more time
I'll . . .

4 Teenagers often protest that they are treated like children. Imagine, then, that you could suddenly be treated like an adult, but that you also took on an adult's responsibilities.
   a In small groups, make a list of all the positive and negative things that you can think of about suddenly becoming an adult. For example:

Positive	Negative
have independence	*completely responsible for yourself*
have certain freedom	*have to pay bills*

   b Share your group's list of positives and negatives with the rest of the class. Create a class list.

A particular language used by a particular group is called **discourse**. For example, doctors and lawyers use certain words and phrases in their discourse. What other professions or groups can you think of that use a particular discourse?

Teenagers and their subcultures use a particular discourse. It's natural for teenagers to want to belong to a special group, set apart by the language they use: the language of 'Teenspeak'. Like fashion and music, language allows teenagers to express their individuality. Sometimes it's also a form of rebellion.

Activity **5.6**

1 a In groups, make a list of current words and sayings you or your friends use which could be called 'Teenspeak'. For example: *awesome, unreal, sick, cool*....

 b Beside each word or saying, give a brief explanation of what it means.

2 Still in your groups, write a 'Teenspeak' poem using ideas from the words in your list, then share it with the class.

3 Teenagers are often concerned with how they appear in the eyes of others, especially people of their own age. Explain how television, magazines and newspapers try to shape people's identities by telling them to be certain things, do certain things and wear certain things. Use examples to support your answer.

4 Reflection. Select a memory that was, or is, important to you. Write a list of details about the event/memory and include how you felt about each detail. The memory may be a happy or a sad one. Use the format of the following table:

Details	Emotions/feelings	Physical feelings
When I was 13 I was caught cheating in an exam	embarrassed ashamed seemed like everyone was staring at me	hot temples throbbing flushed, red cheeks
I had to hand in my paper. I knew I wouldn't get any marks for it. Everyone knew.	humiliated felt small and stupid	heart beating fast sick feeling in my stomach
After the exam I was told to visit the Principal	scared upset remorseful	cried, sobbed couldn't talk shaking body and legs

Details	Emotions/feelings	Physical feelings
I had to tell my parents	terrified of the consequences more shame relief after confessing couldn't explain why I'd done it	cried again sick in stomach thought I'd vomit felt very drained after the 'confession'

5   Write a poem about the memory, using the details from your table.

Not in India

'I want a proper bag,' I cried.
'But this is a proper bag.
In India we always took these to school.'
'We're not in India!'
'Go on, go to school, Craig is here,' ordered Mum.
Craig, his clean pink face beaming a smile,
had his bag across his back.
My satchel laboured at my hip,
constantly trying to get away,

We arrive in school, late for prayers again. Good.
Spelling test. Easy. Full marks.
'This boy came to Britain when he was six.
He couldn't speak English.
Now he's a better speller than all of you.'
Maths, just long division and fractions.
'Indians are always good at Maths,' Mum used to say.
Geography. Maps. Places I haven't seen.
'Sadi came to Wales two years ago and now he knows
all the countries in the world.'

Leaving school for another day.
A boy runs shouting 'Chocolate!'
Craig defends me, 'Then you're a Milky Bar!'
'But I'm not chocolate, I'm just like you!' I think.
'Home already?
In India we didn't come home 'til five,' said Mum.

'But we're not in India, are we?' I cried,
running upstairs and locking the door behind me.

Sadi Husain

Activity **5.7**

1 Describe how the boy in 'Not in India' feels about his identity.

2 Suggest reasons why he wants to forget his old culture.

3 Describe the identity he is trying to construct for himself now, in his adopted country. Why do you think he feels this way?

4 How difficult do you think it is for someone to 'fit in' when they are trying to live within the expectations of two different cultures? Explain.

People

Some of us eat
Birds' meat or
Escargots or
Candied bees or
Each other –
    But we are all people.

Some of us carry
Bibles or
Rifles or
Swastikas or
Spears or
Bows and arrows or
Love signs –
    But we are all people.

Some of us wear
Sarongs or
Feathers or
Cheongsams or
Muu-muus or
Nothing –
    But we are all people.

Some of us dance
Waltzes or
Ballets or
Corroborees or
Hulas or
Bossá nova or
Flamenco –
    We are all people.

Bobbi Sykes

Activity **5.8**

1 What is the message Bobbi Sykes is trying to get across in her poem 'People'?

2 Write a poem like Bobbi Sykes's, substituting her ideas for your own about the ways in which we are different – but in the end, the same.

Don't talk about your childhood

Don't talk about your childhood.
Anyone can do that.
We were all sensitive once,
and most of us hated school.

That man who made his millions
from guns: even he
can recall the smell of his mother's dress,
rain on leaves.

And as for the dark cupboard
and what you did to the cat,
confession of childish guilt
is a form of boasting.

You risk nothing, singing
your song of a small ghost.
Don't talk about your childhood:
say what you are now.

Vicki Raymond

Activity 5.9

1   This poem evokes memories of childhood. What point is the poet making about these experiences?

2   Explain the meaning of the second stanza.

3   Suggest what is meant by 'confession of childish guilt is a form of boasting'.

4   'Singing your song of a small ghost' is a metaphor.
   a   What is the comparison being made here?
   b   Why use the word 'small'?

5   The poet seems to be suggesting that our identities are more than just the sum of our childhood experiences. Quote the lines which tell us this.

6   Why do you think she says we 'risk nothing' by talking about what we *used* to be?

7   How difficult do you think it is for us to 'say what we are now'? Are there risks we take when opening ourselves up to others? Explain.

8   a   Write a poem in which you describe yourself as you are now.
   b   Did you find it difficult? Explain why or why not.

School

I might enjoy it

If a teacher
was reading
over my shoulder
I'd write
I like school,
I enjoy it.
But if a friend
was reading
over my shoulder

I'd write
I hate school,
school really stinks.
But seeing
I'm by myself
I'll write
I like school,
I think I might enjoy it.

Student

Activity **5.10**

1 Draw up a table like the one below and list everything your senses tell you
during a typical lesson. Then write down an image – something that reminds
you of what you are sensing – beside each observation. An example has been
done for you:

In class	What you see, hear, smell, touch, taste	An image: what do these observations remind you of?
Sight	chairs lined up in neat rows	dominoes waiting to be knocked down
	teacher talking, annoyed face	a roaring lion with a bad headache
	students busy, moving, working	moths flapping round a lightbulb
Sound	students talking; joking; laughter	a flock of squawking parrots
	teacher giving instructions, directions	a drill sergeant barking orders at his troops
	trucks driving by on a nearby road	thunder rolling off into the distance
Smell	wafting smells from a nearby tuckshop	my little sister's attempt at cooking
	pies, sausage rolls	pastry is a coffin for dead meat
Touch	my arm on the hard desk	a pitstop for tired limbs
Taste	breakfast - Vegemite on toast, which keeps regurgitating	an oil well ready to blow

2 Use your list of observations and images as 'starters' to writing a poem called 'In class'. It's not necessary to use every idea or image you listed in the table – as you draft your poem you may think of better images or you may leave some out altogether. If you were to use the list provided as an example, your poem might look something like this:

In class

The room is full of roaring students
a platoon of youthful soldiers
with the drill sergeant leading the pack:
barking, instructing, commanding.
We sit restlessly –
wriggling,
uncomfortable
in our rows of too-small chairs
like dominoes which, at any moment,
will be knocked down.
We are thunderous lions, screeching parrots
drowning each other in a tidal wave of
conversation,
stilled for a moment by the sudden gunshot of
laughter.
In the midst of nouns, verbs and adjectives
I think of my breakfast
the Vegemite on thickly-buttered toast,
regurgitating . . .
an oil well I hope will not erupt.
My arms, sore from writing, take a pitstop
on the graffitied desk before me.
I smell the tuckshop aromas of
meat pies, long dead
and the pastry which is their coffin.
The clock takes too long to reach
its destination
we fidget and squirm in our seats
like hand-held worms
hoping for a painless release.
'No one is leaving 'til there's quiet!'
And, just for a moment, we are subdued.
Like bank robbers we make our escape –
fast and furious and not looking back,
leaving the classroom
empty and eerily silent.

Barbara Ellis

There are always people at school who like to rule over others. In this case, a boy named Maurice puts his stamp of authority on the younger students by treating – of all things – a toilet block as his territory!

King of the toilets

Maurice was King of the Toilets,
The ones by the wall – by the shed,
He ruled with the power and conviction
Of a king with a crown on his head.

He entered them first every morning
And he'd sit on the wall by the gate
And wait for the grumpy schoolkeeper
To unlock them – at twenty past eight.

Then he'd rush in with great shouts of triumph
And he'd slam all the doors one by one
And he'd climb on the caretaker's cupboards
And he'd pull all the chains just for fun.

He'd swing on the pipes by the cistern,
And he'd leap from the top of the doors,
And he'd frighten the new little infants –
With bellows and yellings and roars.

He always ate lunch in the toilets,
And he'd sit with his food on the floor,
And check who was coming (or going) –
And kick at the catch on their door.

He once burst the pipe by the outflow
By climbing right up on the tank,
And flooded the lower school library,
With water that gushed out and stank.

He once jammed the door on the end one
With five juniors stuck fast inside,
And bombed them with piles of old comics
Whilst they struggled and shouted and cried.

He was useless in class –
And at lessons.
He couldn't do hardly a thing
But when he was out in the toilets
THEN MAURICE THE USELESS WAS KING!

Peter Dixon

Activity 5.11

Draw a flow chart like one below. In the boxes, use information from the poem 'King of the toilets' to tell the story of Maurice.

Start

Finish

Maurice was 'king' of the toilet block, which was situated where?

Even though the poem is humorous, there is an underlying message. What do you think it is?

Describe the character of Maurice in your own words.

When did Maurice arrive at school every morning and what did he have to wait for?

Apart from 'King of the Toilets', what other name was Maurice known by?

Maurice's behaviour in the toilets, when he was finally allowed in, included . . .

The poem gives a reason for Maurice having to be 'king' of something. What is it?

Did Maurice play with the other children at lunchtime?

How did these children react? Do you think their reaction was understandable?

How did he spend his lunch breaks?

Maurice caused some nasty accidents involving the outflow pipe and library. Describe what happened.

How do we know Maurice picked on children younger and smaller than him?

The colour of my dreams

I'm a really rotten reader
the worst in all the class,
the sort of rotten reader
that makes you want to laugh.

I'm last in all the readin' tests,
my score's not on the page
and when I read to teacher
she gets in such a rage.

She says I cannot form my words
she says I can't build up
and that I don't know phonics
and don't know c-a-t from k-u-p.

They say that I'm dyxlectic
(that's a word they've just found out)
but when I get some plasticine
I know what that's about.

I make these scary monsters
I draw these secret lands
and get my hair all sticky
and paint on all me hands.

I make these super models,
I build these smashing towers
that reach up to the ceiling
– and take me hours and hours.

I paint these lovely pictures
in thick green drippy paint
that gets on all the carpet –
and makes the cleaners faint.

I build great magic forests
weave bushes out of string
and paint pink panderellos
and birds that really sing.

I play my world of real believe
I play it every day
and teachers stand and watch me
but don't know what to say.

They give me diagnostic tests,
they try out reading schemes,
but none of them will ever know
the colour of my dreams.

Peter Dixon

Writing and sums

When the teacher asks us to write,
The words dance in my head,
Weaving neat patterns,
Gliding into their places,
Before flowing down my pencil
In an orderly procession.
But. . .
When the teacher tells me to do sums,
The figures fly round my head,
Fluttering like birds
Trapped behind glass,
Before tumbling down my pencil
In frightened confusion.

                                        Derek Stuart

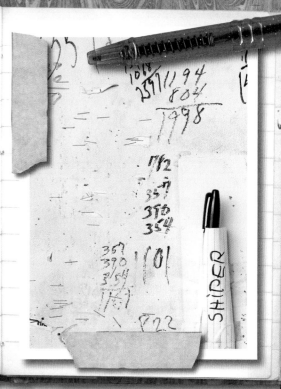

Activity 5.12

1   For each of the previous two poems, answer the following questions. Present
    your answers in a chart with two columns, headed 'The colour of my dreams'
    and 'Writing and sums'.
    a   Describe what the writer of the poem is not very good at. Quote the lines
        that tell you this.
    b   Make a stick figure sketch of the person in each of the poems. Around the
        sketches write a collection of words and phrases from each poem that
        show the person's special talent.
    c   Explain how you think each person is seen by his teachers.
    d   Imagine you are the student in each poem. Describe your feelings about
        your problems with reading/maths and your talent for art/writing. Use
        quotes from the poem to support your answer.

2   Imagine you are a teacher. Write report cards for the students in the two
    poems.

3   a   What is your favourite subject at school?
    b   Explain why you like it and why you are good at it.
    c   What subject don't you do well in at school?
    d   Explain why you dislike it or why you don't do very well.

4   In pairs, role-play a parent–teacher interview with the teacher of your
    favourite and least favourite subjects.

5   Write a poem along the lines of 'The colour of my dreams' or 'Writing and
    sums' in which you set up a contrast between what you are good at at school
    and what you are not so good at.

'Excuses, excuses!'

Late again Blenkinsopp?
What's the excuse this time?
Not my fault sir.
Who's fault is it then?
Grandma's sir.
Grandma's? What did she do?
She died sir.
Died?
She's seriously dead alright sir.
That makes four grandmothers this term Blenkinsopp
And all on P.E. days.
I know. It's very upsetting sir.
How many grandmothers have you got Blenkinsopp?
Grandmothers sir? None sir.
You said you had four.
All dead sir.
And what about yesterday Blenkinsopp?
What about yesterday sir?

You were absent yesterday.
That was the dentist sir.
The dentist died?
No sir. My teeth sir.
You missed the maths test Blenkinsopp!
I'd been looking forward to it sir.
Right, line up for P.E.
Can't sir.
No such word as 'can't' Blenkinsopp.
No kit sir.
Where is it?
Home sir.
What's it doing at home?
Not ironed sir.
Couldn't you iron it?
Can't sir.
Why not?
Bad hand sir.
Who usually does it?
Grandma sir.
Why couldn't she do it?
Dead sir.

Gareth Owen

1 Create a list of all the excuses you can find in the poem.

2 **a** In small groups, make up your own 'Excuses' poem, this time about not doing your homework. Be as outlandish as you can!

   b Write a list of instructions entitled 'How to make excuses to your teacher'.

A child who is in trouble at school may have other, more important things to think about:

Coming late

Isabel comes late to school.
Tight as a bud in winter
into herself she curls
when our teacher reprimands her.

You are a slack and lazy girl.
You won't be any good . . .
(The voice has risen to a howl
of wind above a frozen wood)

. . . until you learn to come on time
and take more pride and show you care.
Isabel hides a living pain
beneath her blank and frosted stare.

She cannot say her dad has gone,
her mum is ill, she has to dress
and feed her brothers, copes alone
without complaint, will not confess

her courage in a shrivelled life,
will not admit to anyone
that deep inside her is a fragile leaf
craving some warmth to open into sun.

                              Barrie Wade

1 a How does the poem 'Coming late' make you feel about Isabel and her situation?
   b Use adjectives to describe Isabel's qualities.
   c If you were to draw something which symbolises her qualities, what colours would you use? What shapes?

2 The poet uses a variety of images in the form of similes and metaphors to describe Isabel and her life.
   a Complete the following table:

Imagery used	What is being compared?	What meaning is conveyed?	How does it make us feel?
'Tight as a bud in winter into herself she curls' (simile)			
'The voice has risen to a howl of wind above a frozen wood' (metaphor)			
'A living pain' (metaphor)			
'Her blank and frosted stare' (metaphor)			
'A shrivelled life' (metaphor)			
'Deep inside her is a fragile leaf craving some warmth to open into the sun' (metaphor)			

   b Describe how these images help us to 'know' Isabel?
   c The poet suggests that Isabel's life has not yet been fully lived. In which lines is this implied?

3 a How are we made to feel about her teacher?
   b What message is being given in the poem about being understanding of others' situations?

4 Imagine you are Isabel. Write a journal entry in which you describe your life.

5 Sum up what school means to *you* by writing an acrostic poem about it (see page 73).

6 a Give 'School' a personality and human qualities. Write a poem about it, using personification, in which you describe:

- its job
- where it lives
- its favourite colour
- its favourite food
- its hobbies and interest
- its favourite song
- its ambitions

- the sports it likes to play
- the problems it has
- what it does on a Saturday night
- its memories
- its feelings
- its favourite film.

   b Sketch your impressions of school using your poem. Try to include both literal and metaphorical images.

7 Write a metaphor poem in which you state that school is something else. For example: *'school is a battle'*; *'school is peak-hour traffic'* . . .

8 Write the word 'School' at the top of a blank piece of paper. Choose someone in the class to start, with 30 seconds to write a line. Then pass it on to someone else to write the next line. Repeat this until everyone in the class has written something about school. You have just written a class 'add-on' poem.

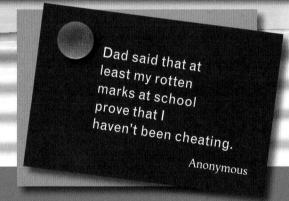

Dad said that at least my rotten marks at school prove that I haven't been cheating.

Anonymous

Friendship

Friends

I fear it's very wrong of me
and yet I must admit,
When someone offers friendship
I want the *whole* of it.
I don't want everybody else
To share my friends with me.
At least, I want *one* special one,
Who, indisputably

Likes me much more than all the rest,
Who's always on my side,
Who never cares what others say,
Who lets me come and hide
Within his shadow, in his house –
It doesn't matter where –
Who lets me simply be·myself,
Who's always, *always* there.

Elizabeth Jennings

Silences make the real conversations between friends. Not the saying, but the never needing to say is what counts.

Margaret Lee Runbeck

Friends . . . are God's apology for relations.

Hugh Kingsmill

The only reward of virtue is virtue; the only way to have a friend is to be one.

Ralph Waldo Emerson

Activity **5.15**

1 According to Elizabeth Jennings, friendship is:
- a special kind of love
- gentleness and understanding
- made better by trust and mutual respect
- giving
- something that cannot be measured.

Write lines from the poem that describe each of these characteristics.

2 Describe what friendship means to you by writing an acrostic poem in which you describe your feelings about it. For example:

F riendships
R emain
I ntact:
E nduring,
N ever
D ying.
S ecrets are shared.
H appiness comes from true friendship.
I t is real, not
P retend.

3   **a** Make a list of the five most important qualities you look for in a friend, and arrange them in order of importance.

    b Explain why each of these qualities is important to you.

    c Imagine you are conducting interviews to find a new best friend. Write ten questions you would ask to find out if the interviewees would be suitable.

    d Explain how you would judge whether a friend is a good one or not.

4   Write a short poem about your best friend. The poem should describe their qualities and the reasons you like them. Begin your poem with: *'My friend is . . .'* or *'[Name] is . . .'*

The poem 'Best friends' deals with the memories of a childhood friend, now dead.

Best friends

(for Elizabeth Ewer, 1942–51)

The day my daughter turned ten, I thought of the
lank, glittering, greenish cap of your
gold hair. The last week of
your life, when I came each day after school,
I'd study the path to your front door,
the bricks laid close as your hairs. I'd try to
read the pattern, frowning down
for a sign.
      The last day – there was not
a mark on that walk, not a stone out of place –
the nurses would not let me in.

We were nine. We had never mentioned death
or growing up. I had no more imagined
you dead
than you imagined me
a mother. But when I had a daughter
I named her for you, as if pulling you back
through a crack between the bricks.
      She is ten now, Liddy.
She has outlived you, her dark hair gleaming like
the earth into which the path was pressed,
the path to you.

                             Sharon Olds

1 a Who is the poem 'Best friends' for?
   b What made Sharon think of her?
   c In what way does she still 'live'?

2 There are two images in the poem which are used to connect the past and the present. What are they?

3 Explain what the poet means by the following:
   a 'The last day'
   b 'I had no more imagined you dead than you imagined me a mother.'
   c 'I named her for you.'
   d 'She has outlived you'.

4 a What do you think Liddy died of?
   b Describe the feelings you get about this friendship after reading the poem.
   c Imagine you are talking to Liddy. What ten things would you tell her about the world today?

Sometimes, friendships are fragile . . .

It is a puzzle

My friend
Is not my friend anymore.
She has secrets from me
And goes about with Tracy Hackett.

I would
Like to get her back,
Only do not want to say so.
So I pretend
To have secrets from her
And go about with Alice Banks.

But what bothers me is,
Maybe *she* is pretending
And would like *me* back,
Only does not want to say so.

In which case
Maybe it bothers her
That *I* am pretending.

But if we are both pretending,
Then really we are friends
And do not know it.

On the other hand,
How can we be friends
And have secrets from each other
And go about with other people?

My friend
Is not my friend anymore,
Unless she is pretending.
I cannot think what to do.
It is a puzzle.

Allan Ahlberg

Activity 5.17

1   Describe the problems that exist in the friendship in 'It is a puzzle'.

2   Explain why you think the words 'pretend' and 'pretending' are used so often throughout the poem.

3   Allan Ahlberg describes the friendship in the poem as a 'puzzle'? Suggest some possible reasons for this.

4   Suggest some ways in which the friendship in this poem could be improved.

5   Draw speech and thought bubbles for the characters based on the information in the poem.

Remember me?

Remember me?
I am the boy who sought friendship;
The boy you turned away.
I am the boy who asked you
If I too might play.
I the face at the window
When your party was inside,
I the lonely figure
That walked away and cried.
I the one who hung around
A punchbag for your games.
Someone you could kick and beat,
Someone to call names.
But how strange is the change
After time has hurried by,
Four years have passed since then
Now I'm not so quick to cry.
I'm bigger and I'm stronger,
I've grown a foot in height,
Suddenly I'M popular
And YOU'RE left out of the light.
I could, if I wanted,
Be so unkind to you.
I would only have to say
And the other boys would do.
But the memory of my pain
Holds back the revenge I'D planned
And instead, I feel much stronger
By offering you my hand.

Ray Mather

Activity **5.18**

1 The poem 'Remember me?' gives us two contrasting pictures of the one person.
   a The rejected boy: Use words and phrases from the poem to describe his feelings and experiences.
   b The popular boy: Use words and phrases from the poem to describe what his life is like now that he is older.

2 What is the boy's decision at the end of the poem? Quote the lines that tell us.

3 What has the boy learned from the experience of being bullied?

Kimberley

The kids at my primary school were all white
and no one ever called them *whitey*.
They used to shout things like *Kunta
Kinte, Kunta Kinte* running after me.
If I was with a friend crossing the burn,
I found these names even more embarrassing.
My friend could watch my cheeks burning.

But one day, a new girl arrived from Hong Kong.
Kimberley Lee. I was eleven and so was she.
The children in the playground descended
on her as if she was good prey;
vultures swooping down with *Chinky
Chinky, Yellow face, Slanty eyes.*
I watched the names bruise on Kimberley's skin,

full of pity and of relief –
which made me feel I was full of sin.
And once I tried the terrible name myself.
Chinky. I felt the word sizzle on my tongue.
That night I couldn't sleep for guilt.
And the next day I was full of sorrow.
I tried a new word out. S-sorry.

Jackie Kay

1 After reading 'Kimberley', rewrite the following, filling in the spaces with words you think are the most suitable.

The poet is telling the story about a new student, _____, during a time when they were both at _____ school. The poet felt different to the other students because _____ . She felt _____ by the names she was called by her classmates. We know this because she states that '_____'. One day, Kimberley, a girl, arrived from _____ . The children treated her _____ by _____ . The poet was no longer _____ . 'I watched the names bruise on Kimberley's skin' means that _____ .

The poet felt both _____ and _____ but, because of this, she felt _____ . This is seen in the line: 'Which made me feel I was full of sin'. The possible reasons for the poet calling Kimberley a nickname may have been _____ . She felt _____ about it, and the words 'I tried the terrible name myself' tell us this. The line 'I felt the word sizzle on my tongue' means _____, and gives the impression that the poet felt _____ .

The other effects of being _____ towards Kimberley were that the poet couldn't sleep because of _____ . The next day she was also _____ . The poet decided to _____, which tells us that she _____ .

2 a Imagine you are the poet. Write down your conversation with Kimberley when you go to her to apologise.

   b Imagine you are Kimberley. Make a list of impressions you now have of your primary school experience. Present them in a table like this:

Saw	Heard	Thought	Felt (emotions)

1 After reading 'Remember me?' and 'Kimberley', write a poem either about a friend you have let down or about forgiving a friend who has let you down. Follow this plan for your writing:

   a Start with a description of what happened between you.

   b Make a list of images that you remember about the incident. You could divide these images into:
   • what you saw
   • what you heard
   • what you thought
   • what/how you felt.

   c Say whether the friendship suffered or was improved by the experience.

   d Arrange the images in any order you like, and you have the first draft of a poem.

    e   Redraft your poem, adding to it or changing it where necessary.

    f   Share your poem with the class.

2   The theme of friendship is important, because we all like to have friends. Write a short explanation (one or two paragraphs) on the importance of friendship in our lives.

3   **a**   What are the things that make friendships last?

    b   Write an 'Instruction manual' explaining the requirements for a lasting friendship, using the following format:

Title: How to make your friendships lasting ones
Requirements of a friend:
Instructions:
Do s: **Don'ts:**
Any recommendations:

Love

Love is like the measles; we all have to go through it.

Jerome K. Jerome

How do I love thee? let me count the ways.
I love thee to the depth and breadth and height
My soul can reach . . .

Elizabeth Barrett Browning

Let no one who loves be called altogether unhappy.
Even love unreturned has its rainbow.

J.M. Barrie

Life has taught us that love does not consist in gazing at each other but in looking together in the same direction.

Antoine de Saint-Exupéry

If I speak in the tongues of men and of angels, but have not love, I am a noisy gong or a clanging cymbal. And if I have prophetic powers, and understand all mysteries and all knowledge, and if I have all faith, so as to remove mountains, but have not love, I am nothing. If I give away all I have, and if I deliver my body to be burned, but have not love, I gain nothing.

Love is patient and kind; love is not jealous or boastful; it is not arrogant or rude. Love does not insist on its own way; it is not irritable or resentful; it does not rejoice at wrong, but rejoices in the right. Love bears all things, believes all things, hopes all things, endures all things.

1 Corinthians 13

What is love?

Love: to regard with affection; to like; to delight in; to be in love; to be tenderly attached; warm affection

Cambridge English Dictionary

Love: to hold dear; bear love to; to be in love with; to be fond of; to care; to admire or be glad of the existence of; endearment

Concise Oxford Dictionary

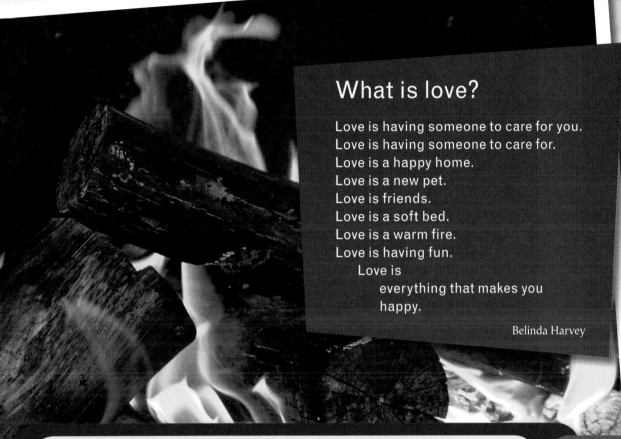

What is love?

Love is having someone to care for you.
Love is having someone to care for.
Love is a happy home.
Love is a new pet.
Love is friends.
Love is a soft bed.
Love is a warm fire.
Love is having fun.
    Love is
        everything that makes you
        happy.

Belinda Harvey

Activity 5.21

1   Explain what the word 'love' means to you. It may be all of the things you have read so far, and more. Write your own list, starting each line with *'Love is . . . '*

2   Write the word 'Love' at the top of your page. Next, write down:
    •   an object
    •   a feeling
    •   a mood
    •   an action
    •   a taste
    •   a sound
    •   a smell
that you associate with love. For example:

Love
A merry-go-round
Butterflies in the stomach
Happiness, excitement, being scared
Laughing together
A burger shared at McDonald's
A velvet voice
The scent of your skin

Love is often so powerful that we are not afraid to let the world know it! Poetry can let us do this; it's a 'public' way of letting others know how we feel about things, but can also be a very private expression of our deepest, strongest emotions. The poem below was written by a student for his girlfriend, and clearly shows the strength of his feelings.

Powerless

When a boy sees a girl
He will do anything to get her,
lay his life on the line
for the affection of that girl,
place his life in the palm of her hand,
buy her anything her heart desires
for the sake of her love.

Her eyes will sparkle with silver,
her golden hair equally matched
by her beauty and her smile.
He will take his time with every glance
Praying, hoping for its return.
Her femininity will lock him in her spell
Her smile will offer comfort
and understanding.
His devotion will be never-ending.

Men are powerless
to control their feelings.

Fabian Jenkin (student)

Activity 5.22

1 Write a series of short poems, or a longer poem if you prefer, about someone you love. These are personal, so don't feel you have to share them.

2 Songwriters also like to explore the theme of love. Think about your favourite singer or songwriter. How do they express their feelings about love? Share your thoughts with the rest of the class.

Tonight the phone

Tonight the phone is warm
and you come soft to me and brush me with
   your voice.
The timbres caress me gently
and carry me there.

A robin sings.

Listen to the thaw as the ice reaches to the sun
and dies as water a little bit closer.

In the wet air there is a rainbow.

The sky speaks and tonight I listen to the
touch of you.

Lisa Freinkel

Little poem

I call you on
the 'phone &
we chat, but
the way tele
is missing from
'phone is the
way it makes me
feel, wishing
the rest of
you were here.

Ron Padgett

Activity 5.23

1   Describe how you think the phone calls made each person feel.

2   Explain what you think is meant by:
   a   '… brush me with your voice'
   b   'The timbres caress me gently and carry me there.'
   c   'In the wet air there is a rainbow.'
   d   '… I listen to the touch of you'
   e   '… the way tele is missing from 'phone is the way it makes me feel, wishing the rest of you were here'.

3   In her poem, Lisa Freinkel creates strong images by combining two senses. For example, 'brush me with your voice' combines the sense of touch with the sense of hearing.
   a   Write down another line from the poem where senses are combined.
   b   How did Lisa Freinkel use elements of nature to describe her feelings? Do you think they are effective images? Explain.

4   Different senses can be put together to create strong images, such as:
   •   a smile in his voice (seeing and hearing)
   •   the touch of her perfume (touching and smelling)
   •   the flavour of your touch (tasting and touching).
   a   In groups, think of other combinations of senses.
   b   Write a short poem about love, using some of these combinations.

Sometimes it takes a lot of courage for us to reveal our feelings to others.

Indecision

I know not where I stand.
Have I the right to demand possession?
Or should I leave her to those who claim her?
Should I cover my thoughts with thin jest
Instead of expressing them?
Would she be embarrassed,
Look for a gentle way to say 'stand off'?
A way that hurts more than an insult.
Is it easier to step aside and watch
As others, more confident than I, move in
And make her smile and laugh?
See how each laugh makes the distance between
Grow, and with it, my resignation?

Andrew Bolt (student)

Activity 5.24

1 In 'Indecision' Andrew likes a girl, but is uncertain about what she thinks of him. Identify the line that tells you this.

2 There are many things going through Andrew's mind as he wonders what he should do about the girl. Explain these questions in your own words, in a table like the one below. (An example has been done for you.)

Andrew's worries	Explanation
Have I the right to demand possession?	
Should I leave her to those who claim her?	*should he forget the idea of desiring her, as other boys do?*
Should I cover my thoughts with thin jest instead of expressing them?	
Would she be embarrassed, Look for a gentle way to say 'stand off'?	
Is it easier to step aside and watch As others, more confident than I, move in And make her smile and laugh?	

3   Suggest why the possibility of being rejected by the girl worries Andrew so much.

4   Describe the effect that the girl's laughter with her other admirers has on Andrew.

5   'Resignation' means a sense of giving up or giving in. Predict his likely decision.

6   a   Imagine you are Andrew. Write a letter to an advice column asking for help with your problem.
    b   Write the response to Andrew's letter.
    c   What would *you* do in this sort of situation?

7   At times, Andrew sees the girl as something to be won and owned. Identify the words in the poem that show this. Do you think it's possible to 'own' a person?

8   Imagine you are the girl, and you know Andrew is interested in you. Write a diary entry about him.

9   Have you ever been in a situation where you liked someone but you couldn't tell whether they liked you? What happened, and how did you feel?

Goodbye

He said
goodbye.
I shuffled
my feet
and kept a close
watch on my
shoes.
He was talking
I was listening
but he probably
thought I was
not
because I never
even lifted my
head.
I didn't want him
to see
the mess mascara
makes when it
runs.

Carol-Anne Marsh

Activity 5.25

1   Summarise what has happened in the poem 'Goodbye'.

2   **a**   Describe the girl's reaction to the boy's news.
    b   Suggest the impression you think this would have given the boy.
    c   Suggest how the girl might have felt after this meeting.

3   Write and illustrate a poem from the point of view of the boy.

4   Write thought bubbles to show what each character is thinking.

5   Who is the stronger character in the poem? Why do you think so?

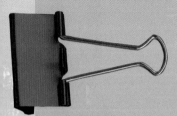

Intimates

Don't you care for my love? she said bitterly.

I handed her the mirror, and said:
Please address these questions to the proper person!
Please make all requests to headquarters!
In all matters of emotional importance
please approach the supreme authority direct!
So I handed her the mirror.

And she would have broken it over my head,
but she caught sight of her own reflection
and that held her spell-bound for two seconds
while I fled.

D.H. Lawrence

Miriam

So great was my joy
when I received your letter
that on reading it the first time
I didn't realise
that in it you had written
that you didn't love me.

Modesto Silva

First love

I remember
last July
in Jindabyne,
when I saw
him,
with another
girl,
in
Maxims.
I stood,
in the
lightly falling
snow,
and watched
him,

through a
big window.
He was
hand in hand
with her.
I felt
my heart beat
so fast,
and my hands,
came down
empty.

Elizabeth Mitchell (student)

Activity **5.26**

1   Summarise the story behind each of these three poems in a table like the one below. In the last column of the table, write down what you think the poets would say about love, rejection and hurt. An example has been done for you.

Poem	Subject matter	What the poet would say about love, rejection, hurt
'Intimates'	A fight/argument Woman accuses man of not wanting her love. He hands her a mirror and tells her to ask the question of the person she sees in it. She vainly looks at her own reflection while the man quickly leaves.	D.H. Lawrence may say that, in love, there is no room for being vain. You should love others more than you love yourself. The woman in the poem is rejected, because the man leaves her. He appears to be happy with that, however. Gives the impression that the relationship was not very good to start with.
'Miriam'		
'First love'		

We know that the ending of a relationship is intense and, for most people, incredibly painful. Consider how the painting below captures the break-up of a relationship in which one person has obviously cared more than the other.

Joshua Dowling, *She Just Wanted to Be Friends*, 1989

1 In groups, look at the painting at the left and brainstorm your initial impressions. Record them on a graphic organiser like the one below. Compare your responses with those of other groups.

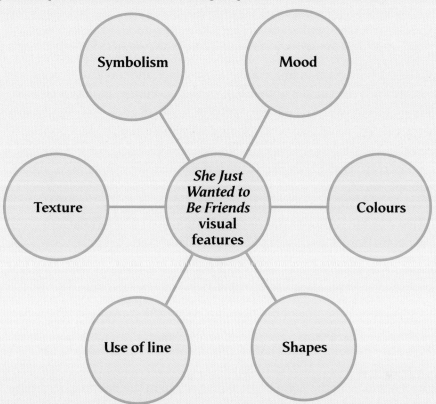

2 Describe the mood of the painting. How does it make you feel?

3 Where is your eye initially drawn to in the painting? Why does this particular image or focal point have an impact?

4 Analyse the artist's use of symbolism:
   - What do the colours suggest?
   - Why is a ghostly image used to portray the man?
   - Why do you think he is draped over a coathanger?
   - Suggest why a coat has been included in the painting.
   - What do you think the woman is holding in her left hand and what might this mean?

5 Look closely at the faces of each person, as well as how their bodies are depicted.
   a What impressions do you get of the woman? The jilted man?
   b Describe their different reactions to the break-up.
   c The artist creates bias in the way the figures are represented. For whom does he evoke our sympathy? How?
   d Do you think the woman ever loved him? Explain.
   e How do we know that he loved her?

6 The texture of the painting and the artist's use of line are reminiscent of Vincent van Gogh, especially during his periods of mental and emotional upheaval.

   a Why do you think the artist may have done this?

   b How does the swirling use of line add to the mood? (Think of the emotions one experiences when relationships come to an end.)

7 Colours are important in influencing our feelings and mood. Culturally, we associate different colours with different things. Purple, for instance, has connotations in western culture of royalty, sophistication and dignity. In negative terms, it can also be associated with mourning, melancholy and suffering.

   a Offer reasons as to why the artist has painted the woman wearing a purple dress.

   b What is the effect of using mainly dark colours?

   c Describe the contrast between the colours used for the man and the woman. How does this emphasise the artist's message?

8 Consider the personal context of the artist. Do you think this painting is a response to a personal experience or a universal one? Explain.

9 a Do you think the title of the painting effectively conveys its theme of rejection? Explain.

   b Give the painting an alternative title and explain your reasons for choosing it.

10 Write a poem from the point of view of the man in the painting describing how he feels.

Marriage

I like our teacher
Ms Ginola.
She tells us about her husband Tony,
how he brings her breakfast in bed on Sunday
and flowers on Monday night
and on Tuesday they go to the movies
on Friday he cooks dinner
and every day he kisses her
when she goes off to school.
Over dinner, I tell Mum and Dad
all about Ms Ginola and Tony.
Mum doesn't say a word,
and Dad
offers to wash the dishes.
He's never done that before.

Steven Herrick

Activity **5.28**

1   Describe the Ginolas' relationship.

2   Why do you think the father offers to do something for his wife that he's never done before?

3   Sometimes we become so accustomed to things that we take them for granted. Explain how Steven Herrick shows this in his poem.

4   How does using the viewpoint of a child make the poem more effective?

5   **a**   What do you think are the important things in a relationship?
    b   Suggest some of the ways in which we can keep relationships 'alive'.

Family

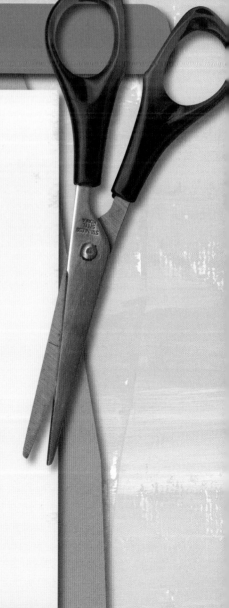

Who is you?

Let's all climb the family tree
See who's you and who is me.

If you are your brother's brother,
Your grandad's daughter is your mother.
But while we're finding who is who
Your grandad's little girl's little girl's you.

If you're a girl climbing family trees,
Your father's brother calls you niece.
He calls you nephew if you're a lad,
But says 'Hi brother!' to your dad.

Now the family tree is buzzing,
Your brother's sister's kid's your cousin.
Your nephew's uncle's you you see,
And my father's brother's nephew's me.

The more we climb the more the fun,
Your great grandma's grandad's mum.
And here's something else you'll find is true,
Your sister's baby's uncle's you.

Up the tree, oh this is the life,
Grandma's daughter-in-law's uncle's wife.
Let's all climb the family tree,
If you're your mum's only child, you're me.

Rony Robinson

Activity 5.29

1   Check your understanding of the poem 'Who is you?'. Copy out the sentences and fill in the blanks with the appropriate word:

a   Your grandfather's daughter is your _____ .

b   Your grandfather's daughter's daughter is your _____ or _____ .

c   Your grandmother's son is your _____ .

d   Your father's brother is your _____ .

e   If you're a girl, your uncle calls you his _____ .

f   If you're a boy, your uncle calls you his _____ .

g   Your uncle is your father's or mother's _____ .

h   Your father or mother's sister is your _____ .

i   Your parents' other daughter is your _____ .

j   The children of your uncles and aunts are your _____ .

k   Your niece's or nephew's uncle is _____ .

l   Your father's brother's nephew or niece is _____ .

m   Your great-grandmother is your mother or father's _____ .

n   Your grandmother's daughter-in-law could be your _____ or your _____ .

2   Draw your own family tree that shows the relationships in your family.

On children

Your children are not your children
They are the sons and daughters of Life's longing for itself.
They came through you but not from you
And though they are with you yet they belong not to you.
You may give them your love but not your thoughts,
For they have their own thoughts.
You may house their bodies but not their souls,
For their souls dwell in the house of tomorrow, which you cannot visit,
    not even in your dreams.
You may strive to be like them, but seek not to make them like you,
For life goes not backward nor tarries with yesterday.
You are the bows from which your children as living arrows are sent forth.

Kahlil Gibran

Activity 5.30

1 **a** For whom was 'On children' written?
  b In a sentence, write down what you think is the main point of the extract.

2 Decide whether Kahlil Gibran would agree or disagree with the statements in the table below. Support your decisions with examples from the extract. (Some have already been done for you.) Give your responses in a table like this one.

Statement	Agree/ Disagree	Supporting example from extract
A child belongs to its parents.	*Disagree*	*'They come through you but not from you'*
Parents are simply the means by which their children come into the world.		
Parents should give their children love.		
Parents should allow their children to develop their own thoughts about things.		
Parents own their children, body and soul.	*Disagree*	*'You may house their bodies but not their souls.'*
Children have their own futures which can't be foreseen by their parents.		
Parents should try to 'mould' their children's identities.		
It's not good to live in the past.		
Children are the products of their parents' desire to be immortal.		
Parents can learn a lot from their children.		

3 Some people say that parents should have a licence to have children. Do you agree or disagree? Discuss your answer with the class.

The poems below and opposite talk about the very strong bond of love which exists between parent and child:

Yesterday

It seems only yesterday
I balanced a tiny foot
on my palm
and marvelled
that anything
so perfect
could be so small.
Now I can fit my hand in
when I clean your shoes.

I can remember
when I was centred
round you
feeling your feet
strong and determined
testing the strength
of my rib cage
your hard heels
distorting my belly.

Now I wave you off
in the morning
and turn away
to continue
with my work
unhindered by your
eager face
grateful to be able
to make my own pace.
Yet tuned
to your return.

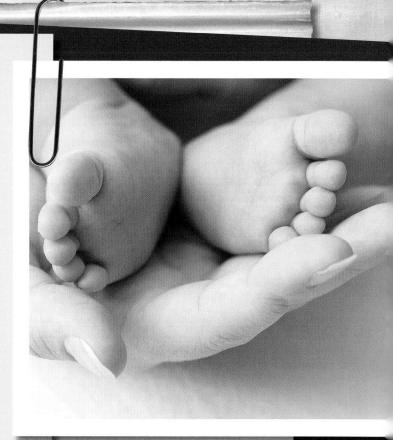

In time the distance
we put between us
will deprive me
of your grace.

Until then
each simple homely act
like rubbing this polish
into your shoes
will focus
    my imperfect love.

Patricia Pogson

First born:

to Christopher

It took
moments to conceive you
nine months to carry you
nineteen hours to deliver you
an eternity till I held you
and I didn't cry,
as I thought I would:
I felt, instead, a private calm.
Your eyes looked at mine,
saying 'I've been here before'.
You were exquisite –
beyond secret hopes.
I spent hours just gazing
at you beside me
in your see-through cot.
Those eyes:
content, familiar, wise
even at a few hours old
in your new, bright surroundings.
Funny that the first word you heard
(apart from primal groans
and 'Here he comes')
was 'Cricket!'
Now, here you are,
Dad's backyard bowling prodigy –
nimble, athletic, invincible;
a ceaseless orator and
tireless explorer.
When I gaze at you
sleeping, angel-like,
you never fail
to melt my heart
and make me smile.

This is for you:
so you'll know
        what you mean to me;
so you'll know that
I can't help but love you.

Barbara Ellis

Activity 5.31

1 List the clues in each poem that tell you they were written by mothers.

2 Find and write down ten words or phrases that show loving, tender or caring images.

3 Patricia Pogson uses memories of her child when very young as a contrast to her feelings for him or her now. Make a list of the comparisons she makes.

4 **a** Who is 'First born' written for?
   b Why did the mother write this poem for her child?

5 Describe how you imagine the children would feel if they were to read these poems.

The family is the most basic unit in our society. It may exist in different forms, but the people within a family believe they have closer ties with each other than with anyone outside the family unit.

Activity 5.32

1 In small groups, make up your own definition of the word 'family'. Try to consider the different types of families that exist in society today when deciding on your definition.

2 Share your definition with the class and discuss the different responses.

3 Do you think being part of a family is important? Why?

4 Present a written discussion of the positive and negative aspects of being in a family. A discussion allows you to present both sides of an issue and sometimes to make recommendations. Prepare your notes first, using the structure below as a guide. Aim for at least five points on either side.

Issue: Being in a family	
PLAN	
Positive	**Negative**
Point 1: Supporting facts:	Point 1: Supporting facts:
Point 2: Supporting facts:	Point 2: Supporting facts:
Recommendations:	

5 In a poem, describe your family. For example:

My family is expanding:
Two parents
Five children
The children have children
We become bigger
and better
It doesn't stop here –
We have become a
spreading mass
of descendants.

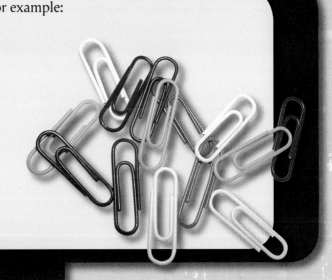

I went to my uncle's wedding
but I got sick so I don't suppose
he'll ask me to his next
one

Mario

The father's off inventions

I bet you my dad would have mistrusted
the steam engine when it first came in,
or Mr Bell's telephone; Mr Baird's television.

I remember he thought the fax
was a figment of my imagination.
What a scream.

I remember him freaking out
when he had to feed us at my aunt's house.
He went green when he saw the microwave.

He held the potatoes at arm's length,
then, panicking, threw them in,
shutting the door with a bang,

sent us children to sit in the garden
and wait for the noise *ting.*
I mean, imagine.

Once someone bought him an ansamachine
for his birthday and he burst into tears.
I had to leave the message.

Now, he said. *Hurry. Before the Bleep.*
All he wanted me to say was: This is
802 9 triple 3. I am sorry.

Then he crouched by the machine
for hours waiting for someone to ring.
There was me wanting to go iceskating.

'We can go out now. That's the whole point.'
I shouted, frustrated. *Just one message*, he said.
My dad won't move with the times.

He refuses to get a plastic hip
even though he's got arthritis
and he'd have a fit if he had to press

the pause button on the video.
Some people are just slow, slow.
'Leave me,' he says, 'off you go.'

Jackie Kay

Why is it?

Why is it
That when we go to the park
to fly my kite
the string always gets tangled
in the trees
and the kite gets torn,
while other kids' kites
go soaring and swooping?

Why is it
that when we play cricket
on the beach
my dad always drops catches
and is out first ball,
while other kids' dads
hit the ball
over the breakwater
into the sea?

Why is it
that when my mum asks my dad
to put up a picture
on the wall,
he drills a hole
that's far too big
and gets plaster everywhere?

But when my dad
tells my brother and me stories
in the dark,
Why is it
I can almost see
the creatures
and feel their hot breath?

Derek Stuart

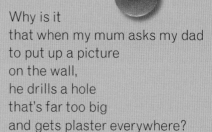

Activity 5.33

1   Summarise the characters of the fathers in 'The father's off inventions' and 'Why is it?', and their relationships with their children.

2   a   In what ways are the poems similar?
    b   In what ways are they different?

3   a   Make a list of the particular 'faults' of their fathers that the poets describe to us.
    b   Do you think these are serious faults to have? Explain.

4   Describe how you think the poets really feel about their fathers.

5   Imagine that the father in 'Why is it?' is being interviewed by his son for a homework task. Make a list of the things he would say about himself, under the headings: 'Things I'm good at' and 'Things I'm not good at'.

6 Imagine that the father in 'The father's off inventions' is tired of being ridiculed about his fear of technology. Write a poem from his point of view in which you outline either:

   a the reasons for his dislike of electronic 'gadgets'; or

   b his good qualities, previously not mentioned.

7 Based on the information in the two poems, and using your imagination, answer the following about the fathers in the poems:

   • How old are they?

   • What type of clothes do they wear?

   • What are their jobs?

   • What are their hobbies?

   Share your answers with the class and be prepared to justify your responses.

8 Are there things your father is good at? Things he isn't so good at? Make lists. (If this is difficult to answer, choose somebody you think of as a father figure.)

9 What does the fact that our parents are not always good at everything teach us about them?

First lesson

The thing to remember about fathers is, they're men.
A girl has to keep it in mind.
They are dragon-seekers, bent on improbable rescues.
Scratch any father, you find
Someone chock-full of qualms and romantic terrors,
Believing change is a threat –
Like your first shoes with heels on, like your first bicycle
It took such months to get.

Walk in strange woods, they warn you about the snakes there.
Climb, and they fear you'll fall.
Books, angular boys, or swimming in deep water –
Fathers mistrust them all.
Men are the worriers. It is difficult for them
To learn what they must learn:
How you have a journey to take and very likely,
For a while, will not return.

Phyllis McGinley

Activity 5.34

In 'First lesson', Phyllis McGinley creates an affectionate description of fathers as they learn to 'let go' of their daughters. Copy and complete the diagram below by quoting lines from the poem that support the statements in the boxes. The first one has been done for you.

Fathers

- sometimes like to be heroic
  They are dragon-seekers, bent on improbable rescues.

- have doubts about change and are fearful for their daughters

- will try to protect their daughters from certain experiences

- don't always trust some of the things they consider 'dangerous' for their daughters

- worry about their daughters

- sometimes find it difficult to let their daughters grow up and become independent

Caroline Ball was born with cerebral palsy and has never been able to walk, read or write as 'abled' people do. She is able to speak clearly, and works with another writer who puts her thoughts onto paper. She says: 'I began writing less than two years ago, but it is now very important to me. I have so many stories to tell.'

Shopping

I've never been alone in a butcher's or a baker's shop,
where your head's below the counter
and you can't catch their eye.

Shopping alone was a long time ago
with a bicycle basket on the side of my chair;
down the tarmac drive and over the dyke,
across the bridge with no sides
where Mum used to worry sky-high,
but Dad would say
'Let her go and see if she comes back'.

Outside the supermarket
butterflies funny in my stomach,
I squeezed the hooter on my chair,
the black hooter to call the man
to read the list in my purse
to bring the goods from the shop shelves,
where I could not go.

Shopping in the basket,
butterflies now flown,
electric as my chair
I whizzed along the quiet lane
home:
to Mum – anxious with barriers of love,
to Dad – loving by letting me go
to grow up,
to try it alone.

Caroline Ball

Activity **5.35**

1   What impressions do you get of the mother and father in the poem 'Shopping'?

2   Describe the things the mother might have worried about after letting her daughter go shopping alone.

3   Suggest why you think the father wants to allow his daughter this particular freedom.

4   Describe the feelings the poet's parents have for her and the different ways they show these feelings. Quote lines from the poem to support your answer.

5   Describe how the poet felt about being given the chance to be independent.

6   Write a paragraph about a time when someone in your family trusted you enough to let you try some new challenge alone.

I'm starting to wonder . . .

I'm starting to wonder what my folks were up to at
my age that makes them so doggoned suspicious
of me all the time.

Margaret Blair Johnstone

Mementos

In a box in her mother's room she found them then:
the spaghetti-legged girl, in the drawings from infant school,
with hair like water-buffalo horns, the pudding-shaped cat
with currant eyes, the lop-sided house,
the gawky pastel flowers still staring out at the world,
the clothes-peg doll, the comb,
each in its tissue-paper wrapping thus preserved
from every hazard, especially that of the dust
which rose, so it seemed, from the very land itself,
infiltrating the house, the throat, the heart,
so that no word of what mother felt could ever be said
– even *I love you* folded away with infinite care,
for which she would have exchanged all else that was there.

Bruce Dawe

Activity 5.36

1　A 'memento' is a souvenir or keepsake, usually treasured because it reminds us of someone.
   a　Draw the mementos of her daughter that the mother kept.
   b　What is the importance of her keeping them?
   c　What do you think is the significance of the last two lines?

2　The mother found it hard to express her feelings for her daughter in words. Identify and write down the lines from the poem which show this.

3　Suggest why you think we sometimes find it hard to express our love to members of our family.

4　Imagine that the mother and daughter have a conversation after the daughter's discovery of the mementos. In small groups, write a dialogue between the two women in which one or both of them finally express feelings that have remained hidden.

5　Describe your favourite memento that was given to you by a family member. Why is it so special to you?

This poem is, in itself, a memento of a mother.

Living on

My mother died eight years ago
When I was five, but still awake,
Asleep, I see her summer face
And feel her living hand on mine.
No ghost, but there and meeting need
And helping me to know there are no dead.

John Kitching

Activity **5.37**

1   What has happened to the mother in 'Living on'?

2   Why do you think the poet says that his mother died when he was 'still awake'?

3   Explain the comparison he makes about being awake and being asleep.

4   Even though she is no longer living, the poet talks about his mother in the present tense. Suggest why you think this is so.

5   Describe the feelings he has for his mother.

6   Why does the poet believe 'there are no dead'?

One-parent family

My mum says she's clueless
not, as you'd imagine,
at wiring three pin plugs or
straightening a bicycle wheel,
but at sewing buttons
on a shirt, icing names and
dates on birthday cakes,
preparing a three course meal.

She's not like other mothers;
although she's slim and neat
she looks silly in an apron,
just great in dungarees.
She'll tackle any household job,
lay lino, fix on tiles, does
all the outside paintwork, climbs
a ladder with practised ease.

Mind you, she's good for
a cuddle if I fall and
cut my knee. She tells me
fantastic stories every night,
laughs at *my* disasters, says
that she's as bad when she
reads a recipe all wrong and
her cakes don't come out right.

I know on open evenings
she gives a bad impression
at the school. She doesn't wear
the proper clothes. 'Too bad,'
the others sometimes say,
'You've got such a peculiar mum.'
'It's just as well,' I tell them.
'She is my mother *and* my dad!'

Moira Andrew

Activity **5.38**

1 Choose three verbs, three adjectives and three nouns to describe the mother in the poem.

2 In what ways does Moira Andrew say her mother is 'different' from most other mothers?

3 Describe the mother's personality, supporting your answer with lines from the poem.

4 What do you think the mother would say if someone told her she was 'peculiar'?

5 Identify the reason given for her uniqueness. Do you agree that this makes a person unique? Explain.

6 Describe with the help of a diagram what the poem tells you about the poet's relationship with her mother.

7 In a table, list the mother's special talents, as well as the things she is not so good at. Use two columns, headed 'Things she does well' and 'Things she doesn't do well'. Which of your lists tells you more about the mother?

A sense of love

The grandchildren haven't turned out the way we thought they would. Their parents, my children, are hurt and angry, ashamed and worried about it. I'm not. I like these kids the way they are: open and honest, disorganised and gentle, scruffy and kind. They don't seem to mind spending time with me. We talk about real things: dreams, peace, the sky. They tell me that living is more important than accomplishing things. I agree.

Their parents are outraged by this so I don't go into it. I say, 'The kids came.' The parents say, 'Good, at least they have a sense of duty.' I think they have a sense of love.

Readers' Digest

1 **a** The grandparent in 'A sense of love' seems to understand the grandchildren better than their parents do. Give reasons for this.

  b What things does the grandparent like about his/her grandchildren?

2 Imagine you are the grandparent talking to your son or daughter about his or her children and the relationship they share. Role-play in small groups, focusing on solutions for improving the relationship.

3 Explain how you would like people to treat you when you are old.

4 Interview one of your grandparents, or another person of their generation, asking them about their life, then write a character profile describing the type of life they have had.

5 Choose a member of your family and draw a 'character card' for them. Use the following layout, or make up one of your own.

CHARACTER CARD

Affix photo here

Name: ....

Age: .... Place of birth: ....

Job/career: ....

Physical description: ....

....

....

Personality: ....

....

....

Special features: (unusual hobbies or interests, physical or speech mannerisms, something interesting in past, etc.) ....

....

....

A 'traditional' family is often described as consisting of a mother, a father and two children, but there are many families that don't fit this picture. Family units differ for a variety of reasons, but they are, nonetheless, still families.

George

George said:
sometimes my dad doesn't shave
and his face is all prickly.

The new teacher said:
what does your mother say about that?

And George didn't say anything.

Clare said:
his mum don't live with his dad.

And the new teacher said:
Don't say don't
say doooon't.

And Clare said:
I live with my auntie.

Michael Rosen

Alex, on holiday?

I'm sure glad Mr Carey
didn't ask us to write
about our holiday.
How do you write an essay
on helping your dad move out
to go and live in a little flat
around the corner?
And spending half the time
sitting in the bedroom
listening to your parents
argue
over what Dad can take
and what has to stay behind?
And every argument ends
with one of them saying,
'As long as Alex is happy.'
That's when I put the pillow
tight over my ears
so I couldn't hear any more
and so I wouldn't shout,
'I'm *not* happy!'

I spent exactly twenty days
at Dad's place,
and twenty days
at our house with Mum,
which I think is my parents' idea
of being fair and even.
I couldn't wait for school to start.
How weird is that?

Steven Herrick

Activity **5.40**

1   Explain what happened to the families in 'George' and 'Alex, on holiday'.

2   What do you think the child in each of the poems is feeling?

3   Choose a partner and find out about each other's family.

Monologue

He, my lonely Father
    Sits alone
        with no lights on.
His cigarette glows in the dark.
Smoke melts
    up into the privacy
        of his nothingness.
He is still.
She, my lonely Mother
    sits propped up in bed alone,
    nervously shuffling through
        well-read magazines.
I tiptoe past
    and hold my breath.
    'Sweet dreams', she calls,
But I have forgotten how to dream.
    Just like her.
I'll leave them to
    their silent moons
    their tearful nights
    their fearful dawns.
We hate them for what they are.
They hate themselves for what they are not.
Bury the wound. Close the scar
    to other prying eyes.
But I am not deaf nor blind.
I live here. I see it as it is.
And all I am is the tape
    that tethers them to time.
But I have my life to live.
And now
    their private melodrama
        makes me weep
            no more.

Cathy Newell (student)

Activity **5.41**

1   A monologue is a scene in a drama in which a person speaks alone, without the presence of others. Suggest why the poem has been given this title.

2   **a**   Describe the kind of family life shown in the poem. Quote lines to support your answer.
    b   'We hate them for what they are.
           They hate themselves for what they are not.'
           Suggest what the poet means by this.

3   Identify the only thing keeping the parents together. Quote the lines from the poem that tell you this.

4   Describe, in your own words, the attitude of the poet to her parents' situation.

5   In groups, act out a family meeting with the people in the poem working on solutions to improve the family relationships.

6   Describe the kind of 'scars' you have heard about in families who have experienced separation or divorce. Do you think these things *do* scar people? Explain.

Going through the old photos

Me, my dad
and my brother
we were looking through the old photos.
Pictures of my dad with a broken leg
and my mum with big flappy shorts on
and me on a tricycle
when we got to one of mum
with a baby on her knee,
and I go,
'Is that me or Brian?'
And my dad says,
'Let's have a look.
It isn't you or Brian,' he says.
'It's Alan.
He died.
He would have been
two years younger than Brian
and two years older than you.
He was a lovely baby.'

'How did he die?'

'Whooping cough.
I was away at the time.
He coughed himself to death in Connie's arms.
The terrible thing is,
it wouldn't happen today,
but it was during the war, you see,
and they didn't have the medicines.
That must be the only photo
of him we've got.'

Me and Brian
looked at the photo.
We couldn't say anything.
It was the first time we had ever heard about Alan.
For a moment I felt ashamed
like as if I had done something wrong.

I looked at the baby trying to work out
who he looked like.
I wanted to know what another brother
would have been like.
No way of saying.
And Mum looked so happy.
Of course she didn't know
when they took the photo
that he would die, did she?

Funny thing is,
though my father mentioned it every now and then
over the years,
Mum – never.
And he never said anything in front of her
about it
and we never let on that we knew.
What I've never figured out
was whether
her silence was because
she was more upset about it
than my dad –
or less.

Michael Rosen

1 Describe the family in the poem, 'Going through the old photos'. Quote lines from the poem to support your answer.

2 Explain what happened to Alan.

3 The poet says, 'For a moment I felt ashamed, like as if I had done something wrong'. Suggest reasons for this.

4 Offer suggestions as to why the mother and father had never told their sons about Alan.

5 Who do you think was more upset about his death – the mother or the father? Explain your answer.

6 Imagine you are the boy in the poem. Write a letter or poem to Alan telling him about his family.

Forgotten

It's sad when my children want to know
Of Aboriginal legends of long ago,
Of Dreamtime stories and corroborees,
Things that should have been taught to me.
But how do I tell them that I missed out
Simply by being shuffled about
From one white home to another?
And that's how nobody came to bother
To tell me that I had a family tree,
Or even that I was part Aborigine.

I had to wait until I was grown,
To find my people on my own.
It's impossible to learn in a very short time
The language and culture of these people of mine.
I feel I am selling my own kids short,
But how can I teach them what I wasn't taught?
So have patience, my kids, I'm anxious too,
To know these things as much as you.
Maybe in time we'll still this yearning
But remember, my kids, I too am still learning.

Margaret Brusnahan

Activity 5.43

1   Explain what has happened to the children in 'Forgotten'.

2   Identify the lines in the poem where Margaret Brusnahan describes the importance of belonging to a family.

3   The person in the poem was one of the 'stolen generation'. Research the 'stolen generation' and try to find out how many families were affected and why so many families were torn apart. How did the government of the time justify this policy? What have been the consequences for those involved?

Conflict

Benjamin Zephaniah is a rap poet of Jamaican origin. In his poem about a bully at school he presents us with a one-sided, but interesting, conversation:

Beyond de bell

Yu push
Yu shove
Believing
School moves around **yu**,
Yu spy an lie
Believing
Tings control by **yu**,
What mek **yu** tink like dat?
Never mind
Academic ability
Concentration span
I.Q. business
Yu big in de playground,
Never mind
People who
Don't push an shove
Yu do.

Table may turn
Yu may be pushed,
An macho boy
Yu may lose **yu** watch
Yu ill gained sweet money
Yu bigheadedness,
Table may turn
Yu may be shoved
Den walked over
By an army
Of carers
Teaching lessons,
We don't want dat now
Do we.

Yu are not respected
Yu are other tings,
People do talk behind yu back
Whatever **yu** say,
We all have problems

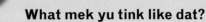

But
Dere are people who will talk to **yu**
If **yu** won't talk to yuself.

Yu grab an slap
An won't give back
Believing
It's over at four,
By day **yu** taunt
At night **yu** haunt,
Believing
Yu rule OK,

What mek yu tink like dat?
Is it
Parents,
Dreams,
Bigger bullies
Or television,
Who do we blame,
An
What mek yu tink like dat?

Benjamin Zephaniah

Activity 5.44

1   Write 'true' or 'false' for each of the statements below. (They may be worded
    differently in the poem.) Justify your answers.
    a   The poet is speaking to himself.
    b   The person being spoken to is a boy.
    c   The bully pushes, shoves, lies, grabs, slaps and teases others.
    d   The bully thinks a lot of himself.
    e   The bully does many bad things, but he doesn't steal.
    f   The poet repeats a question throughout the poem.

2   Write 'true' or 'false' for each of the statements below. (The statements may be
    implied in the poem – they may be what the poet is meaning to say, but not
    actually stated in the same words.) Justify your answers.
    a   The bully is well respected.
    b   The bully has little ability when it comes to academic subjects.
    c   The bully doesn't care about others.
    d   One day the bully himself may be bullied by someone bigger and better.
    e   The poet thinks that teachers are caring.
    f   Teachers try to help the bully.
    g   The bully wants to improve his behaviour.
    h   The bully has no-one to talk to about changing his ways.
    i   The bully is not interested in school.
    j   The bully doesn't try to make excuses for the way he behaves.
    k   The poet blames the bully's behaviour on television.
    l   The poet can't understand what makes the bully behave the way he does.
    m   The poet wants to get to the reason for the bully's behaviour.

3   With which of the statements below do you think the poet would agree?
    Justify your answers.
    a   Bullying is a negative activity.
    b   Bullies are usually under-achievers at school.

c   Bullies try to have power over others because they are insecure and have to look 'big' in front of others.
d   Bullies cannot change their behaviour into good behaviour.
e   Bullying is something that is copied.
f   Bullies are influenced by violent television shows.
g   There are many reasons why bullies act the way they do.
h   Bullies need someone to help them change their behaviour.
i   There are people who can help bullies if only they would talk to them.
j   Bullies have to want to change their behaviour and stop making excuses for it.
k   Bullies must admit that their behaviour is wrong.
l   Bullies are usually boys.

4   Discuss your responses to questions 1–3 as a class. Try to support your choices by using examples from the poem, where possible.

5   Write down what you think is meant by the following:
    a   'Believing school moves around **yu** . . . believing tings control by **yu**.'
    b   'Never mind people who don't push an shove . . . '
    c   '**Yu** may be . . . walked over by an army of carers teaching lessons. We don't want dat now do we.'
    d   'Dere are people who will talk to **yu** if **yu** won't talk to yuself.'
    e   '**Yu** grab an slap an won't give back believing it's over at four.'

1   The cartoon seems to be a warning. Describe the cartoonist's message. What is he trying to tell us?

2   Look at the visual elements and complete the following:
    a   Use adjectives to describe the tone of the cartoon.
    b   What meaning is conveyed by the position of the shadow in relation to the child? Which one is the dominant image and what does this suggest?
    c   Describe the facial expressions of the boy and the shadow. Likewise, look at the objects each one holds. Explain the transformation and the point being made.
    d   Explain the significance of the boy drawn in white and the shadow in black. Describe how the use of the contrasting black and white contribute to the cartoonist's message.
    e   The lines in the drawing are very distinct, bold and strong. How does this add to the tone of the cartoon?

3   Does the cartoon rely on our understanding of particular cultural experiences, or do you think its message can be universally understood? Explain your answer.

4   Is this a stereotypical representation of bullies? Discuss and give reasons for your answer.

5   a   Write a list of the various ways in which bullies cause conflict.
    b   Suggest why you think there are bullies in our society and describe the different forms can they take. Explain your answer.

Mart's advice

If someone's acting big with you,
if someone's bossing you about
look very hard at one of their ears.
Keep your eyes fixed on it.
Don't let up.
Stare at it as if it was
a mouldy apple.
Keep staring.
Don't blink.

After a bit
you'll see their hand
go creeping up to touch it.
They're saying to themselves
'What's wrong with my ear?'

At that moment
you know you've won.

Smile.

Michael Rosen

Activity 5.46

1   Have you ever been bullied or bossed around so that you felt helpless and 'small'? In a table, list all the details you can remember. Here's an example:

Details	Emotional feelings	Physical feelings
Bailed up by a gang on the bus Took my bag, emptied all its contents, stole my money	embarrassed and humiliated – everyone looking helpless; weak; frustrated angry that no-one helped me when I needed them	forehead and palms sweating red-faced; hot and flushed knees trembling heart beating very fast

2   Now write a poem about the experience, using your list to help you.

Bullying is one form of conflict, but conflict can take many forms.

A formal apology

To whom it may concern, I say we're all
dreadfully sorry over here that we
dropped those bombs on you all
over there, well, you know how it is.
We didn't mean to hurt you or anything,
didn't mean to demolish your houses or scorch your feet.

You know, we're really feeling bad over here,
but we just wanted to shake you up a bit,
you know, just to make peace over there –
with all that fighting and everything, you see.
We didn't mean to hurt you or anything,
didn't mean to tear your bodies or cremate your children.

I say, I hope there are no hard feelings or anything.
Needless to say, if we can do anything to help at all,
you'll let us know, won't you?
Well, don't be afraid to ask, will you? Because after all,
we didn't mean to hurt you or anything,
didn't mean to silence your babies or cripple your hearts.

Karyn Healy (student)

Terribly sorry

Shuffle through the motions
Next!
Poverty for you –
Next!
Wealth for you –
Third door on the right
You there! – death
No refunds
Or exchanges
Get what you're given and
Don't forget to say 'thank
      you'
You don't like it?
That's too bad
Next!
Disease for you
Terribly sorry
Just doing my job.

Debbie Frandsen (student)

Land that itself does not change

Land that itself does not change,
      Land where my people once dwelt –
Its peace has been broken by the roar of bulldozers
      Uprooting our sacred trees,
      Scarring our sacred places . . .
      And the hearts of my people
      have broken with it.

Alison Gurramu

Complete a chart like the one below, summarising the poets' attitudes to the issues in the poems 'A formal apology', 'Terribly sorry' and 'Land that itself does not change' in the first column. In the last column, briefly summarise your own attitudes to the issues.

Activity **5.47**

Issue	Attitudes	
	The poet's	**Yours**
War ('A formal apology')		
Poverty and disease ('Terribly sorry')		
Heritage ('Land that itself does not change')		

War

Most of us would agree that war is a terrible thing, involving tragic loss of lives, yet wars continue to occur. Ironically, the First World War (1914–1918) was called 'The Great War' and 'The war to end all wars' but was followed by the Second World War only twenty years later. The two poems that follow, written during the First World War, vividly express anger and disillusionment about the waste of human lives that war brings.

Wilfred Owen served in the British Army. He wrote with striking truth of the horrors of that war, from seeing it firsthand. Owen was killed in France, one week before the Armistice, at the age of 25. His parents received the news of his death on the day that peace was declared in Britain, 11 November 1918.

The Latin phrase *Dulce et decorum est pro patria mori* was coined by the Roman poet Horace over 2000 years ago. It means: 'It is sweet and fitting to die for one's country'. Many soldiers, including Owen, became increasingly disillusioned by the war, particularly by the continuing demand for patriotic poetry which talked of 'valour', 'honour' and 'sacrifice'. Owen's anger against those who sent young men to war and hid the realities of it from those at home was simple and strong. He wanted 'the old lie', that it was glorious to die for your country, to be destroyed, by telling civilians what war was really like. The poem below gives an account of a gas attack and is a bitter take on Horace's motto:

Dulce et decorum est

Bent double, like old beggars under sacks,
Knock-kneed, coughing like hags, we cursed through sludge,
Till on the haunting flares we turned our backs,
And towards our distant rest began to trudge.
Men marched asleep. Many had lost their boots,
But limped on, blood-shod. All went lame, all blind;
Drunk with fatigue; deaf even to the hoots
Of gas-shells dropping softly behind.

Gas! Gas! Quick, boys! – An ecstasy of fumbling,
Fitting the clumsy helmets just in time,
But someone still was yelling out and stumbling
And floundering like a man in fire or lime. –
Dim through the misty panes and thick green light,
As under a green sea, I saw him drowning.
In all my dreams, before my helpless sight,
He plunges at me, guttering, choking, drowning.

If in some smothering dreams, you too could pace
Behind the wagon that we flung him in,
And watch the white eyes writhing in his face,
His hanging face, like a devil's sick of sin;
If you could hear, at every jolt, the blood
Come gargling from the froth-corrupted lungs,
Obscene as cancer, bitter as the cud
Of vile, incurable sores on innocent tongues, –
My friend, you would not tell with such high zest
To children ardent for some desperate glory,
The old Lie: Dulce et decorum est
Pro patria mori.

Wilfred Owen

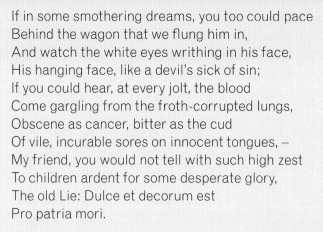

'Dulce et decorum est': three-level guide

Activity **5.48**

1   Level 1: Write out the statements below and beside each one identify whether it is true or false. Be prepared to justify your choices using quotes from the poem.
    a   The soldiers are walking through mud.
    b   Because many men have lost their boots, their feet are covered in blood.
    c   The soldiers are lame, blind, deaf or drunk.
    d   The soldiers are retiring from battle to get some much-needed sleep.
    e   They are too tired to notice what is going on around them.
    f   They are excited at the thought of putting their gas masks on quickly.
    g   One of the soldiers doesn't put his mask on in time and is overcome by mustard gas.
    h   The gas is like thick fog.
    i   The soldier's death is quick and painless.
    j   He is coughing up blood from his lungs.

2   Level 2: Write out the statements below and beside each one identify whether it is true or false, according to the poem. Be prepared to justify your choices using quotes from the poem.
    a   The war has gone on for a long time.
    b   The soldiers are well equipped.
    c   Everyone is alert and at the ready for battle.
    d   The soldiers have to march behind a wagon full of sick and injured.
    e   It is the innocent who are victims of war.
    f   To die for your country in war is a wonderful thing to do.
    g   Owen has become used to the pain and suffering he has seen.
    h   War not only leaves physical scars, but it also scars the mind.

3   Level 3: Copy the statements below and identify those that you think Wilfred Owen would agree with as 'true' and those that you think he would disagree with as 'false'. Quote from the poem, and any other information you have, to support your choices.

   a   Soldiers who fight in wars take risks of which they should be fully aware.
   b   Death in war is the most unselfish and greatest of sacrifices.
   c   Serving one's country means being prepared to fight on its behalf.
   d   War makes soldiers become 'anti-war'.
   e   War is ugly and senseless.
   f   The victims of war are those who don't start them.
   g   There is nothing 'sweet' about dying slowly and painfully.
   h   We should not brainwash our children into thinking that war is glorious and a good way of solving conflict.
   i   If we could experience war we would not think of it as 'sweet'.
   j   War poetry can do much to increase our awareness of what soldiers actually experience in war.

Siegfried Sassoon, a friend and mentor of Wilfred Owen, also wrote about the realities of war, condemning the men who sent the young to their deaths. His first reactions to the outbreak of war in 1914 were like those of many others at the time who saw it as an heroic adventure. However, his experiences of fighting in the trenches in France, and seeing his friends die, deeply affected him, and his feelings changed radically. Sassoon, unlike Wilfred Owen, survived the war.

Attack

glow'ring: to look angrily

scarred: the ridge is pock-marked by battle fire

barrage: heavy artillery fire

furtive: stealthy, sly

flounders: fumbles, struggles

massed: dense

dun: dull or greyish-brown

shroud: covers or conceals

bristling: gunfire comes in short, stiff bursts

grappling: clutching, grabbing

At dawn the ridge emerges massed and dun
In wild purple of the glow'ring sun
Smouldering through spouts of drifting smoke that shroud
The menacing scarred slope; and, one by one,
Tanks creep and topple forward to the wire.
The barrage roars and lifts. Then, clumsily bowed
With bombs and guns and shovels and battle-gear,
Men jostle and climb to meet the bristling fire.
Lines of grey, muttering faces, masked with fear,
They leave their trenches, going over the top,
While time ticks blank and busy on their wrists,
And hope, with furtive eyes and grappling fists,
Flounders in mud. O Jesus, make it stop!

                                    Siegfried Sassoon

1   Describe what is happening in the poem 'Attack'.

2   How would you describe its tone?

3   The poem relies heavily on sight and sound imagery.
    a   Identify the lines where such imagery occurs.
    b   In what ways is each image powerful?

4   What image is evoked in the lines 'clumsily bowed with bombs and guns and shovels and battle-gear'? How does the repetition of 'and' add to this?

5   Write out the lines that suggest a frenzy of movement.

6   'Time ticks blank and busy' is a metaphor. To what could 'blank' and 'busy' refer?

7   Hope is personified in the poem.
    a   What human qualities is it given?
    b   Explain the poet's point in saying that it 'flounders in mud'.

8   The last sentence is a forceful, almost violent, plea.
    a   What does it tell us about the impact of the war on the poet?
    b   How did you feel when you read it? Explain.

Erich Maria Remarque was a German soldier who fought in France during 1917 and 1918. His novel *All Quiet on the Western Front* is told through the eyes of a narrator, Paul Baumer, who is 19 when he enlists. Remarque prefaced his novel by saying that it was an account of 'a generation that was destroyed by the war – even those of it who survived the shelling.'

All Quiet on the Western Front

I am young, I am twenty years of age; but I know nothing of life except despair, death, fear, and the combination of completely mindless superficiality with an abyss of suffering. I see people being driven against one another, and silently, uncomprehendingly, foolishly, obediently and innocently killing one another. I see the best brains in the world inventing weapons and words to make the whole process that much more sophisticated and long-lasting. And watching this with me are all my contemporaries, here and on the other side, all over the world – my whole generation is experiencing this with me. What would our fathers do if one day we rose up and confronted them, and called them to account? What do they expect from us when a time comes in which there is no more war? For years our occupation has been killing – that was the first experience we had. Our knowledge of life is limited to death. What will happen afterwards? And what can possibly become of us?

Erich Maria Remarque

1 Describe your feelings about war after reading this extract from *All Quiet on the Western Front*.

2 What lessons do you think the writer wants us to learn?

3 Various reasons are provided for killing others in wartime. What are they?

4 'I see the best brains in the world inventing weapons and words to make the whole process that much more sophisticated and long-lasting.' As a class, discuss whether these words are still true today.

5 Explain what you think is meant by 'What would our fathers do if one day we rose up ... and called them to account?'

6 Interestingly, Remarque rarely uses the word 'enemy' in his novel. Instead, the narrator refers to 'the others' or 'those over there', or those 'on the other side'. Identify the lines that convey that war affects entire generations, regardless of the countries they come from.

7 Referring to the extract, if 'the enemy' is not other people, then suggest what it could be.

8 Describe the impact of the lines 'For years our occupation has been killing – that was the first experience we had. Our knowledge of life is limited to death.'

9 Transform the extract into a poem, while still retaining the mood.

10 Imagine you are a soldier. Write a letter home expressing your experiences of war.

During the Second World War (1939–1945) Adolf Hitler ordered the mass extermination of millions of Jews throughout Europe. Lily Brett's poem shows us that even the survivors were scarred for life.

The questions

the questions
that tormented
my mother

were
the same questions
every day

did she do
anything
at anyone else's

expense
to save
herself

did
her mother know
she'd have preferred

to go
with her
to the ovens

did
her sister hear
her crying

did
her niece
die quickly

another question
that tormented
her

was
why was she
saved

why
was she
spared

she wasn't sure
she was
saved

she wasn't sure
she was
spared

Lily Brett

Activity 5.51

1 Explain why the poet's mother in 'The questions' was haunted by her memories.

2 Describe the connection between Rowel Frier's cartoon on page 242 and this poem.

3 The word 'tormented' is a powerful one. What are the feelings evoked by this word?

4 The use of short and, often, single-word lines in the poem creates emphasis, and therefore a particular mood. Explain what you think Lily Brett is trying to highlight.

5 Often survivors of war, conflict or other traumatic events are overlooked; we tend to focus on those who have lost their lives. What do you think the poet could be saying about 'living' when you have lost those you love under terrible circumstances?

6 Explain why you think the mother did not feel 'saved' or 'spared'.

7 Write a journal entry from the mother's point of view, reflecting upon her life, her experiences and the loss of those she loved.

Gulf war

When I looked out and saw
three Navy officers in dress uniform at my door
I knew why they were there.

'It's nothing,' I said quietly to our two
children crowding close, the way young children do:
'Some friends of Daddy with some time to spare,'
'Beg pardon, ma'am,' said the first,
'We have some bad news for you, I'm afraid – the worst . . .
May we come in?' he said.

'Of course,' I told him, and my mouth went dry.
They were so kind, I could not let them see me cry.
'You've come to tell me that my husband's dead . . . ?'

'Yes, ma'am. He was unfortunately shot down
by a SAM missile over an Iraqi town
– for security reasons, we cannot say which one.'

'I understand,' I said, although
Of course I didn't altogether, but I know
all our lives are on a vast loom spun.

* * *

I've told the children Daddy's on a cruise
– they're getting used to that (and why refuse
the white lie that must cover the black fact?).

His graduation photo smiles at me;
friends help me learn to smile back, and to see
his memory honoured with each future act.

On a cruise . . . And in a sense that's true
from the *Saratoga*'s flight-deck to the blue
infinity of all our unspent years.

No gulf of loss can separate me still
from you, my love, you did your country's will
– out of the well of duty spring these tears . . .

Bruce Dawe

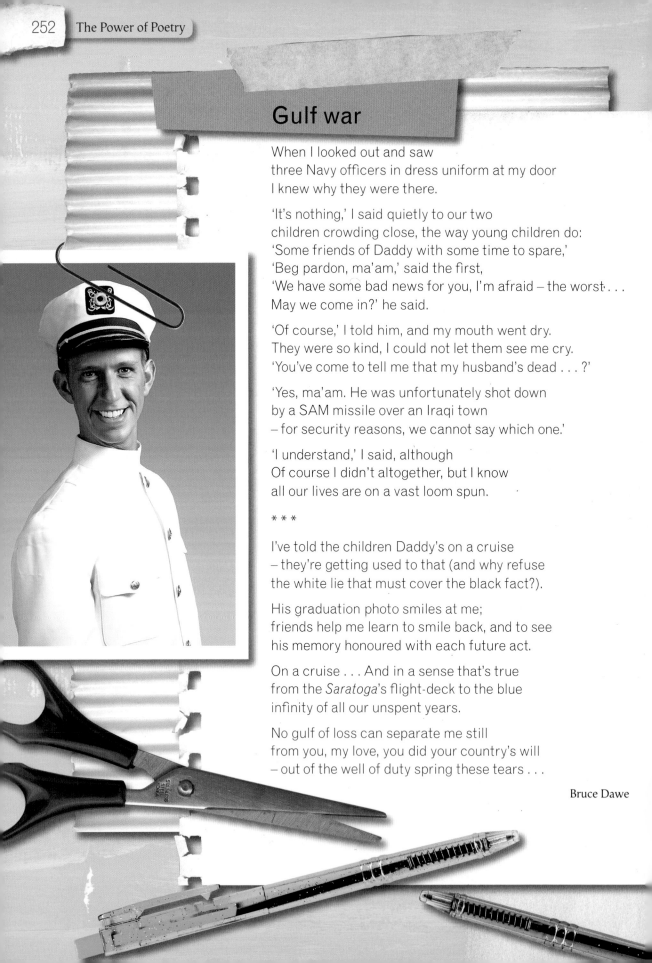

1   There is a tone of acceptance in the poem, yet Dawe is using irony to highlight a serious message. Where does the irony occur and what do you think his message is?

2   'I've told the children Daddy's on a cruise' is both metaphoric and ironic.
   a   How does the wife justify telling them this?
   b   List other metaphors used in the poem and explain what they mean.

3   'Why refuse the white lie that must cover the black fact?'
   a   Under what circumstances do some people normally tell a white lie?
   b   Explain what is meant by the 'white lie' as opposed to the 'black fact'.
   c   Do you think it is fair of the mother to hide the truth from her children about the death of their father? Explain.

4   The phrases 'your country's will' and 'the well of duty' suggest that the wife's grief seems to be eased by the idea of sacrifice and honour. Is 'a country's will' ever a justification for the death of those who follow it? Explain your answer.

5   Research Australia's involvement in global wars and conflicts. Draw a timeline of this involvement, starting from the Sudan War in 1885 to today.

Walt Whitman, an American poet, was very concerned with social issues, and the connections we have to each other. The poem 'I sit and look out' presents a commentary on the confusion and helplessness that individuals may feel when confronted by the ills of our society – 'the sorrows of the world'.

I sit and look out

I sit and look out upon all the sorrows of the world, and upon all oppression and shame;
I hear secret convulsive sobs from young men, at anguish with themselves, remorseful after deeds done;
I see, in low life, the mother misused by her children, dying, neglected, gaunt, desperate;
I see the wife misused by her husband – I see the treacherous seducer of young women;
I mark the ranklings of jealousy and unrequited love, attempted to be hid – I see these sights on the earth;
I see the workings of battle, pestilence, tyranny – I see martyrs and prisoners;
I observe a famine at sea – I observe the sailors casting lots who shall be kill'd, to preserve the lives of the rest;
I observe the slights and degradations cast by arrogant persons upon labourers, the poor, and upon negroes, and the like;
All these – All the meanness and agony without end, I sitting, look out upon,
See, hear, and am silent.

Walt Whitman

1 How would you describe the tone of the poem 'I sit and look out'?

2 Whitman conveys his impressions using a 'listing' technique. Explain how this contributes to our understanding of the poem.

3 The speaker is more an observer than a participant.
   a How is this reflected in the poem?
   b Does he arrive at a conclusion?
   c Why do you think he is 'silent'?

4 'I sit and look out' was written in 1860.
   a Even though the poem has its own historical context, how is it a text 'before its time'?
   b What is contemporary about the poem?
   c What is universal?

5 Whitman is prophetic when he says 'All these – all the meanness and agony without end . . . '. This suggests that there will always be terrible things that occur in society. Write your own poem which lists the things that are socially and politically important now – the things you could say we 'sit and look out upon' at this time.

6 Our ability to be an individual is not always an easy choice; sometimes it is easier to be 'silent' than to stand against those who contribute to society's ills. However, Martin Luther King Jnr once wrote: 'Our lives begin to end the day we become silent about things that matter'.
   a With which of these sentiments do you agree? Explain.
   b In groups, brainstorm and suggest some ways in which we can contribute to making society better.

7 Choose an issue which is important to you. For example:
   - death
   - poverty
   - AIDS
   - destruction of the environment
   - problems of the elderly
   - war
   - development of technology
   - destruction of the ozone layer
   - street kids
   - prejudice
   - violence
   - abuse.

   Write a poem that reflects how you feel about the issue. Create a display – a mixture of visual and written texts – on the issue. You can use photographs, illustrations, artwork, poems, song lyrics, articles, quotes – whatever you think conveys a message about your chosen issue. Present it to the class and explain your chosen texts.

Chapter 6

'Westfield creek' by Steven Herrick

Study of a poet: Steven Herrick

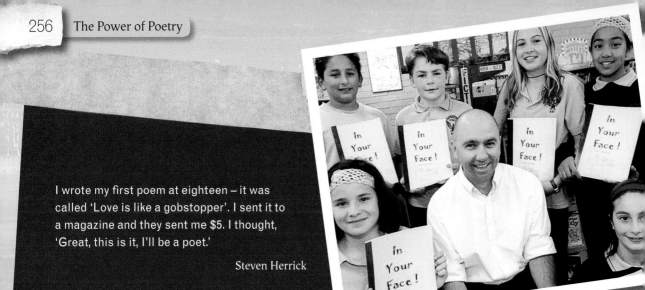

I wrote my first poem at eighteen – it was called 'Love is like a gobstopper'. I sent it to a magazine and they sent me $5. I thought, 'Great, this is it, I'll be a poet.'

Steven Herrick

Steven Herrick

Steven Herrick is one of Australia's most popular poets. He has published award-winning books of poetry and verse novels for children, young adults and adults.

I was born in Brisbane on New Year's Eve, 1958. While everyone celebrated the New Year, Mum was left holding the baby. I was the youngest of seven children – Mum wanted a girl. She got me instead. I went to Coopers Plains State School, where I was good at English and soccer, and where I got punched in the eye by a girl one year older than me – I ran home!

From the age of eight to fifteen I was obsessed with soccer – I spent every spare moment kicking a ball against the house, or trying to knock the branches off trees from twenty metres with a well-aimed right foot drive. At Acacia Ridge High School I decided to concentrate on a life of soccer instead of education, so I failed Year 10. The Principal suggested I not return for Year 11, so I didn't. I worked instead – fruit picker, storeman, clerk. And I played soccer on the weekend – still dreaming of football glory. After three years of hard work and no chance of making the FA Cup Final at Wembley, I decided to go back to school as an adult. This time I passed all my subjects and went to university, where I studied poetry.

. . . I liked poetry as a teenager. It was good for someone with a limited attention span like me at 18 . . . All my friends were in rock bands, and I couldn't sing or play an instrument. So I decided to get up on stage before they played, and read some of my poems. It went down a storm so I kept writing, and performing.

Steven Herrick

Steven Herrick has performed his poems throughout Australia in schools, pubs, universities, at festivals, rock venues and on radio and television. He has also toured Canada, the United Kingdom, the United States and Singapore. He is one of Australia's most travelled and widely heard poets. He lives in the Blue Mountains with his partner and two sons.

Themes

In his poems and verse novels, Steven Herrick communicates his own ideas, experiences, knowledge, attitudes and beliefs through his characters and subject matter. His works deal with such themes as:

* growing up; coming of age
* personal journeys; emotional transformation
* identity and belonging
* escape
* community
* freedom versus restriction
* representations of home
* the idea of hope
* heroism, courage, overcoming adversity
* friendship which spans age, gender and other differences
* love – familial; romantic; love which brings people together
* representations of family
* father–son relationships
* coping with grief, loss and leaving
* empathy and understanding of others' situations
* acceptance of others
* helping others.

'The colour of my town', from the verse novel *by the river*, is told from the point of view of Harry, a boy growing up in a small country town in the 1960s. The poem acts as a prologue to the novel, foreshadowing Harry's experiences and memories, and establishes the complex nature of the people in his community. Note how the poem is written in the past tense to give a feeling of 'reminiscing':

The colour of my town

Red
was Johnny Barlow
with his lightning fists
that drew blood in a blur.
Yellow
was Urger,
who stood behind,
with crooked teeth,
spitting and cursing.
Blue
were Miss Spencer's eyes,
pale and shining,
and fading distant grey
as the taxi drove away.
Green
was my dad's handkerchief,
ironed,
pressed into the pocket

above his heart;
a box of handkerchiefs
Mum gave him on his birthday
two weeks before she died.
Brown
was dry grass all summer,
a dead snake,
cane toads squashed flat,
our house smeared in oil;
nothing that lives,
nothing that shines.
White
was Mum's nightgown,
the chalk Miss Carter used
to write my name,
hospital sheets,
and the colour of Linda's cross.

by the river, pp. 3–4

Activity 6.1

1 Describe the mood of the poem.

2 Colours have an emotional significance – they can influence our moods and feelings, and often have an important role in our memories.
   a Make a list of the colours in the poem.
   b With whom or what are these colours associated?
   c Which colours are presented positively and negatively by Harry? Explain how you know this.

3 Draw or paint a visual representation of the people or things described in the poem.

4 The colours and images work together to create a picture of Harry's past.
   a What information are we given on a literal level? (What do we know?)
   b What references to events and people allow us to make predictions? (What do we have to infer?)

5 Steven Herrick says 'I feel comfortable in writing poetry because I see a different set of rules – or fewer rules . . . all the white space makes it less intimidating. The reader can see themselves progressing with the story as it has so few words. Then they do get involved in the story. They see my stories less as poetry and more as a narrative . . .'. How is 'The colour of my town' not only poetry, but narrative?

6 'The colour of my town' is a 'list' poem which uses strong visual language to construct images. Write your own list poem using colours to describe a place or event that has personal significance for you now, or that you remember from your past.

Settings

Herrick's use of settings are important in his poetry. They situate us, not just in place, but in time, and contribute enormously to atmosphere and mood. It is the characters' responses to their environments – either positive or negative – which allow us to get to know them.

I always get a location before I get the character. I then put the character in the location and wait for something to happen . . . I remembered staying in a disused railway carriage in Ballarat, Victoria when I was a young person hitching around the country. It was probably the best place I slept – warm and comfortable (and free!) . . . I spent time travelling around the country, working as a fruit picker, or in a cannery, and I slept and stayed where I could. I felt incredibly lucky . . . Most of the characters in my novels are fictional, but all the locations are based on places I know well . . .

Steven Herrick

In the verse novel *The simple gift*, 16-year-old Billy describes his favourite place, which he visits one last time before leaving home for good:

Westfield Creek   Billy

I love this place.
I love the flow of cold clear water
over the rocks
and the wattles on the bank
and the lizards sunbaking,
heads up, listening,
and the birds,
hundreds of them,
silver-eyes and currawongs,
kookaburras laughing
at us kids swinging on the rope
and dropping into the bracing flow.
I spent half my school days here
reading books I'd stolen
from Megalong Bookshop
with old Tom Whitton
thinking I'm his best customer
buying one book
with three others shoved up my jumper.
I failed every Year 10 subject
except English.
I can read.
I can dream.
I know about the world.
I learnt all I need to know
in books on the banks
of Westfield Creek,
my favourite classroom.

The simple gift, p. 6

Activity 6.2

1   Identify the reasons Billy gives for his love of this location.

2   What one word can you think of which sums up Westfield Creek for Billy? Compare your response with others' and discuss.

3   Consider what Billy's description of the creek tells us about his character. In a paragraph, write a description of Billy, based on what we learn about him in the poem.

4   Do *you* think that we can often learn more about life outside the classroom? Explain.

In *Tom Jones Saves the World,* Steven Herrick sets his main character in a 'gated' community in a new suburb.

I hate the things. They are packaged as specific communities when in fact they are the opposite of a community; they are trying to make the residents safe by shutting out the world. I wanted my main character to be a boy who came from a town where he had always felt safe because he was known by everybody – that's the true sense of community.

Steven Herrick

A gated community

To get into our suburb
you drive
down Cherrywood Avenue
and at the end of the street
is a sandstone wall
and a massive iron gate.
To get through this gate
you reach out of
the car window and punch your
Personal Entry Number (PEN)
into the keypad on the pole.
The gate slides open,
you drive through,
and it closes behind you.
Often there is a Security Guard
in the office beside the entrance.
He sits at his desk
reading the paper
waiting for something to happen.

After two months
of living here
I realised it was
like a prison that
parents paid lots of money
to live in so
they could say things like
   "I feel so secure now.
    Thomas can walk the streets
    and I know he's safe."

In our old town
I used to walk to the shops
    to the river
    to the school.
I knew everyone.
At Pacific Palms, I know only
Mrs Johnson
who keeps trying to show me
her garden.
I live in Camellia Prison.

Tom Jones Saves the World, p. 9

1   Explain the differences in location between the two poems 'Westfield Creek' and 'A gated community'. How does the location affect the atmosphere of each poem?

2   The tone of Tom's character in 'A gated community' is deliberately sterile.
   a   Explain why you think Steven Herrick has done this.
   b   Quote the words and lines which convey this sterility.
   c   What other words would you use to describe Tom's environment?

3   a   How does the simile 'like a prison' make us feel about Tom's existence?
   b   Sketch the gated community as described in the poem. Try to incorporate the 'prison' metaphor.

4   a   If the gated community is so secure, why does it need a security guard?
   b   In pairs, write a list of ten rules you think should be compulsory in a gated community. Give reasons for your answers.

5   a   Explain the point being made in the lines 'In our old town I used to walk to the shops, to the river, to the school. I knew everyone.'
   b   In which community does Tom feel more secure and happy? Why?

6   Describe what you think Steven Herrick could be saying about urbanisation and suburbia, and their effects on freedom.

Characters

I read a lot, and am probably influenced by everything I read. I like poetry that tells a story. I love writing verse novels. They allow me to get into the characters and tell the reader all about their lives: it's often just one or two characters in a story telling you all their secrets in their own voice, which I think is really intimate and enjoyable. Because I write from real-life incidents a lot of my main characters tend to be boys – I have two teenage boys. I really have to work hard with my female characters. I often have my two main characters as sounding boards for each other, and that way I find I can write a female character more easily.

Steven Herrick

Tom and Cleo

Walking back to class
Cleo says "Thanks for the game."
I ask her where she learnt about snakes.
      "It's the only thing
      my Dad taught me,
      unless you want to know
      about 400-year-old vases
      and building tools from the eighteenth century."
I tell Cleo her Dad
should look at Arnold's Bottle Top Collection.
      "Why are parents like that?" she asks.
"That's what happens when you get old.
Dumb things become important." I say.
      "Yeah, that's why we have to live behind
      a huge stone wall, I reckon."
"I hate that wall.
Every time I go for a bike-ride
Mum says, 'Stay within the wall.'
So I ride around in circles,
like a circus animal."
      "It's a prison. A prison for kids."

Tom Jones Saves the World, p. 44

Activity **6.4**

1   What do Tom and Cleo have in common?

2   Explain how the use of dialogue in the poem gives us an insight into their characters.

3   Many of the friendships in Steven Herrick's verse novels exist between a main male character and his female best friend – Tom and Cleo in *Tom Jones Saves the World*, Harry and Linda in *by the river*, Jack and Annabel in *Love, ghosts and nose hair* and *A place like this* and Billy and Caitlin in *The simple gift*. Suggest reasons why Herrick constructs his friendships in this way.

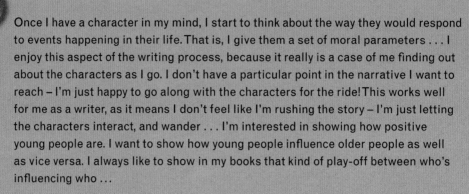

Once I have a character in my mind, I start to think about the way they would respond to events happening in their life. That is, I give them a set of moral parameters . . . I enjoy this aspect of the writing process, because it really is a case of me finding out about the characters as I go. I don't have a particular point in the narrative I want to reach – I'm just happy to go along with the characters for the ride! This works well for me as a writer, as it means I don't feel like I'm rushing the story – I'm just letting the characters interact, and wander . . . I'm interested in showing how positive young people are. I want to show how young people influence older people as well as vice versa. I always like to show in my books that kind of play-off between who's influencing who . . .

Steven Herrick

Sleep   *Billy*

Occasionally
I find Old Bill
asleep on the gravel
beside the carriage,
an empty bottle beside him.
I try to wake him
and help him inside
into the warmth.
He swears
and coughs
and his breath smells
of beer
and cigarettes.
We stumble into the carriage
and he falls on the seat
still swearing
at me for waking him
and at his luck for
being found
smelling badly
asleep
on the gravel
beside the train tracks
by a kid
who can't leave well enough
alone.

The simple gift, p. 84

1   What are the 'moral parameters' Billy faces in this poem, and how does he respond to them?

2   **a**   Billy has left home to escape an abusive relationship with his father. Given that his experiences with his father – an older male – are negative, why do you think he helps Old Bill?
   b   Explain how the lines 'by a kid who can't leave well enough alone' relate to this.

3   One of Steven Herrick's main themes is 'heroism', and how it is tied up with the nature of 'good': having ethics and courage, overcoming adversity, influencing others in a positive way, having hope, accepting others' vulnerability and giving of oneself.
   a   Explain how Billy's actions in the poem 'Sleep', and the attitudes behind them, are 'heroic' in this sense.
   b   What does 'heroism' mean to you? Explain your answer.

Loss, grief and leaving

Another recurring motif in Steven Herrick's work is that of loss, grief and leaving.

One of my continuing themes is to explore how men and boys deal with losing their significant other (Mum, wife) – I'm interested in how we males sometimes bottle things up, sometimes externalise pain, sometimes try to ignore it . . .

Steven Herrick

In *by the river*, Harry's mother dies when he is seven. In 'One Sunday at a time' we see the effect of this loss on Harry's father:

one Sunday at a time

I knew
because
he was quieter than usual
on Sunday
and he swept Mun's gravestone
slowly
and I saw him
touch his lips
with his good hand
and ran it gently
over Mun's name.
He gave us money
for ice-cream.
Keith ran to the shop.
I ~~stay lost~~ behind
the tiered headstone
of some ~~long-~~dead
rich man
out of Dad's view
and I watched. ~~his~~
~~wipe his eyes~~ —
in the distant quiet,
I saw his lips moving
telling Mun
of Keith's cleaning
and my ~~coshing~~
and his ~~twenty~~ drinks
at the bar.
~~And Aunt Alice~~
~~am still coshing~~
~~His marri~~age anniversary.

with the merciless sun
heating the cool stone
where I sat
watching my Dad
~~grow old~~
~~one ~~~~on the~~
~~one Sunday~~
~~at a time~~
with his gentle hands
~~and the naughty boy~~
~~and~~ grow old
one Sunday
at a time.

Steven Herrick's draft of the poem
'One Sunday at a time'

One Sunday at a time

I know
because
he's quieter than usual
on Sunday,
and he sweeps Mum's gravestone
slowly,
and I see him
touch his lips
with his good hand
and run it gently
over Mum's name.
He gives us money
for chips.
Keith runs to the shop.
I hide behind
the tiered headstone
of some long-dead
rich man,

out of Dad's view,
and I watch.
In the stillness
I see his lips moving,
telling Mum
about the adventures
of our days.
Their wedding anniversary,
The merciless sun
heating the cool stone
where I sit
watching my dad –
his gentle hands
tracing this special day
through his other life,
through his memory.

by the river, p. 136

The final, published version of 'One Sunday at a time'.

Activity 6.6

1 In what way does the title of the poem convey how Harry's father deals with the death of his wife?

2 a How do the words 'slowly', 'gently', 'stillness' and 'gentle' create mood?
   b What do these words convey about the father's feelings towards his wife and how he deals with the strong emotions of loss and grief?

3 Harry's father visits his wife's gravestone with his two sons every Sunday. What is the line which tells you that this Sunday is special?

4 Suggest what you think Harry means in the lines 'tracing this special day through his other life, through his memory.'

5 Harry deals with the loss of his mother by watching how his father handles it. What lessons do you think he is learning from his father, not only about loss, but about love?

6 Compare the draft and published versions of the poem. Choose three differences and suggest why Steven changed or deleted the lines.

In *Love, ghosts and nose hair*, Jack's mother dies when he is eight. 'The earthquake' shows us the pain still experienced by Jack's father, particularly when events occur to remind him:

The earthquake

The earth moved last night
the ancient plates under our mountain shifted
    as windows spooked and rattled
      the lampshade cracked
and our wedding photo
    fell off the dresser.
Desiree slept
Jack snored

I fastened the window
  turned off the lamp
    picked up the photo
and spent an hour holding the frame
    getting married all over again
while the earth
    threatened.
This morning
    the papers reported
    3.5 on the Richter Scale
    and no damage
I didn't mention the wedding
    but all morning I felt
      the cruel aftershock.

Love, ghosts and nose hair, pp. 76–77

Activity 6.7

1   What has happened in 'The earthquake'?

2   Explain how the father's sense of loss is communicated in the lines 'and spent an hour holding the frame getting married all over again'?

3   How is the earthquake a metaphor for the father's pain? What do these things have in common?

4   Suggest the irony in the lines '3.5 on the Richter Scale and no damage'.

5   What do you think is meant by 'but all morning I felt the cruel aftershock'?

6   Even though the wives and mothers in the two poems 'One Sunday at a time' and 'The earthquake' are absent, in what ways can we see that they were – and remain – positive influences in their families' lives?

7   The fathers in the two poems deal tenderly with grief. In what ways do you think this would have a positive impact on their children?

8   Suggest why you think it's important for both boys and girls to have positive female *and* male influences in their lives.

Steven Herrick says:

I'm also interested in the whole question of male-on-male influence. We adults think we can influence our sons – I prefer to think of it as an enormously gratifying two-way-street . . . I know my two teenage sons are a wonderful positive influence on my own life. It seems to me that the world of young people is becoming increasingly marginalised by mainstream media. As adults, we need to accept, encourage, and indeed, embrace the world of young people.

Interestingly, in Herrick's poetry father–son relationships are generally ones of mutual love. In the following poems we see the notion of fathers 'letting go' of their children – having enough courage, faith and trust to allow them to make their own decisions and their own way in the world.

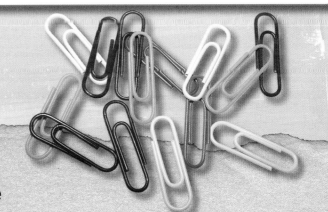

For once in my life

When Jack told me last night
about leaving
what I really wanted to say
was *NO*.
Like a father should.
NO.
And I had all the words ready,
all the clichés loaded
but I couldn't do it.
He looked so hungry,
so much in need of going
that I gave him my first big speech in years,
only this time it was one he wanted to hear.
So that's it.

When Jack was asleep last night
I went into his room.
I sat beside his bed
    and listened to his breathing.
I don't know for how long.
I listened,
and with each breath
I felt his yearning, and confidence,
and strength.
I walked out of his room
sure I'd said the right thing
maybe not as a father
but as a Dad.
I'd said the right thing,
for once in my life.

A place like this, pp. 10–11

Directions out

My dad once said,
'You go left at the grocery.
Follow that road for a mile,
sharp right where the sawmill
sends the dust high.
Then left, after the river.
That leads you through the Kelly farm.
Those cows, dairy mainly,
and a few prize bulls
living the life . . .
Okay, take a left at the T-junction.
You go along that road,
new bitumen,
no potholes for a few years,
even gutters for the stormwater,
until you see the dry-stone wall
on the right,
built years ago,
and still standing.
Turn right,
follow that for a few miles
until you reach the major intersection,
then . . .
well, you can turn left or right,
it doesn't matter,
because, by then
you're miles
and another world away
from here.'

by the river, pp. 144–145

Emma and the right way

I've been thinking hard.
It's all I can do right now.
Think. And wait.

I needed Jack and Annabel
on this farm two months ago.
They came out of nowhere,
and gave me hope.
The way they were, together.
Everything they do is positive.
They're not like the kids at school.
I needed them.
I needed help with birth classes.
But now,
I've been thinking about Dad.
I've never thought about him.
He just was.
I worried about Mum, wherever she is.
I worried about Beck and Craig, without Mum.

But Dad, look at him.
Three children, no wife,
a farm that barely pays
and he gets up every morning
sits on the veranda
watching the sunrise
and he counts himself lucky.
And when I come home pregnant
he doesn't yell, or rant, or blame.
He just keeps on going.
He looks almost proud of me.
Now he worries I'll leave.
He worries Jack and Annabel leaving
will mean I'll follow,
maybe not after them, but away,
anywhere.
But he's not saying anything.
He's going to let me choose,
I know.
It's his way.
It's the right way.

A place like this, pp. 113–114

1 a Explain why you think the fathers in these poems give 'permission' for their children to make their own journeys in life.

   b In what ways does it take courage to do this?

2 Describe the impressions you get about each father.

   a List adjectives using the information we are given in the poems.

   b Write a description of them that goes beyond what we are told by the poet.

3 In the poem 'For once in my life' (page 269) what makes Jack's father certain that he has given the right advice to his son?

4 Draw or map out the locations as described by Harry's father in 'Directions out'.

5 Explain what you think he means when he says 'it doesn't matter, because, by then you're miles and another world away from here'.

6 As Emma, write a letter to your father which captures the sentiments in the poem 'Emma and the right way'. How will you convey the respect you have for him?

7 Find information about and read interviews with Steven Herrick on his website http://acay.com.au/~sherrick/.

   a Make a list of the impressions you have about the author through reading about him. Compare your responses with others'.

   b Read any reviews you can find on Steven Herrick's verse novels or poetry books and suggest whether you think there is a common thread running through his work. If so, how would you describe it?

   c Imagine you were asked to write a letter to Steven Herrick or conduct an interview with him. Write five questions you would ask him.

   d Children and young adults are used to short 'grabs' of visual and written information in the world of computer games, text messaging, fleeting images in advertising and television programs. Suggest ways in which Steven Herrick's poetry and verse novels may appeal to such an audience.

Activity 6.8

Activity 6.9

Research task. On your own or with a partner, research Steven Herrick or another poet. While you are researching, consider these questions to help you select your information:

- Briefly outline the poet's life and describe their personal, cultural and historical context. How has the country of their birth, the time in which they lived, and their own experiences influenced their work?
- What are the issues about which the poet feels strongly or writes about often?
- Does the poet have a particular style which is seen in many of the poems? Describe this style.
- Which of his/her poems is your favourite? Explain your choice.

You could present your research in one of the following ways:

- conduct an imaginary interview
- write a magazine article
- complete a PowerPoint presentation
- compile a collage or display of one of their themes which combines written and visual texts
- write and present a persuasive speech about the value of their poetry today
- write a review of one of their books of poetry
- present a dramatic reading of a selection of their poems and use songs or music to accompany it
- paint a piece of artwork which reflects one of their poems or themes. Write an analysis of this artwork which explains how you have responded to the poem
- choose a character from one of their poems and write their autobiography
- create a board game which provides information about the characters and events in one of the poems.

Chapter 7

'Integration as a process' by Liam O'Connor

Analysing poetry

Unlocking the poem

When we seek to analyse or 'unlock' a poem, we are looking for the key to appreciating more fully what the poem means. We can treat poems very casually, reading them just once and not thinking about them any more. Alternatively, by exploring a poem more deeply, we can immerse ourselves in the poet's experience. The more we explore a poem, the clearer it becomes. Unlocking the poem is like unlocking the mind and heart of the poet.

Sometimes it is surprising how much we relate to the poetry of others. We discover that beauty, sadness, excitement, grief and all the other emotions in the poetry are part of our own lives.

We can never be sure that we understand and feel everything that a poet meant to include in a poem. Sometimes, however, we may see things that the poet was not even aware of. Australian poet Bruce Dawe once said: 'I had no idea how clever I was until I heard other people analysing my poetry.'

When we want to fully appreciate a poem, we can critique or analyse the poem by looking at its poetic features and thinking about its social and cultural context. Critiquing (or analysing) a poem involves a series of steps.

Step one: What is the subject matter of the poem?

Ask yourself what the poem is about and what event, experience or issue it describes. There is no need to elaborate on everything that happens in the poem. You should be able to describe the subject matter in one sentence.

Step two: What is the theme or message?

Ask yourself what comment the poet wants to make to the reader. Themes can be simple, such as the beauty of nature, or can address a particular issue, like prejudice or the poor treatment of particular people or groups. Some common themes include love, sorrow, adolescence, friendship, death and war.

Step three: What is the form of the poem?

Is the poem a ballad, an ode, a sonnet? Or perhaps free verse, a lyric or blank verse? You should be able to justify your answer by referring to particular features of the poem.

Step four: What is the tone or mood of the poem?

Does it have a positive or negative atmosphere? How would you describe the mood? Joyous? Melancholy? Uplifting?

Step five: What poetic techniques have been used and to what effect?

The language used by poets helps the reader to feel the full impact of the poem. Poetic techniques can be the use of visual images (metaphors, similes, personification, symbolism) or sound devices (alliteration, assonance, onomatopoeia, rhyme and rhythm). You need to ask yourself how the poem and its message are enhanced by these techniques.

Step six: What social comment is the poem making?

Ask yourself what this poem is saying about society or a particular aspect of society. Has the poet experienced the events or emotions in the poem? How could the poem influence or change the reader's opinion?

Poetry and critical literacy

While it is important to look at the textual features of a poem (subject matter, theme, mood, form, visual images and sound devices) it is also important to question the poem's message about our world.

Many poets use poetry as a medium to make a comment about the world and its people. Sometimes the comments may be about social or political issues, such as the environment, equality or the treatment of particular groups in society. When we analyse a poem and consider its comments about society and culture, we are using critical literacy. This can make us more aware of the world around us. Critical literacy takes us out of the poem and allows us to explore the society in which it was created.

When poets explore serious issues and voice their opinions or concerns they may come from the perspective of a disadvantaged or marginalised group. Sometimes the poet may be writing on behalf of a particular group in society, or they may have experienced injustice themselves. These groups may include those who are less powerful or less dominant in society: the poor, the voiceless, or those who are discriminated against due to race, class or gender.

It must be remembered that a poem is not neutral, in that its creation has been influenced by a number of factors.

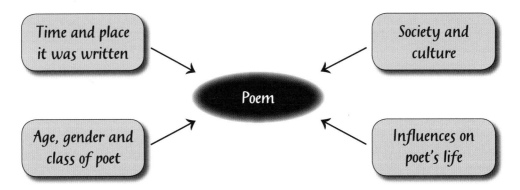

To analyse a poem using critical literacy, use the following questions as a guide:

- How has the poet's race, class, gender or age influenced the poem? How old is the poet? Is the poet male or female? Do they have a disability? Are they from a privileged or poor background? Do you know the poet's race or religion and would this information help you to understand the poem more? Knowing a little bit about the poet can help us understand the poem at a deeper level.

- When and where does the poem come from? A poem from 16th-century Shakespearean England would be quite different from a modern poem from Australia. This is because the societies and cultures are quite different. Poetry can give us insight into another world or into the past.

- What is my reaction to the poem? Your background (age, class, gender, race and experiences) can also affect the way you understand the poem. This is because you have adopted a reading position depending on your background and your beliefs and values as a person. For example, if you have been unfairly treated because of your age or gender, you will empathise with a poet who has written of similar experiences.

Activity **7.1**

Let's analyse a poem using the guidelines opposite.
1 First, read the poem carefully thinking through the first five steps (pages 274–275).
2 Then read the short biography on Wilfred Owen and work through step six of the analysis.

Anthem for doomed youth

What passing bells for these who die as cattle?
   Only the monstrous anger of the guns.
   Only the stuttering rifles' rapid rattle
Can patter out their hasty orisons.
No mockeries for them from prayers or bells,
   Nor any voice of mourning save the choirs, –
The shrill, demented choirs of wailing shells;
   And bugles calling for them from sad shires.

What candles may be held to speed them all?
   Not in the hands of boys, but in their eyes
Shall shine the holy glimmers of good-byes.
   The pallor of girls' brows shall be their pall;
Their flowers the tenderness of silent minds,
And each slow dusk the drawing down of blinds.

Wilfred Owen

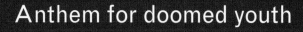

Biography of Wilfred Owen

Wilfred Owen

Wilfred Owen stated, 'My subject is War, and the pity of War. The Poetry is in the pity.' This phrase encapsulates the main theme and subject of Wilfred Owen's poetry: war. Owen was born on 18 March 1893 in England. His family were religious and Christian imagery is evident in much of his poetry.

    Owen failed the university entrance exam so he worked as an assistant to a local vicar. During this time, he saw poverty and death that made him more aware of the less fortunate, but more critical of the Church. After a second attempt, he passed the university entrance exam and studied literature and botany. After a short career as an English teacher in France, he enlisted in the Artists' Rifles on 21 October 1915.

It was the First World War, the most brutal and bloody war in history. After training for 14 months, in 1917 Owen was sent to fight in France during the worst winter ever. After four months of battle experience he was wounded and shocked by the horrors of war. He spent some time recuperating in a hospital in Scotland where he met the other great war poet, Siegfried Sassoon, who had also been severely injured in battle. It was during this time that he wrote 'Anthem for doomed youth'.

Wilfred Owen believed he had a duty to help other soldiers so he returned to the war front in France. On 4 November 1918, just seven days before the end of the war, he was caught in German machine gun fire and killed. He was twenty-five years old.

Activity 7.2

Look at the analysis of 'Anthem for doomed youth' below and identify the six steps used.

Analysis of 'Anthem for doomed youth'

Wilfred Owen's poem, 'Anthem for doomed youth' is a lament for the dead soldiers of war. As a response to his experiences in the First World War, Owen highlighted the futility and cruelty of war through religious imagery and powerful sound techniques. This sombre poem explores the pain of war and the loss of so many young men.

'Anthem for doomed youth' explores the subject matter of Owen's experience of war and the poem makes a strong statement on the useless nature of war and the youths who are 'doomed' to die on the battlefield. The poem reflects on the horror of trench warfare and the brutality of the First World War.

Wilfred Owen skilfully explores the theme of war and its social effects on the soldiers and their families and loved ones left behind. The 'passing bells' ring for the death of the soldiers and this reinforces the message that war is death, useless and futile.

The poem is written as an elegy, a lament for the dead. An elegy is a sad poem that explores loss and death. Owen does not personalise or individualise death; instead he maintains a detached view that highlights more strongly the issue of death and the multitude of its victims. The first eight lines, the octet, sets the scene of the destruction and madness of warfare set against the more subdued and sombre images of the church.

At the opening of the poem, the tone is one of bitter passion and then moves to a more quiet thoughtful tone. By the end of the poem, the mood is sombre and solemn. This is reinforced by the 'drawing down of blinds' as loved ones are informed of the death of a family member or friend. The poem quietly closes.

Wilfred Owen uses poetic techniques to enhance the horrific images of war and its effects. The simile 'die as cattle' in the first line shocks us with the image of a slaughterhouse, the soldiers likened to animals. The octet shows the sounds of war, the weapons of destruction, the guns, rifles and shells that are all linked to religious imagery. The use of onomatopoeia, alliteration and personification create a brilliant image in the line, 'Only the stuttering rifles' rapid rattle'. The contrast of 'choirs' and 'wailing shells' is a startling image. The bugles sounding in the eighth line leads into the next stanza (sestet) with the muted, silent sound of the Last Post. As dusk falls in the last line, the poem has a feeling of finality and sadness. The 'slow dusk' haunts the ones who mourn for the dead soldiers.

'Anthem for doomed youth' shows the injustices of war and how people in society are cruelly affected by the deaths of their young men. Owen has chosen to silence the people who send these young men to war: the politicians and leaders. Instead he has placed in the foreground the soldiers and their loved ones, and the senseless nature of war. Through his use of poetic techniques, Owen has highlighted the theme that the young are doomed in war.

Now read the song below about Australians fighting in a war 50 years later, the Vietnam War.

I was only nineteen

Mum and Dad and Denny saw the passing out parade
At Puckapunyal. (It was a long march from cadets.)
The sixth battalion was the next to tour – and it was me who drew the card.
We did Canungra and Shoalwater before we left.

Chorus 1
And Townsville lined the footpaths as we marched down to the quay.
This clipping from the paper shows us young and strong and clean.
And there's me in my slouch hat with my S.L.R. and greens.
God help me, I was only nineteen.

From Vung Tau riding Chinooks to the dust and Nui Dat,
I'd been in and out of choppers now for months.
But we made our tents a home, V.B. and pinups on the lockers,
And an Asian orange sunset through the scrub.

Chorus 2
And can you tell me, doctor, why I still can't get to sleep?
And night-time's just a jungle dark and a barking M-16?
And what's this rash that comes and goes, can you tell me what it means?
God help me, I was only nineteen.

A four-week operation, when each step can mean your last one
On two legs; it was a war within yourself.
But you wouldn't let your mates down 'til they had you dusted off,
So you closed your eyes and thought about something else.

Chorus 3
Then someone yelled out 'Contact', and the bloke behind me swore.
We hooked in there for hours, then a god-almighty roar.
Frankie kicked a mine the day that mankind kicked the moon.
God help me, he was going home in June.

I can still see Frankie, drinking tinnies in the Grand Hotel
On a thirty-six hour rec. leave in Vung Tau.
And I can still hear Frankie, lying screaming in the jungle,
'Till the morphine came and killed the bloody row.

Chorus 4
And the Anzac legends didn't mention mud and blood and tears.
And the stories that my father told me never seemed quite real.
I caught some pieces in my back that I didn't even feel.
God help me, I was only nineteen.

Chorus 5
And can you tell me, doctor, why I still can't get to sleep?
And why the Channel Seven chopper chills me to my feet?
And what's this rash that comes and goes, can you tell me what it means?
God help me, I was only nineteen.

John Schumann

Activity 7.3

1 Complete the following table for 'I was only nineteen':

Analysis	'I was only nineteen'
Subject matter	
Theme	
Form	
Mood	
Poetic techniques	
Social comment	

2 Using this information, write a poetic analysis. Don't forget to add an introduction and conclusion. Refer to the example on pages 278–279 to help you.

Appreciation, not destruction

The only reason we explore a poem is to understand and enjoy it more. In our explorations, it is important not to destroy the poem's beauty or power. We have to learn how to combine our analysis with an overall understanding of the whole poem, whatever form it takes. Sometimes we need to step back and take a fresh look at something we thought we understood. Read 'Integration as a process' with this thought in mind.

Integration as a process

I once saw a man
Sneaking up on butterflies.
He caught them,
Quietly killed them,
And pinned them to a board.
I saw the man again,
Analysing poetry.
Piece by meaningless piece,
He cut it up,
Catalogued it,
Until it died.
Like an old photograph,
Studied closely,
Merely a collection of dots.
But step back!

Liam O'Connor

1 How could the processes involved in killing butterflies and in analysing poetry be similar?

2 Explain the message in the last line: 'But step back!'

3 The poet A.E. Housman once said that 'even when poetry has a clear meaning, it may be a mistake to analyse it. Perfect understanding will sometimes almost extinguish pleasure.' What message is Housman giving us?

Activity **7.4**

This poem by Michelle Williams describes a very moving experience in her life. Read the poem, and then her analysis which follows.

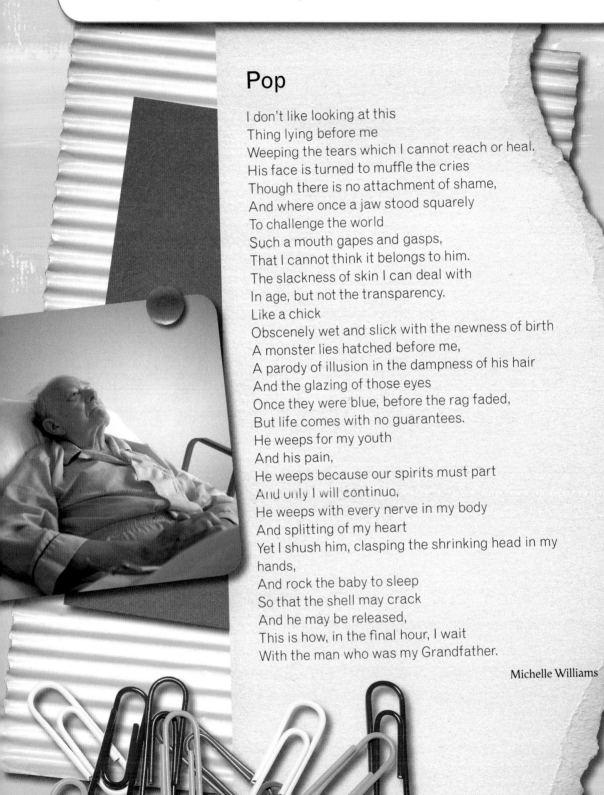

Pop

I don't like looking at this
Thing lying before me
Weeping the tears which I cannot reach or heal.
His face is turned to muffle the cries
Though there is no attachment of shame,
And where once a jaw stood squarely
To challenge the world
Such a mouth gapes and gasps,
That I cannot think it belongs to him.
The slackness of skin I can deal with
In age, but not the transparency.
Like a chick
Obscenely wet and slick with the newness of birth
A monster lies hatched before me,
A parody of illusion in the dampness of his hair
And the glazing of those eyes
Once they were blue, before the rag faded,
But life comes with no guarantees.
He weeps for my youth
And his pain,
He weeps because our spirits must part
And only I will continue,
He weeps with every nerve in my body
And splitting of my heart
Yet I shush him, clasping the shrinking head in my
hands,
And rock the baby to sleep
So that the shell may crack
And he may be released,
This is how, in the final hour, I wait
With the man who was my Grandfather.

Michelle Williams

'Pop': an analysis

This was a painful poem to write, because it describes the dying moments of my grandfather. The way he seemed to physically change as death approached, and his own sadness at his coming death, are things I will never forget.

The subject matter of the poem deals with my shock at seeing my grandfather, my discomfort at having to face his grief, and my urgent desire to release him from his pain. The man I once knew had vanished, replaced instead by something which resembled a newborn child. The tragedy was that it was like a birth in reverse. The journey led to death in our world, not life.

My purpose in writing this poem was simply to share the experience with others. Sooner or later we must all face the death of someone we love, and it helps to know that when we feel intense grief and pain, we are not alone.

Imagery is the focus of the poem. In describing exactly what I saw and felt, I tried to reach the heart of anyone reading my words. The images of a wet chick are purposefully horrific, since I couldn't come to terms with how the man I loved so much was transforming. Even the colour of his eyes gave way as death worked in. The image of the shell cracking is a positive one. It represents Pop's release from suffering and fear, and freedom for his spirit to begin a new life.

The atmosphere of grief in the poem is reinforced by writing in free verse. There was no point in trying to make my emotions fit a particular rhythm pattern or rhyming scheme. Letting the feelings flow, and integrating them with the visual images seemed to best suit the mood of this poem. Repetition of the word 'weeps' and the sound of 'shushing' as one would soothe a baby, show our shared pain as we waited for the end to come.

Michelle Williams

Activity 7.5

1   Which steps of the guidelines has Michelle Williams followed in her analysis?

2   Which step do you feel is the most important to understand the poet's experience? Explain.

The following two poems are similar in terms of their subject matter and themes. Read the poems carefully remembering the six steps of analysis on pages 274–275. Then look at the analysis that critiques both poems on page 286.

The child who walks backwards

My next-door neighbour tells me
her child runs into things.
Cupboard corners and doorknobs
have pounded their shapes
into his face. She says
he is bothered by dreams,
rises in sleep from his bed
to steal through the halls
and plummet like a wounded bird
down the flight of stairs.

This child who climbed my maple
with the sureness of a cat
trips in his room, cracks
his skull on the bedpost,
smacks his cheeks on the floor.
When I ask him about the burns
on the back of his knee,
his mother tells me
he walks backwards
into fireplace grates
or sits and stares at flames
while sparks burn stars in his skin.

Other children write their names
on the casts that hold
his small bones.
His mother tells me
he runs into things,
walks backwards,
breaks his leg
while she lies
sleeping.

Lorna Crozier

A poem for Darcy

Is there a Darcy at your school?

Darcy Leveridge was the poorest kid in school.
He walked to school without shoes
and wore the same clothes most days,
kids called him Smelly Darcy.
Darcy was the last boy picked
for soccer games
and basketball
and even tug-a-war games.
No-one wanted to be near Darcy.
He lived with his Aunt
in a shack by the creek
with lots of dogs, and cats,
and chickens, and geese.
Darcy was the suburb's paperboy.
He said he could throw each paper
onto the verandah of every house
in the suburb.
And he could too.
I always got the paper for Dad,
right at the doorstep.
Darcy was an expert at paper-throwing.
The money he earnt
he gave to his Auntie
and I think she spent it
feeding the cats and dogs and
everything but feeding Darcy
who was also the skinniest kid in school.
Darcy sat up the back in Year 6
and never answered one question right all year.
He stared out the window,
throwing papers in his head probably.
He failed every exam.
The teachers stopped asking Darcy questions.
They left him to his window.
I never talked to Darcy.

One day I got punched by
a Year 7 girl.
I was so hurt and surprised
I ran out of the schoolyard
and all the way home
to a lunch of embarrassment
alone on the back stairs.

When I finally returned
to school
everybody in class called me
'scaredy-cat' or
'chicken' or
'weakling, weakling'.
Everyone except Darcy.

After school, on the way home,
Darcy told me to ignore them
and do what he did
when people called him
'smelly' or 'poorboy Darcy'.
He told me to look out the window
and think of the one thing
you're good at,
paper-throwing or
kicking a ball or
writing a story
and
to do that one thing in your head
over and over
until you did it perfect.

That's what Darcy said,
and that's what I did.

Steven Herrick

An analysis of 'The child who walks backwards' and 'A poem for Darcy'

The poems 'The child who walks backwards' by Lorna Crozier, and 'A poem for Darcy' by Steven Herrick explore the issue of child neglect. In each poem, the neglected boys are seen through the eyes of onlookers, a next-door neighbour and a classmate. The conversational tone of the poems and the realistic images highlight the stark reality of child abuse in society.

The subject matter of the poems is similar; both poems deal with the serious problem of child neglect. In 'The child who walks backwards' it is suggested that the young boy is physically abused by his mother who makes excuses for his 'accidents'. 'A poem for Darcy' tells of 'the poorest kid in school', neglected by his aunt with whom he lives. His clothes are dirty and he is malnourished and is also rejected by the children and teachers at school.

The themes of the two poems are quite similar. The message is that it is a sad reality that there are poor and abused children in our society. The poems also highlight that nothing seems to be done about this terrible problem. In Crozier's poem, the neighbour doesn't act on her suspicions of abuse and in 'A poem for Darcy', even though the teachers and the community know Darcy is neglected, nothing seems to be done about it.

Both poems are free verse in form. There is no set pattern, rhythm or rhyme. 'A poem for Darcy' by Steven Herrick is almost conversational in its style. 'The child who walks backwards' also has a fluency of speech. It is as if you can hear the people in the poem speaking to you. This helps to make the poems more realistic.

There is a mood of detachment in both poems and this is enhanced by the conversational tone. There is a sense of sadness in Crozier's poem as if the child had experienced a time when there was no abuse and he played freely with the other children. Steven Herrick's poem has a mood of forgiveness and understanding, particularly towards the end of the poem when the poet connects with Darcy and understands his reasons for detachment.

The poems use different poetic techniques to add realism and emotion. In 'The child who walks backwards', the simile 'plummet like a wounded bird' used to describe the boy effectively depicts the helplessness of the child. The alliteration in 'cupboard corners' is hard and unfriendly. Onomatopoeia is used to startling effect. The words 'cracks' and 'smacks' highlight the cruelty and abuse suffered by the boy. 'A poem for Darcy' uses little imagery, adding to the realism of the poem. The window is used as symbol of escape and this secret is shared between Darcy and the persona. This shows the human side of Darcy, his kindness and sadness despite his hardship.

'The child who walks backwards' and 'A poem for Darcy' both make a serious social comment. They highlight the issue of child abuse and neglect and show how little support appears to be given to those in need or distress. Steven Herrick asks, 'Is there a Darcy at your school?' This shows how we might all know someone who is abused, neglected or ignored and makes us question our own actions.

Choose one of the three poems that follow, and write an analysis. Begin by drawing up a table of guidelines as in Activity 7.3 on page 280. Remember that these poems deal with poor or rejected people in society. You will need to include this in your social comment.

Activity **7.6**

Ballad of the landlord

Landlord, landlord,
My roof has sprung a leak.
Don't you 'member I told you about it
Way last week?

Landlord, landlord,
These steps is broken down.
When you come up yourself
It's a wonder you don't fall down.

Ten bucks you say I owe you?
Ten bucks you say is due?
Well, that's ten bucks more'n I'll pay you
Till you fix this house up new.

What? You gonna get eviction orders?
You gonna cut off my heat?
You gonna take my furniture and
Throw it in the street?

Um-huh! You talking high and mighty.
Talk on – till you get through.
You ain't gonna be able to say a word
If I land my fist on you.

Police! Police!
Come and get this man!
He's trying to ruin the government
And overturn the land!

Copper's whistle!
Patrol bell!
Arrest.

Precinct station.
Iron cell.
Headlines in press:

Man threatens landlord
Tenant held no bail
Judge gives Negro 90 days in county jail

Langston Hughes

The hunchback in the park

The hunchback in the park
A solitary mister
Propped between trees and water
From the opening of the garden lock
That lets the trees and water enter
Until the Sunday sombre bell at dark

Eating bread from a newspaper
Drinking water from the chained cup
That the children filled with gravel
In the fountain basin where I sailed my ship
Slept at night in a dog kennel
But nobody chained him up.

Like the park birds he came early
Like the water he sat down
And Mister they called Hey mister
The truant boys from the town
Running when he had heard them clearly
On out of sound

Past lake and rockery
Laughing when he shook his paper
Hunchbacked in mockery
Through the loud zoo of the willow groves
Dodging the park keeper
With his stick that picked up leaves

And the old dog sleeper
Alone between nurses and swans
While the boys among willows
Made the tigers jump out of their eyes
To roar on the rockery stones
And the groves were blue with sailors

Made all day until bell time
A woman figure without fault
Straight as a young elm
Straight and tall from his crooked bones
That she might stand in the night
After the locks and the chains

All night in the unmade park
After the railings and shrubberies
The birds the grass the trees the lake
And the wild boys innocent as strawberries
Had followed the hunchback
To his kennel in the dark.

Dylan Thomas

First day at school

A millionbillionwillion miles from home
Waiting for the bell to go. (To go where?)
Why are they all so big, other children?
So noisy? So much at home they
must have been born in uniform
Lived all their lives at playgrounds
Spent the years inventing games
that don't let me in. Games
that are rough, that swallow you up.

And the railings
All round, the railings.
Are they to keep out wolves and monsters?
Things that carry off and eat children?
Things you don't take sweets from?
Perhaps they're to stop us getting out
Running away from the lessins. Lessin.
What does a lessin look like?
Sounds small and slimy.
They keep them in glassrooms.
Whole rooms made out of glass.
Imagine.

I wish I could remember my name
Mummy said it would come in useful.
Like wellies. When there's puddles.
Yellowwellies. I wish she was here.
I think my name is sewn on somewhere
perhaps the teacher will read it for me.
Tea-cher. The one who makes the tea.

Roger McGough

Reading for meaning

When poetry is read aloud there is a real opportunity to give it life and character. You can achieve this by choosing the right pace, tone and rhythm for each poem. Sometimes it is important to vary these vocal features so that the best atmosphere or mood is created.

The following poems are quite different in purpose, mood and style. Practise reading each one aloud by performing in small groups. Allow the notes provided to guide you in your delivery. Perhaps you could read one of these to the class.

Reynard the fox

The fox was strong, he was full of running.
He could run for an hour and then be cunning.
But the cry behind him made him chill.
They were nearer now and they meant to kill.
They meant to run him until his blood
Clogged on his heart as his brush with mud.
Till his back bent up and his tongue hung flagging
And his belly and brush were filthed from dragging.

alliteration: repeating first letters of words

regular rhythm and rhyme contribute to telling of the story

Like a rocket shot to a ship ashore.
The lean red bolt of his body tore.
Like a ripple of wind running swift on grass:
Like a shadow on wheat when a cloud blows past.
Like a turn at the buoy in a cutter sailing.
When the bright green gleam lips white at the railing.
Like the April snake whipping back to sheath.
Like the gannets' hurtle on fish beneath.
Like all things swooping, like all things sweeping.
Like a hound for stay, like a stag for swift,
With his shadow beside like a spinning drift.

repetition adds rhythm; builds sight images

pace of poem becomes more rapid. Emphasis is on the powerful verbs – builds tension

And here, as he ran to the huntsman's yelling,
The fox first felt that the pace was telling;
His body and lungs seemed all grown old,
His legs less certain, his heart less bold,
The hound-noise nearer, the hill-slope steeper,
The thud in the blood of his body deeper.
The pride in his speed, his joy in the race.
Were withered away, for what use was pace?
He had run his best, and the hounds ran better.

assonance: repeating vowel sound

mood change – the race seems lost for the fox

At the second attempt he cleared the fence,
He turned half right where the gorse was dense,
He was leading the hounds by a furlong clear.
He was past his best, but his earth was near.

Within, as he reached the soft green turf,
The wind, blowing lonely, moaned like surf.
Desolate ramparts rose up steep
On either side, for the ghosts to keep.
He raced the trench, past the rabbit warren,
Close-grown with moss which the wind made barren;
He passed the spring where the rushes spread,
And there in the stones was his earth ahead.
One last short burst upon failing feet –
There life lay waiting, so sweet, so sweet,
Rest in a darkness, balm for aches.

The stars grew bright as the yews grew black,
The fox rose stiffly and stretched his back,
He flaired the air, then he padded out
To the valley below him, dark as doubt.
The stars grew bright in the winter sky,
The wind came keen with a tang of frost,
The brook was troubled for new things lost.
The copse was happy for old things found,
The fox came home and he went to ground.

John Masefield

> onomatopoeia: sound image creating the noise of the wind

> repetition emphasises relief

> mood becomes more relaxed

Masefield's poem demands that we read it in a certain way with varying speeds, and it creates a strong mood of suspense. Read the poem again and answer the questions overleaf.

1   Would the poem 'Reynard the fox' be as interesting if it had been written as free verse, without regular rhythm or rhyme? Explain your answer.

2   List as many examples of alliteration as you can. Describe how the use of alliteration helps the poem's rhythm.

3   Explain how the sight imagery creates the pace and atmosphere in the poem.

4   Write down any words you don't understand. Try to guess a meaning, based on the story of the poem. Confirm or change your answers by discussing the words in class or checking their meaning in a dictionary.

5   Read a section of this poem, as powerfully as you can, to the class.

Decide on your tone of voice for the next poem. How do you imagine the poet is speaking? Practise reading this poem with just the right 'voice'. Notice the regular rhythm and rhyming pattern, even though the verses are not regular in form.

Christmas 'thank you's

Dear Auntie
Oh, what a nice jumper
I've always adored powder blue
and fancy you thinking of
orange and pink
for the stripes
how clever of you.

Dear Uncle
The soap is
terrific
So
useful
and such a kind thought and
how did you guess that
I'd just used the last of
the soap that last Christmas brought

Dear Gran
Many thanks for the hankies
Now I really can't wait for the flu
and the daisies embroidered
in red round the 'M'
for Michael
how
thoughtful of you

Dear Cousin
What socks!
and the same sort you wear
so you must be
the last word in style
and I'm certain you're right that the
luminous green
will make me stand out a mile.

Dear Sister
I quite understand your concern
it's a risk sending jam in the post
But I think I've pulled out
all the big bits
of glass
so it won't taste too sharp
spread on toast.

Dear Grandad
Don't fret
I'm delighted
So don't think your gift will
offend
I'm not at all hurt
that you gave up this year
and just sent me
a fiver
to spend.

Mick Gowar

Activity **7.8**

1   Which lines would you emphasise when reading 'Christmas thank you's'?

2   What tone of voice would you use – humorous, serious, aggressive, relaxed? Explain.

3   Would you read this poem slowly or quickly? Explain.

4   What do you think the poet is really wanting to say in this poem?

Feel the rhythm of the waves as you read 'Song of the humpback'.

Song of the humpback

I am the keeper of the deep
In watery warmth and calm
Where peace lies still and undisturbed
On ocean's wrinkled palm.

I have seen the shadows dance
Round campfires' amber glow,
And heard the yearning in the songs
As embers crackled low.

I have been the red of blood
On stained and virgin sands,
And tasted salty dying tears
That crusted white-man's hands.

And now once more without the fear
I watch a white-washed shore,
And see a thousand flickering eyes
Light darkness as before.

For I am now the 'gentle giant'
The wisdom and the key;
Secrets of the restless deep
Mankind must learn from me.

Shelley Robinson

Activity 7.9

1 Describe or sketch the scene in the first verse of 'Song of the humpback'.

2 Describe the atmosphere created by the assonance in the last two lines of the second verse.

3 **a** Explain why the mood changes in the third verse.
   b What has happened to the whale?

4 **a** Describe how the alliteration in the fourth verse helps to build the watery rhythm.
   b Suggest what could be meant by 'a thousand flickering eyes' that 'light darkness'.

5 In what way is the message in the last verse similar to the idea expressed in the first verse?

6 **a** In your opinion, what are the poet's feelings about the environment and its creatures?
   b Summarise the social comment of this poem in one sentence.

Sharing ideas

The previous activities asked you to create as much meaning as you could from a poem by reading it to other members of your class or group. The experience of sharing poetry with others goes beyond simply reading a poem. By discussing a poem with group members, you will gain a wider variety of insights than by relying only on your own ideas.

Like 'Song of the humpback', the following poem also has a whale as the subject. However, David Gill has chosen a very different aspect for his focus.

Killing a whale

A whale is killed as follows:
A shell is filled with dynamite and
A harpoon takes the shell.
You wait until the great grey back
Breaches the sliding seas, you squint,
Take aim.
The cable snakes like a squirt of paint,
The shell channels deep through fluke
And flank, through mural softness
To bang among the blubber,
Exploding terror through
The hollow fleshy chambers,
While the hooks fly open
Like an umbrella
Gripping the tender tissue.

It dies with some panache
Whipping the capstan like
A schoolboy's wooden top,
Until the teeth of the machine
Can hold its anger, grip.
Its dead tons thresh for hours
The ravished sea,
Then sink together, sag –
So air is pumped inside
To keep the corpse afloat,
And one of those flags that men
Kill mountains with is stuck
Into this massive death.

Dead whales are rendered down,
Give oil.

David Gill

Activity **7.10**

1 Form groups and select one member of your group to read 'Killing a whale' to the others. Allow time for each person to re-read the poem silently, then discuss the questions below. Select another group member to be responsible for reporting your findings to the class. This person will need to take notes.

Remember that every person in a group discussion is entitled to a fair say and to have their opinion reported to the class. If all members of a group hold the same opinion, then this must be clearly stated when the report is given. Your teacher will decide whether the groups are to discuss all of the following questions, or be responsible for one question each.

a What attitude does the poet have towards the killing of whales? Explain your answer with evidence from the poem.

b Suggest why the poem is written in a very 'matter of fact' way. How does this tone help the message to be very clear?

c Identify the sight imagery in the poem, and show how this makes the reader become involved in the event being described.

d This poem is free verse. Why is this an appropriate form for the poet to have used? Suggest what effect a regular rhyming scheme and rhythm pattern might have had on the poem.

e What impact do the last two lines have on the reader, in the light of the rest of the poem?

2 Write a poetic analysis of both poems – 'Song of the humpback' and 'Killing a whale' – similar to the one on page 286.

Comparing poems

Often poets discuss similar subjects in very different ways, and with totally different attitudes. Step into the lives of the poets who wrote the poems below, and be aware of their emotions and the social issues they are highlighting as you read.

She's leaving home

Wednesday morning at five o'clock as the day begins,
Silently closing her bedroom door,
Leaving the note that she hoped would say more,
She goes downstairs to the kitchen clutching her handkerchief;
Quietly turning the backdoor key,
Stepping outside she is free.
She (We gave her most of our lives)
is leaving (Sacrificed most of our lives)
home (We gave her everything money could buy).
She's leaving home after living alone
For so many years. Bye-bye.
Father snores as his wife gets into her dressing gown,
Picks up the letter that's lying there,
Standing alone at the top of the stairs
She breaks down and cries to her husband,
'Daddy, our baby's gone.
Why would she treat us so thoughtlessly?
How could she do this to me?'
She (We never thought of ourselves)
is leaving (Never a thought for ourselves)
home (We struggled hard all our lives to get by).
She's leaving home after living alone
For so many years. Bye-bye.
Friday morning at nine o'clock she is far away,
Waiting to keep the appointment she made,
Meeting a man from the motor trade.
She (What did we do that was wrong?)
is having (We didn't know it was wrong)
fun (Fun is the one thing that money can't buy).
Something inside that was always denied
For so many years. Bye-bye.
She's leaving home. Bye-bye

John Lennon and Paul McCartney

Growing up

It must be, oooh,
a month or more
since they last complained
about the way I eat

or crisps I drop
on the kitchen floor

or not washing my feet

or the TV left on
when I go out

or the spoon clunking
against my teeth

or how loudly I shout

or my unmade bed,
mud on the stair,

soap left to drown
or the state of my hair. . .

It *must* be
a month or more.
Have they given up
in despair?

For years
they've nagged me
to grow up,
to act my age.

Can it be
that it's happened,
that I'm ready
to step out of my cage?

Wes Magee

Activity 7.11

'She's leaving home' and 'Growing up' present differing viewpoints about that special moment when children finally leave home.

1   Explain why the moods of these two poems are so different. Describe the message each poet is communicating to the audience. Choose words from each poem to back up your answer.

2   Suggest why Lennon and McCartney's song lyrics are much wordier than Magee's poem. Consider the thoughts in brackets as you decide on your answer.

3   Which of these poems on the theme of leaving home do you prefer? Explain your answer by considering the style, mood and form of the poems, and which one feels more relevant to you.

Activity 7.12

Research one of the poets included in this chapter. Select two of his/her poems which do not appear in the chapter and write – or present as a speech – a comparative analysis of these poems, following the examples given on pages 278–279 and 286. Your analysis should include quotes from the poet and from the poems. You should also show where your information came from (see 'Hints for researching and writing' below). In writing your analysis, refer to the guidelines on pages 274–276. Remember to include a personal response.

Hints for researching and writing

Always write down the title of any book, magazine or other reference material you use, including the author, publisher and date and place of publication. Also write the page numbers that your information came from.

For example:

Herrick, S. (2000) The simple gift. *University of Queensland Press: St Lucia. p. 3*

When using reference material, rewrite the information in your own words. If you use someone else's exact words, then it should be made clear that it is a direct quote. When you cite a quote, you must actually tell the reader who wrote or said these words, and when and where they were published.

Take notes, then write a first draft. Ask your teacher to read this, and any subsequent drafts, before you complete the final version.

Don't forget to include a bibliography. This is a list of any reference material consulted in the course of your research, set out in alphabetical order according to the authors' surnames.

Forms of poetry glossary

Ballad

- narrative verse: a poem that tells a story
- strong regular rhyme, rhythm, and repetition
- emphasis on action/the telling of events
- may have a refrain or chorus
- usually written in four-line stanzas
- common rhyme schemes: - a b a b
  - a a b b
  - a b c b
- originally sung to accompany dances

Elegy

- any poem, regardless of its form, which is written to lament or commemorate the death of a loved one, or which reflects on our mortality in general
- 'elegy' comes from the Greek word for 'a mournful poem'
- can have any structure, but is always sad and serious
- personal and subjective (i.e. The poet expresses personal grief at the loss of a loved one)
- can be objective (i.e. The poet ponders the issue of death and how it affects us)

Blank verse

- verse with no rhyme but with a regular metre
- each line has roughly the same number of syllables
- usually about detailed descriptions of events, or characters may reveal a great deal about themselves
- Shakespeare used this form many times in his plays (e.g. *'To be, or not to be'* in *Hamlet*)

Epic

- a long narrative poem (tells a story)
- usually centred around a hero on an important (and long) journey
- gods and other supernatural beings watch over the hero
- arranged into lines of even length, but there is no division into stanzas
- some famous epic poems: the *Iliad* and the *Odyssey* written by the Greek poet Homer

Dramatic monologue

- a form of poetry where we only get a one-sided conversation; we hear the speaker, but not the person to whom he/she is speaking
- like an extended soliloquy in drama
- reveals an incident in the life of the character and his/her temperament (psychological insight)
- no formal structure
- may or may not have rhyme

Free verse

- no formal pattern or structure
- no rhyme
- uses the natural rhythms of ordinary speech, therefore sounds 'conversational'
- the rhythm is based on phrases, sentences and paragraphs, and how lines are put together
- usually not divided into stanzas, but sometimes can be (but still don't rhyme)

Forms of poetry glossary (continued)

Lyric

- emotional and reflective poem, as opposed to telling a story
- characterised by an intensely personal outpouring of the poet's innermost thoughts and feelings
- many poems, regardless of their form, can be lyrical (eg. odes, free verse poems, elegies, pastoral, song lyrics, sonnets, etc.)

Ode

- written to honour a person or object – to praise someone or something
- lyrical poems, therefore have a high level of emotion
- the subject is often 'addressed'
- usually written in stanzas with a definite rhyme scheme, though modern odes are more flexible than traditional odes

Pastoral/nature poetry

- no restrictions in form
- lyrical poems giving a picture of rural life
- depict country scenes, people or events in idyllic ways
- a form usually used by the Romantic poets who worshipped Nature in a reaction to industrialisation

Prose poetry

- a form of free verse
- looks and sounds like a passage from a story as it is written in sentences and sometimes paragraphs
- language is more compact than a story
- intensive use of rich imagery
- appeals to the emotions

Short forms

Acrostic poems

- the first letter of each line, read downwards, spells a word

Alphabet poems

- like acrostic poems but do not spell out a word – each new word or line begins with the next letter of the alphabet

Cinquain

- five lines
- the length of each line can be written according either to the number of syllables or to the number of words per line

Dylan Thomas portraits

- focus on the senses and begin with the question 'Did you ever . . . ?'. The question is then answered with a description.
- always written in couplet form

Ezra Pound couplets

- unrhymed couplets which make comparisons between two things – say that one thing is another (metaphors)
- an image is presented in the first line; a comparison is made in the second line

Haiku

- originated in Japan – a very old form of poetry
- aim is to capture a single moment, idea or feeling, usually to do with nature or the seasons
- three lines long, unrhymed, written in present tense, uses strong visual imagery
- 17 syllables in all: line 1 has 5 syllables; line 2 has 7 syllables; line 3 has 5 syllables

Forms of poetry glossary (continued)

Limericks

- poem of five lines that is meant to be absurd and witty
- rhyme scheme is a a b b a
- 1st, 2nd and 5th lines rhyme with each other and have the same number of beats; the 3rd and 4th lines rhyme with each other and have the same number of beats
- rhyme depends on sound, not spelling
- the humour is contained in the last line – the 'punchline'

Numerical poems

- working with letters and numbers at the same time
- the form can be adapted to indicate not just a poem's length, but its 'value'

Ruptured rhymes

- make fun of traditional nursery rhymes, fairytales, or well-known stories

Shape poems

- visual, written in the shape of the poem's subject matter (e.g. bowling ball, jellyfish)

Spoonerisms

- accidentally or deliberately mixing up the first letters in two or more words

Tanka

- also a Japanese form of poetry
- is really a Haiku with two added lines
- has five lines and 31 syllables used in this pattern: 5, 7, 5, 7, 7

Soliloquy

- like a dramatic monologue; the character is speaking to him/herself – 'thinking out loud' – without the presence of others
- gives insight into the character speaking, who is often in turmoil or faced with a decision
- a form commonly used, among other forms, by Shakespeare in many of his plays

Song lyrics

- have strong rhythm and rhyme because they are meant to be sung
- are often lyrical, focusing on the feelings and ideas of the writer
- language is simple and direct
- often contains a chorus or refrain which is repeated
- themes are usually emotional (love, pain, despair, hope, rebellion, protest, etc.)

Sonnet

- recognised by their length – always 14 lines
- have regular rhythm and rhyme
- often used to tell of the joy and sadness of love and life
- may be written in two ways:
  a with an octave (eight lines) and a sestet (six lines), known as a 'Petrarchan sonnet'
  b with three quatrains (four lines) and a couplet (two lines), known as a 'Shakespearean sonnet'
- although traditional sonnets have a set rhyme scheme, some modern sonnets may or may not use rhyme

Verse novels

- a series of poems which together create a story
- a blend of narrative and poetry
- organised into short sections and are often told by multiple narrators
- we gain an insight into each character as they tell us about events from their own perspective

Glossary of terms for writing a critical response

binary oppositions

words and concepts in a text that are opposed to each other (eg. black/white, good/evil, rational/emotional), whereby one element is privileged over the other

class

a person's position in society based on their birth, wealth, occupation, level of education, etc. Different classes have differing degrees of power and opportunity

context

the personal, situational, cultural and historical background of a text and its composer, which influences both its creation and our reading of it

discourse

the type of language used by particular groups who share a common interest or occupation. Involves not only terms and concepts, but ways of speaking

dominant

a character, person, group or ideology that is given most power in a text

gender

masculine and feminine traits which we learn as we grow up, and which society and culture traditionally expect from us on the basis of our sex

marginalised

a character, person, or group that is given little power in a text

positioning

how readers are invited or encouraged to respond to a text

receptive reader

a reader who agrees with the ideas, issues and values in the text

resistant reader

a reader who disagrees with the ideas, issues and values in the text

silenced

a character, person or group that is given no voice or power in a text

Glossary of poetic terms, techniques and devices

alliteration

when two or more words in a sequence begin with the same consonant(s) (e.g. 'Betty Botter bought some butter...'; 'laughing friends lounged lazily')

assonance

when two or more words in a sequence repeat the same vowel sound (e.g. 'How now, brown cow?'; 'child of silent time')

cliché

a once-clever saying that has lost its power through over-use (e.g. 'as dead as a dodo'; 'as clear as a bell'), and therefore lacks originality

emotive words

words that create or influence the emotional response of the reader

foreshadowing

hinting at or suggesting events or themes that do not occur until later in the text

hyperbole

an excessive overstatement or exaggeration of fact

imagery

a word or group of words that appeal to one or more of the senses: sight, taste, touch, hearing, and smell

irony

saying one thing but meaning another (e.g. calling someone 'modest' when they boast about themselves); a contradiction that points out unfortunate coincidences (e.g. being stranded on a desert island surrounded by the ocean, but having no water to drink); a discrepency between the expected result and actual result (e.g. downloading an anti-virus program to your computer, only to find later that it has a virus)

metaphor

a comparison of two things in which one thing is said to actually *be* another (e.g. 'His mood was a black storm'; 'the sea is a hungry dog')

Glossary of poetic terms, techniques and devices
(continued)

onomatopoeia

a word that imitates the sound an object or action makes (e.g. 'The boom of the thunder'; 'The drip, drip, dripping of the tap')

paradox

a statement that first appears to contradict itself, but makes sense with more thought (e.g. 'Deep down, he's very shallow')

parody

imitating a poem or other literary work closely, but in a humorous or mocking way

personification

describing non-human things – animals, objects or ideas - as though they were human (e.g. 'The sun smiled'; 'the house sagged, bored and lonely')

rhyme

the repetition of the same (or similar) sounds. Rhyme that occurs at the end of a line of verse is called 'end rhyme'; rhyme that occurs within a line of verse is called 'internal rhyme'

rhythm

the flow and beat of a poem, created by the emphasis we place on certain words or parts of words when we read

satire

ridiculing a subject, often as an means of provoking or preventing change. The aim of satire is to expose faults or arouse disapproval through amusement or humour

simile

when two things are directly compared using 'like' or 'as' (e.g. 'she ate like a bird'; 'he was as quiet as a mouse')

symbolism

when an object, character, animal, place, or colour is used to represent a deeper idea or concept (e.g. white as a symbol of weddings in western culture, of mourning in others; the raven as a symbol of death)

Index by author–title

Index by author–title (continued)

Index by author–title (continued)

Index by author–title (continued)

Index by subject

Index by subject (continued)